Epic Voices

Epic Voices

Inner and Global Impulse in the Contemporary American and British Novel

Robert Arlett

Selinsgrove: Susquehanna University Press
London: Associated University Presses

Associated University Presses
440 Forsgate Drive
Cranbury, NJ 08512

Associated University Presses
16 Barter Street
London WC1A 2AH, England

Associated University Presses
P.O. Box 338, Port Credit
Mississauga, Ontario
Canada L5G 4L8

The paper used in this publication meets the requirements of the American National Standard for Permanence of Paper for Printed Library Materials Z39.48-1984.

Library of Congress Cataloging-in-Publication Data

Arlett, Robert, 1943–
  Epic voices : inner and global impulse in the contemporary American and British novel / Robert Arlett.
    p. cm.
  Includes bibliographical references and index.
  ISBN 0-945636-81-4 (alk. paper)
  1. English fiction—20th century—History and criticism. 2. Epic literature—History and criticism. 3. American fiction—20th century—History and criticism. 4. Characters and characteristics in literature. 5. Lessing, Doris May, 1919– Golden notebook.
  6. Mailer, Norman. Why are we in Vietnam? 7. Pynchon, Thomas. Gravity's rainbow. 8. Fowles, John, 1926– Daniel Martin.
  9. World history in literature. I. Title.
  PR888.E6A75   1996
  823'.91409—dc20
                                                    95-49127
                                                    CIP

3397

Contents

For Lyn,
who got me through many a storm
on this project and
countless others

Epic Voices

1

Two Rivers of the Modern Novel

GENRE IS CULTURE BOUND AND CHANGING CULTURES BREED NEW modes of artistic discourse. So we find that the path of the modern novel has been marked by a dialectic of seemingly rival impulses: while certain novelists have sought to deal with wide-scale social and political dimensions of modern existence, others have been principally concerned with the interior sensibility. Zola might be representative of the first tendency, Proust of the other. In *The Struggle of the Modern,* Stephen Spender categorizes these impulses, respectively, as "contemporary" and "modern,"[1] but the dialectic has tended to be dynamic as the rival impulses of the novel have increasingly interacted in the twentieth century so that narrative experimentation has resulted whereby the novelist as personal participant in his narrative competes, or shares space, with the novelist as director of outside characters and plots. Spender's aim for his experimental autobiography *World Within World* "is to create the true tension between the inner and the outer, subjective and objective"[2]—and the second half of this century has seen a number of novels that themselves attempt, with resultant experimentation in form, to achieve Spender's aim by combining thinly disguised confession with examination of political/social—indeed, global—affairs. An intensification of interaction between first- and third-person voices marks a group of novels covering a period from roughly the early 1960s through the mid-1970s. I find the old and sometimes abused term "epic" useful to describe these works that display simultaneously the global reach of contemporary history and a contrary movement demanding the sincerity of inner investigation and revelation. Writers from both sides of the Atlantic—for example, Barth, Bellow, Durrell, Fowles, Heller, Lessing, Mailer, and Pynchon—exhibit a range of polyvocal narrative tendencies as they offer various signals that invite epic consideration.

Clearly, the radicalization of narrative voices in the twentieth

9

century dismays a number of critics—for example, Wayne Booth, who claims that "an author has an obligation to be as clear about his moral position as he possibly can be,"[3] and Roy Pascal, who suggests that "the gain in authenticity and directness of experience" achieved by radical fusions in narrative is accompanied by "a loss of clarity."[4] Others respond that such censure indicates a failure to grasp "temporal and cultural conditions" so that such critics "are willing to blame a man of the twentieth century for not being of the eighteenth or nineteenth."[5] In fact, T. S. Eliot's criticism of a lack of objective correlative notwithstanding, *Hamlet*'s negative capabilities had offered a mirror of the relativity of things long before the twentieth century, and certainly a work like *Billy Budd* echoes that complex mirror of Shakespeare as Melville's "inside narrative" allows us to enter inner consciousnesses for extended periods but is withheld at moments that are keys to knowing.

Just as Auerbach, Booth, and Pascal bemoan the loss of narrative control in the twentieth-century novel, a school of criticism finds this century ill-equipped to achieve epic reach or control (a similar school assumes that drama cannot achieve tragic experience in this century). Though Austin Warren sees the novel as "the modern descendent of the epic,"[6] E. M. W. Tillyard—perhaps because his sensibilities were most in sympathy with pre-twentieth-century moral certainty (one assumes that the mysteries and uncertainties of *Hamlet* don't fit neatly into Tillyard's Elizabethan world picture)—contends that no novel of the epic kind is to be found after *Nostromo* because post-1904 novels lack "the serene security of Conrad's belief in his ideals."[7] Thus Tillyard claims that *Ulysses,* which I assume Joyce thought of as redefining and rejuvenating the epic for the twentieth century, "cannot be epic" because it fails to "embody some positive faith."[8] Finding Tillyard's rigid emphasis on "traditional traits" of the epic ignorant of the "social changes that more or less deflate them,"[9] Mark Spilka agrees with Ian Watt that Fielding, and all novelists after him, extended "epic scale and variety" to "the unexplored immensity of social, personal and domestic life, which gives the novel epic magnitude and which constitutes . . . its epic impulse."[10]

In seeking to lay epicism upon certain novels written in the third quarter of the century, one would do well to align one's approach with that of Brian Wilkie, who, following the lead of such earlier epic liberals as Voltaire, Schelling, and Fielding, suggests that the "basic law of epic throughout its history has been growth"[11] and that, although the epic tradition may be rooted in the past, "the partial repudiation of earlier epic tradition is itself traditional."[12] Thus he asserts that "no great poet has ever written an epic without radically transforming it or giving it new dimensions, and often that intention is specifically declared."[13] Thus he finds a manifestation of Wordsworth's greatness in the breaking with epic tradition and Southey's mediocrity in the strict regard for the rules of the past. One might also turn to Wilkie's recognition of epic history as organic when confronted by such a claim as M. M. Bakhtin's assertion that the epic and the novel are at opposite poles: the former "an absolutely completed and finished generic form";[14] the latter "the sole genre that continues to develop."[15] For Bakhtin, "epic discourse is infinitely far removed from discourse of a contemporary about a contemporary addressed to contemporaries"[16]—a definition that would certainly exclude *The Divine Comedy, The Prelude,* or *Leaves of Grass* from epicism. In fact, recent archaeologically based Homeric studies have revealed the Trojan epics as mirrors of Greek culture contemporary to their writing just as more recent literary analysis has tended to refute Lukács's claim that the Greek epic hero's definition was grounded in position rather than character. But when Bakhtin suggests that, by the "Trojan epic cycle . . . epic is already being transformed into novel,"[17] he on the one hand establishes linkage between the genres surprisingly supportive of Lukács's claim that the novel is prime descendent of the epic and on the other reveals the reactionary nature of his definition of epicism (pre-Homeric)—an exclusiveness necessary for him to claim that all other genres of literature are exhausted and the novel the only one still in a condition of becoming (film, we assume, not being a literary genre).

Certainly the four novels which I will primarily examine—Doris Lessing's *The Golden Notebook,* Norman Mailer's *Why Are We In Vietnam?,* Thomas Pynchon's *Gravity's Rainbow,* and John Fowles's *Daniel Martin*—are not permeated with the certainties that Tillyard requires in claiming that the epic writer must "cause himself to be trusted in a special and profound way" by exhibiting "masterly control seeming to know everything."[18] (Actually, the second half of *Daniel Martin* reaches toward that control and, once one recognizes the complexity of Lessing's scheme, one might attribute masterly control to *The Golden Notebook.*) But the simultaneous intensity of their interior and exterior impulses constitutes a new condition, a new kind of integrity, for the epic novel. Indeed, Wilkie would recognize that these novels reach back to the English and resultant American romantic epic poem—for example, *The Prelude* or *Leaves of Grass*—where the poet employs himself as representative individual to connect individual and universal worlds. The self-reference that reflects the enduring presence of the artist as subject in the epic has resulted in variations of metafiction in the novel (following Lionel Abel's identification of metatheater).

While I have chosen to avoid the rigid requirements of clarity and self-certitude demanded by Booth and Tillyard of novels, I am also liable to face the fashionable censure that I've avoided the new tools available from postmodern, deconstructive, and "literary" or "contemporary literary" theory (to use coinage by de Man and McHoul and Wills). I tend to side with Abel's suggestion that postmodernist and deconstructive criticism follow the footsteps, with increasingly nihilistic shadowing, of the New Criticism and the work of Northrop Frye in that the New Critics and Frye attempted, respectively, to "judge literary works in literary terms alone" and to not judge them at all.[19] Deconstructionists and postmodernist critics (as distinct from writers of postmodern fiction despite the tendency of deconstructive/postmodernist critics to place literature and criticism on at least equal footing) remove themselves from moral judgment of the work by aligning themselves with two Saussurian precepts: the imperfection and arbitrariness of linguistic signs as a way to describe reality and the collective rather than individual ownership of any given language—especially written—output. Thus, on the one hand, Barthes claims that any given text is a "tissue of quotations drawn from innumerable centres of culture"[20] and that "a text's unity lies not in its origin but in its destination"[21] and Foucault claims that all discourses "are objects of appropriation"[22] while, on the other, de Man claims that literature is an unreliable "source of information about anything but its own language."[23]

Abel's assessment of postmodernist/deconstructive appropriations of the text laments not only the implications of Foucault—that "commentary on a text ought to be more interesting than the text itself"[24]—but the appropriation of literature at the university by other disciplines: "the important thing today in connection with any book is to be able to dominate it with some idea drawn not from literature but from some other discipline."[25] Moreover, critics like Benjamin, Jameson, and Baudrillard deny the individuality of a text by imposing dogmatic stencils upon what Lessing would term the "small, personal voice" of the writer; Abel demonstrates how de Man distorts a passage of Proust in order to present rhetorical dissection.[26] So, too, just as New Criticism is generally accepted as being best applied to certain kinds of writing (lyric poetry, for example), it is not surprising that certain writers demonstrate the death of the author better than others—Foucault has a better time with the passivity of Beckett's fidelities to failure than he would with *Why Are We In Vietnam?* or *Daniel Martin*. Abel also points out that an interpreter of Derrida whose work Derrida has praised as "faithful, rigorous in its readings, explication and commentary" claims that Derrida insists deconstruction "applies only to philosophy" and not to literature.[27]

My position toward deconstruction is close to that of M. H. Abrams's 1976 response to deconstructive attacks on his traditional brand of literary historiography. Abrams responds to the ultimate implications of Derridean deconstruction "that no sign or chain of signs can have a determinate meaning"[28] and J. Hillis Miller's stance that all deconstructive reading, finding the work to be deconstructed itself contains its own unravelling, returns continually to a condition of aporia, by suggesting that the deconstructionist's own deconstructions obey the same shared linguistic convention and assumptions of understanding about the spoken and written word that they seek to deny in the texts they examine. Indeed, like the dogmatic criticism of Jameson, deconstruction is a totalitarian criticism in that it denies the legitimacy of critical approaches other than its own nihilism even as, despite Derridean erasure and Lacanian faux-maths, it relies upon the possibilities of meaning contained in combinations of written and spoken words and symbols.

Denis Donoghue noted in 1986 that not all deconstructionists were really deconstructionists—for example, he claimed that Miller was essentially "a phenomenologist, a critic of consciousness" (I'd call Miller an identifier of negative capabilities) and only an "occasional" deconstructionist while Harold Bloom and Geoffrey Hartman don't practice deconstruction at all.[29] His common sense approach, like that of Abrams, is that the "extreme form of skepticism" shared by de Man and Derrida is "enough to induce an occasionally felt scruple, but not a determination to change one's ways"[30] and, like Abel, he suggests that the deconstructionists distort texts in order to triumph over them by rhetorical analysis.[31] In fact, like the best semiotic criticism (for example, Robert Scholes's later exegeses), the most intelligible deconstruction—I think of Hartman's Freud-driven analysis of "A Slumber Did My Spirit Seal" or de Man's negatively capable speculations on "The Fall of Hyperion"—would work as well with traditionalist critical rather than deconstructive apparatus. Indeed, Miller's fine analysis of the inescapable mystery of things rendered in *Heart of*

Darkness might well be no different from a standard critical reading of *Hamlet* as a work that concludes not as a standard Roman salute to the fallen hero or within the stencil marks of some neat Elizabethan world picture, but with the heart of Hamlet's mysteries unplucked. Certain kinds of writing—Keats's "On First Looking Into Chapman's Homer," Browning's "Memorabilia," most of Melville's work, and most of Mailer's—deal in the unknowability and the impossibility of complete articulation about complex matters, but to examine these matters is not necessarily to raise the deconstructive standard. Miller's reading of *Heart of Darkness*, recognizing that Conrad reflects the folly, the horror of European imperialism, surely invites additional and therefore adeconstructive analysis of the symbol in the tale of Marlow's tale—for example that Marlow, looking upriver as he speaks, is named after a town on the upper Thames and therefore connects the horror of current imperialism with that of speculations of pre-Roman British savagery (and the implied savagery of the Roman conqueror) by which he begins his tale.

The pressure that deconstruction has been under, particularly since revelations of de Man's wartime columns, to separate itself from charges of moral nihilism is revealed as recently as Jeffrey T. Nealon's attempt in *PMLA* to distinguish Derridean implications regarding the possibility of interpretation from those of Culler, de Man, and Miller. Yet Nealon's attempt to explain "Derrida's reluctance to criticize de Man or Culler" in terms of the "siege mentality" surrounding language departments[32] strikes me as lame.

A primary source of bafflement regarding the deconstructionist enterprise is the language that its practitioners present in their analyses of language or of a particular piece of language. Lacan's agreement with de Saussure—that access between signified and signifier "cannot . . . have any meaning"[33]—allows both Lacan and Derrida (to say nothing of their disciples) to use language as they wish. Nealon, defending Derrida, admits that the guru "has had considerable trouble defending or explaining certain words" such as "undecidabilty," "différance," or "text."[34] Even Derrida's definition of deconstruction is an evasive exercise.[35] When the disciple begins to use Derridean terms, the language carries its own implosion:

> For Derrida, undecidability is a condition of possibility for reading; reading's impossibility—the impossibility of totalizing reading, of self-identical reading, of self-identical meaning—allows reading to be set in motion.[36]

Lacan's compounding of Freudian examination of linguistic psychoanalysis allows him to declare "the dictatorship of the signified"[37] and to enter into a teasing, imprecise language that is "the condition of the unconscious."[38] This might make for an acceptable single, provocative, if minor, contribution in psycholinguistic analysis, but the influence that Lacan has had on French psychoanalysis has lead to an across-the-board anarchy in French psychology and beyond. Just so, the Derridean influence on the American academy has lead to a species of academic bun-shaking unanticipated in *The Dunciad.* Here are McHoul and Wills in a fantasy threesome with Pynchon: "the figure of the critic is, these days, one which can be as widely known and publicly celebrated as the poet or novelist."[39] Because they can deny that "authors always spoke language," and claim that "discourse . . . *wrote* them,"[40] they can appropriate Pynchon texts, of course deny the legitimacy of previous approaches to Pynchon (though somehow Kermode, McHale, and Tanner are allowed into the heavenly mansions of "contemporary literary theory") and go on to adopt a pretentious approach of "'bookmatching' . . . a relatively esoteric term used by stringed instrument makers" in hopes of avoiding the "theoretically retarded fashion" of previous Pynchon criticism.[41] In fact the "readings" that McHoul and Wills make of the sections of *Gravity's Rainbow* and other Pynchon works are as pedestrian as *Cliff's Notes* summaries, while their increasing relation of matters from their own lives or imposition of Lacanian mathemes into their appropriation of Pynchon's work go beyond pretention in search of tenure. I prefer the clear, scientific exegeses of Lance Ozier on *Gravity's Rainbow* and Joseph Slade on *Vineland* or the social/ historical hermeneutics of Smith and Tololyan.

Alvin Kernan's claim that "deconstruction has been largely the creation of sophisticated mandarins, but their audience has been in large part a group of marginal young academics"[42] follows Donoghue's decade-earlier comment that deconstruction helps graduate students "feel superior not only to undergraduates but to the authors they are reading."[43] It might be more charitable to suggest that deconstruction and its bedfellows have flourished in reaction to the rigid hierarchies of traditional academia, but, as Michiko Kakutani points out in her recent consideration of the implications of invention in Joe McGinniss's *The Last Brother,* the relativity of interpretation and the questioning of authorial authenticity encouraged by the flowering of deconstruction in America has denied the very possibility of plagiarism and moral accountability.[44] Replying to the implications of recent critical trends—that "anything can be said about anything"—Steiner insists that critical theory "is a politics of taste."[45] Steiner, responding to radical deconstruction's destination at nihilism, insists that the primary text must take precedence over its commentary; that, existentially, a text must be read as if it represents "a real presence of significant being."[46]

While Kernan notes that "structuralism and deconstruction are criticism-oriented theories,"[47] I'd suggest that the best of postmodernist critics maintain reverence for the work itself, but that they are more concerned with the formal system of the work than with the writer's transfer of ideas. For example, McHale's post-free indirect discourse is, as he suggests of his work on postmodernism, in the "category of descriptive poetics."[48] Rather than affirm that Pynchon presents us with the proposition that World War II, like other wars, is a system of markets, "a plot by the great international corporations and cartels," he suggests that in this postmodernist work "no conclusion is possible."[49] At its worst, postmodernist criticism presents an odious political correctness, for example when Catherine Stimpson, in an exercise in name-dropping, affirms *Vanity Fair,* where Roseanne Barr and Martha Graham are treated as equals who "both have interest for us, as active creators and not as passive symbols," as a model postmodern organ.[50] Missing is Steiner's politics of taste.

In this country especially, there has been a continuing dialectic between formalism and art as statement. We see this even in individual artists and critics. For example, Susan Sontag, both artist and critic, sided against interpretation and for style so strongly in the 'sixties that she claimed content itself, even in Riefenstahl's films, can play a purely formal role; but a decade later, after her radicalizing trip to Hanoi, she found Riefenstahl's photographs of the Nuba to be fascistic in their formal beauty. In fact, the application of critical instruments often serves as a bad faith way of expressing sympathy of the moment toward works of art. Thus the narrator of Mann's *Death in Venice,* tending to align himself with the aesthetics of the work's principal character (in fact, the only true, rounded character in the work), Gustave Aschenbach, asserts:

> Men do not know why they award fame to one work of art rather than another. Without being in the faintest connoisseurs, they think to justify the warmth of their commendations by discovering in it a hundred virtues, whereas the real ground of their applause is inexplicable—it is sympathy.[51]

Too often now, the impetus for critical approach goes beyond sympathy for the work supposedly at hand and into a Kinbotean rivalry with, or self-immersion in, text. I plead guilty to a traditional sympathy for what I take to be an author's text and a reasonably traditional approach involving close reading of how the subjects of the text relate to its voices and forms.

David Lodge, before Bahktin, speaks of "a special genre, which begins with *Tristram Shandy,* and which is particularly common in our era." Thus he sees Kingsley Amis's *I Like It Here* as an example of "the kind of novel which is not so much turned outward toward the world as inward upon literary art and upon the artist himself."[52] In fact, self-reference can be traced back to an earlier work such as *Don Quixote,* where the central character anticipates the intoxication by romantic literature of an Emma Bovary or a Robert Cohn and where the nominally omniscient narrator's intrusions separate reader from character's fantasy. The self-reference within narrative vectors of those contemporary novels to be scrutinized may be likened to those novels of Fielding, Smollett, and Sterne where the author's intermittent presence, the text's own awareness of itself—equivalent to the self-awareness of the Restoration and eighteenth-century stage—is both a component of the reach toward rendering interior human patterns and a comic means—at least in the eighteenth century—of achieving what Brecht would call "Verfremdungseffekt": distancing from the cathartic lure of the narrative. Thus the resultant impulse is twofold—both inner and outer. A similar transaction occurs in *Gulliver's Travels* and "A Modest Proposal" where heavy authorial irony competes with the narrator's naivete. Swift's legacy may be seen in what we might term a naturalist ironic school, detectable in certain of Blake's songs, the ant war segment of *Walden,* developing in Crane's sardonic short stories, especially "The Blue Hotel," flourishing in *USA* and Dos Passos's subsequent recycling of that trilogy, and remaining in the dour humor of the Canadian writer, David Adams Richards, and in the dark visions of the filmmaker Frederick Wiseman.

An important stage on the way toward the fissions and fusions of contemporary narrative's inner and outer impulse was the growth of "le style indirect libre" or "der erlebte rede"—"free indirect speech" as Roy Pascal translates it, or "free indirect discourse" as Brian McHale terms it[53]—which lies midway between direct and indirect speech or discourse. Pascal defines this phenomenon of the nineteenth-century novel (noticeable, for example, in the concluding episode of *Germinal*) as a stylistic device based upon the form of simple indirect (reported) speech, i.e. using the tenses and person proper to the latter. It injects into this rather colorless form the vivacity of direct speech, evoking the personal tone, the gesture, and often the idiom of the speaker or the thinker reported.[54]

Thus free indirect speech allows the witness of characters not merely through the established framework of a given narrative perspective, but "within their own worlds of perspective understanding."[55] This dual perspective is one of the achievements of William Kennedy in the elegiac Albany trilogy. When John Hersey, in his extreme censure of *The Executioner's Song,* attacks what he terms the perversity of "Mailer's tag lines—touches of prose . . . buffed to such hummingbird-feather iridescence as almost to hurt the eye,"[56] he fails to grasp that Mailer is reaching back to a nineteenth-century stratagem in order to carry out a twentieth-century fusion of the roles of novelist and journalist and thus render the complex circuits of current American experience.

In *Mansfield Park,* a relatively early example of a novel using free indirect speech, Jane Austen fuses voices and perspectives of narrator and character so that narrator/author could not merely identify with a given character, but could also exhibit a range of attitudes, including "irony, sympathy, or negation, or approval."[57] Such irony occurs when Dickens's narrator speaks to his audience in the same "O my brothers" oratory which Slackbridge, a secondary villain of *Hard Times,* uses to manipulate the workers against Stephen Blackpool. Thus free indirect speech is not merely an intensification of inner direction in the evolution of the novel, but represents an accommodation of both inner and outer impulses. It was and remains one means for the modern novel to achieve narrative multiplicity. Indeed, "le style indirecte libre" has been a major way of entry into that "central tradition of the novel . . . constituted by texts which are not unitary in their discourses . . . but multiple, polyphonic, juxtaposing many modes of discourse."[58] What Hugh Kenner—seeming to claim the discovery of the phenomenon—terms the "Uncle Charles Principle"[59] after the character in *Portrait of the Artist as a Young Man* is that free indirect speech that permeates Joyce's fiction. Pascal notes that both Dostoyevsky and Joyce switch back and forth between "normal indirect form (third-person and past tense) to the first-person and present tense."[60] Going beyond that, Kenner notices in Joyce not only a dialectical process of first-and third-person, present and past, but that the apparently outside narrative itself is divided into different narrative voices. Thus in the "Wandering Rocks" episode the "harsh and awkward being" is the "Second narrator . . . a mutation of the Vivid Narrator we have already met."[61] These narrative presences are accompanied by abrupt shifts in perspective as free indirect speech and direct speech merge, resulting in a fragile narrative purchase. The abrupt narrative shifts in the Nighttown episode also constitute a radicalized version of free indirect speech—a technique echoed in the hallucinogenic sequences in *Under the Volcano* where perspectives of character (Geoffrey Firmin), narrator, and author are fused and where other characters—Yvonne, Hugh—share in the vortex of Geoffrey's condition. While Pascal bemoans the twentieth century's failures to discriminate between narrators' and characters' perspectives, such narrative volatility may be viewed as the direct outgrowth of earlier narrative mergers through free indirect speech.

Free indirect speech and narrative multiplicity tend to break down distinctions between author and character. While the last thirty or so years have seen a distinct literary phenomenon as novelists have broken barriers between themselves and their closely investigated characters to exhibit the interaction between personality and society, narrative experimentation after Joyce did not simply wait to resume until the late 'fifties. Thus the multiple interior selves and interweaving of characters' perspectives in a novel like *Mrs. Dalloway* mark the distance traveled from the free indirect speech of *Mansfield Park*. A version of Woolf's narrative fusions may be found in Elizabeth Bowen's *The Death of the Heart* where simultaneous sixteen-year-old and thirty-five-year-old consciousnesses are displayed. A novel with such an initially apparent omniscient stance as *Lady Chatterley's Lover* ("Ours is essentially a tragic age," etc.) gradually displays a symbiotic relationship between speaker/author and character (Mellors) in the attempt to "scramble over the obstacles" of a ruined post-war civilization. Whereas characters such as the short story writer Clifford Chatterley or the playwright Michaelis (GBS?) are as inadequate as literary saviors as they are as sexual saviors, there is a meshing of the narrator with Mellors so that the "tap, tap, tap" of Mellors's hammer operates upon Connie as the novel's prophetic voice operates upon the reader. Thus some promise is offered by what Booth would have us believe is a "confused and pretentious little author"[62] of a reciprocal personal and social deliverance from the ruins of 1914–18. As Lawrence weds himself to character in the act of a civilization's sexual rescue, so Orwell weds himself to

Winston Smith, the budding author, in an attempt to rescue civilization from the smothering of language.

Whereas fusion of character and author in *Lady Chatterley's Lover* seems an attempt to save civilization from acquisitiveness gone mad, authorial intrusions in Beckett's novels are acts of literary devaluation as pantomime self-reference signals surrender to the void of a failed civilization. Beckett's statement that "until recently art has withstood the pressure of chaotic things"[63] suggests that the continual commentaries which interrupt action or narrative in *Murphy, Malloy, Malone Dies,* and *The Unnameable* are set up to fight a continuing war against the possibility of art as an expression of the creative process. When Molloy announces that "sometimes you would think I was writing for the public,"[64] or Malone cuts short a description with "to hell with the fucking scenery,"[65] or when a description of Murphy trying to get more tea for his money is punctuated with "try it sometime, gentle skimmer,"[66] the expression is "that there is nothing to express."[67] Thus Beckett separates himself from Joyce: "He's tending toward omniscience and omnipotence as an artist. I'm working with impotence, ignorance. I don't think impotence has been exploited in the past."[68] If Dos Passos's *USA* fails, despite its use of free indirect speech and "Camera Eye" sections, to match social scope with deep penetration of personality, Beckett fails to counter pressures inward so that there is nothing to be done on the outside. Thus Beckett's usefulness in the devaluation of the author by Barthes and Foucault.

Successive drafts of *The Sun Also Rises* escape the lyric narrative of the Hem, Hadley, and Duff first draft through incremental addition of a lyric/epic symbolic framework borrowed from *Ulysses* and *The Waste Land.* This allows Hemingway to extricate himself from the novel and to wed the personal—the death of love, as Mark Spilka would say—to the outer (the war and its aftermath). While McHale notes the frequent use of free indirect speech in Dos Passos's *USA* trilogy, which allows fusions of narrative and characters' perspectives, a more complex scheme of fusion is achieved by the interrelationships of various components of the work. The autobiographical "Camera Eye" segments of the trilogy coexist with narrative episodes so that, as Donald Pizer notes, "when we read *USA* we are encountering, somewhat as in a familiar kind of romantic poem ('Out of the Cradle Endlessly Rocking,' for example), both an account of the growth of an artist's imagination and the product of that growth."[69] Indeed, while Dos Passos claimed long after the trilogy was written that the "Camera Eye" functioned to "drain away the subjective" from the narrative episodes, it is clear that experience and emotion of the autobiographical sequences spill into the narrative's personalities. For example, the early existence of Richard Ellsworth Savage, which dictates his later failures of character, parallels early experience in "The Camera Eye." A less compartmentalized method of presenting the individual temper than the "Camera Eye" technique is found in Agee's *Let Us Now Praise Famous Men*. A work close to the contemporary nonfiction or "True Life novel," it offers an initially irritating presumption of Agee to impose his own operating sensibility upon an account of Alabama sharecroppers; but this is mitigated by that sincerity of offering up for inspection the lens through which the subject is to be seen—much as Mailer will allow a ladder of his own personality to be erected in Book I of *Armies of the Night*— so that sincerity supersedes the detached grammar of history.

In *The Last Tycoon*, seemingly unfinished but technically Fitzgerald's most interesting and mature novel, there is a dialectic between an intense narrative mode representative of the seductive aspect of the movies (Nathanael West could only achieve this world through subject matter rather than through style) which the British writer Boxley is just beginning to understand and that initial narrative mode of Cecilia Brady pointing to materialistic Hollywood as symbolic of western decadence. Thus the novel's primary strategy is to infiltrate Cecilia Brady's detached, first-person narrative— Fitzgerald's notebooks suggest that she is "*of* the movies but not *in* them"[70]—with a movie-like third-person intensity describing the intense but evanescent experience of the relationship between the producer Monroe Stahr and Kathleen, that apparition of his dead wife, itself punctured by Cecilia "taking up the narrative in person" or "taking up the story."[71]

Although its global reach is slight, J. P. Donleavy's *The Ginger Man* is a forerunner of the novel that becomes representative of the epic kind a decade later. What begins as an omniscient narrative soon slips into Sebastian Dangerfield's recollective free indirect speech at such length and intensity that essentially two competing narrative modes are present. It is a post-war novel—as the American Dangerfield has drifted over to Trinity College, Dublin after serving in the U.S. Army in Europe—and the narrative represents Dangerfield's difficult self-reckoning which involves ridding himself of an overbearing father's long-distance hold as well as a class-conscious marriage to an Englishwoman. While the "I" narrative tends to be confessional, the outside narrative tends increasingly to become an escape valve from self-accounting. The struggle between third and first-person narrative, with dialogue as median, represents a tentative kind of healing process, although the pain of self-revelation in the Dublin scenes seems to give way, in the concluding scenes amid warm Irish arms in London, to the kind of fantasy enjoyed by William Kennedy's perishing characters in *Ironweed*.

In the body of this book I will examine four novels (two American and two British) that I think best represent the phenomenon I see occurring at a particular stage of the novel—at least as far as the English-speaking exponents of the novel are concerned. (To discuss complementary continental examples would require an enterprise tracing a line from Goethe, touching Dostoyevsky, Proust, Kafka, Gide's *The Counterfeiters*, Sartre's *The Age of Reason* and *The Roads to Freedom*, Broch's *The Sleepwalkers*, to reach the ironic polyphany of Milan Kundera.) Lessing's *The Golden Notebook*, Mailer's *Why Are We In Vietnam?*, Pynchon's *Gravity's Rainbow*, and Fowles' *Daniel Martin* offer examples of the assorted ways by which contemporary novelists have sought epic dimension while simultaneously attempting close personal scrutiny through alignment with primary characters: Lessing renders not merely a particular female sensibility with a depth not achieved before, but the political temper of mid-twentieth-century Britain; Mailer, through a dual narrative of the hunting expedition in Alaska of a group from Dallas, presents an inner and outer texture of an America at war with both itself and a people outside of its domain; Pynchon, presenting a panorama of surrealistic World War II endeavor that looms toward present annihilation, achieves, unlike Beckett, global purchase with simultaneous inside and outside consciousness; Fowles, perhaps the least politically preoccupied of the four novelists, intercuts first- and third-person narrative as an epic stooge in the form of a movie about Kitchener is foil to a scriptwriter's attempt to escape the clutches of Hollywood as symbol, as in *The Last Tycoon*, of a declining West. In the following chapters, I'll examine closely how each novel examines social/global concerns, how they examine contemporary inner existence, how these spheres interact, and how this interaction is manifested in the narrative form of the work. In my conclusion, I'll discuss other contemporaneous novels that exhibit epic reach yet balance outer statement with self-analysis; but the four works to be discussed in separate chapters carry a reciprocity of social and personal inquiry, which I think make them most representative of the contemporary epic novel.

2

Real People:
Character and Author in *The Golden Notebook*

IF *THE GOLDEN NOTEBOOK* IS "POSSIBLY THE MOST AMBITIOUS British novel since *Ulysses*,"[1] it is because, as Irving Howe pointed out in his early review of the novel, Lessing "grasps the connection between Anna Wulf's neurosis and the public disorders of the day. . . . "[2] The division of the novel into six distinct texts, themselves staggered by an unidentified editor to make up twenty-two sequences, reflects not only the fragmentation of Anna Wulf, the principal character and narrator of the work, but the fragmentation, the chaos of the world in which she exists. For Lessing, the highest point of literature was the nineteenth-century novel, "the work of the great realists"; yet that literature is separated from our time by the present "confusion of standards and the uncertainty of values."[3]

Early in "Free Women," the short novel that parallels Anna's notebooks, the painter Basil Ryan has decided to stop his work "because the world is so chaotic art is irrelevant" (42). It is a decision that reflects Anna's own writing block. Her first words—"everything's cracking up"—echo throughout the opening section of "Free Women" and seem to reflect Lessing's own response to when an "epoch of our society, and of Socialism, was breaking up. . . . "[4] Thus she could feel that "the Bomb had gone off inside myself, and in people around me. That's what I mean by cracking up."[5] The bomb inside matches the global threat of atomic annihilation, so that we are a good distance from the "serene security" of the author's view that Tillyard has demanded of the epic.

In the novel which Lessing wrote immediately following *The Golden Notebook*, *The Four-Gated City*, the American literary agent Dorothy Sayers pronounces "that only second rate writers dealt with social conditions, or politics, or concerned themselves in any way at all with public affairs. . . . "[6] Anna Wulf, the author of the notebooks that presumably are refined into "Free Women," finds it impossible to be that "real great artist" who for Miss Sayers "creates truth and beauty from within himself. . . ." That, to Anna, would be "a lying nostalgia" (63). Instead, she must devote a whole notebook, the Red, to her relationship with the political world. And just as her personal life infiltrates the political reportage of that notebook, so political affairs become enmeshed into other, ostensibly more personal, notebooks. In the opening section of the Blue notebook Anna compares the "dedicated" order of her psychiatrist's room with the "crude, unfinished, raw, tentative" (236) quality of her own life. And, unlike her Jungian analyst, she cannot ascribe her own problems merely to archetypal patterns of human development. The contemporary world, she will insist, presents new experience and therefore has new problems.

World affairs cause guilt in Anna the writer because, while she has been "wrestling with my precious soul," it is only chance that she is not one who has been "tortured, murdered, starved to death . . ." (250). As Lessing has put it, "I've a sense of the conflict between my life as a writer and the terrors of our time."[7] The conflict between the individual and his relation to society, is, for Lessing, a relatively new encounter for the shared human consciousness—an outcome of the French Revolution.

Lessing's introduction to the paperback edition of *The Golden Notebook* asserts that a principal motif of the novel, Anna's writing block, is caused by "the disparity between the overwhelming problem of war, famine, poverty, and the individual trying to mirror them" (xii). The texture of the novel is thus made up of the collision of the personal, interior life of the artist/individual with the events outside herself. Anna's dissatisfaction with her psychiatrist is rooted in the latter's emphasis upon the personal achievement of balance without taking into account the disharmonies of the outer world. Indeed, it is the public events of the western world (not merely of England) and of Africa that constitute a major frontal assault upon Anna's sensibilities and upon her relationships with men. Her descent "close to" madness in the penultimate sections of the book coincides with the tumultuous political events of 1956. On the other hand, she must reject the stock socialist stance that art should dismiss the personal in favor of "the real."

To Lessing, the "individual and his relation to society" is "a new idea and we don't know how new it is"[8]—and we may see it as Lessing's primary theme in not merely *The Golden Notebook*, but in *Briefing for a Descent Into Hell, Summer Before the Dark,* and the five-volume *Children of Violence* series. It is a preoccupation that, I think, makes Lessing a representative writer for her age. The Red Notebook sets out to record current events and Anna's reactions to them. The notebook begins as a record of Anna's experiences in the British Communist Party, starting in 1950, seven years before the opening sections of "Free Women" take place, and moves up to and through the death of Stalin in 1953, making up a major component of Lessing's attempt to render "the intellectual and moral climate of . . . Britain," which she has suggested was her aim for the Golden Notebook (x). For Lessing, the attempt to achieve an "ideological feel" of the mid-twentieth century necessitates dealing with Socialism and Marxism, for her possibly "the first attempt, for our time, outside the formal religions, at a world-mind, a world ethic" (xiv). But while Marxism might seem a candidate to replace that secure stance of Christian epic writers such as Dante or Milton, the time is one of Marxist disillusionment following revelations of the Twentieth Congress and the suppression of Hungary—as Anna says, "It's not an easy time to be a Socialist" (21). Indeed, Anna recognizes that, while her friend Molly's ex-husband Richard Portmain and his fellow tycoons, living in terms only of "business reasons" and "business friends" (14), are to be scorned, "their opposite numbers are just as irresponsible" (46).

The second section of the Red Notebook picks up chronologically from the first section, with Anna and Molly worrying about whether news of Sino-American contention over Quemoy means that there will be another "big war" (296). This concern leads the two women to discuss the problems they experience as Communist Party members. Both women are at the point of leaving the Party over the leadership's insincerity in dealing with issues of Stalinist repression—so that Molly has said to Comrade Hal:

> Look, you people have got to understand something pretty soon or you'll have no one left in your party—you've got to learn to tell the truth and stop all this hold-and-cover conspiracy and telling lies about things. (297)

But, despite the set piece that Hal offers as a reply, Molly is soon almost to the point of apologizing for her outburst. If the "ideological 'feel' of our mid-century" is to be "set among Socialists and Marxists," the condition of that "feel" is confusion.[9]

The Golden Notebook deals not only with the impact of large public events on human relationships, but also with the undercur-

rents of personal lives, with such acute perceptions as Anna's off-
hand recognition that, when she and Molly part after their reunion,
"there'll be a sudden resentment . . . because after all our real
loyalties are always to men, and not to women" (48). In the Black
Notebook, the final excursion to Mashopi provides a crucible for
the examination of human sexuality: from Anna's affair with Willi
we learn that "two people can be sexually incompatible who are
perfectly happy in bed with other people" (70); in the Boothby's
daughter, June, Anna recognizes her own youthful prowling "state
of sexual obsession that can be like a sort of trance" (96); and
from Willi's behavior towards Mrs. James of the Gainsborough,
towards Maryrose's mother, and towards Mrs. Boothby, Anna
learns "how many women like to be bullied" (98) and yet how
men are "far less honest" about using their sex for gain than are
women (84).

The second section of the Blue Notebook offers an intense first-
person account of one woman's sensibility. Thus we are given striking images of Anna's feelings as she passes through the day: her
delight as her palm strokes the rough chest of her sleeping lover;
her resentment, after her "nipples begin to burn" with excitement
as Michael tries to entice her back to bed, that she must be the
"practical and efficient" woman he complains of and see him off
to work; her recognition that her resentment is a shared condition
of modern women—"the housewife's disease" (333)—an impersonal state that, when unrecognized for what it is, will be turned
against their men; her sorrow that she must wash away the likeable
smell of sex before going into her daughter's bedroom, a mood
that quickly evaporates into the warm feeling she has for the child.

The Yellow Notebook, containing Anna's novel in progress "The
Shadow of the Third," also offers intense scrutiny of modern sexual ways. For example, in the first section of the notebook Ella's
sexual encounter with her editor reveals an awareness of the complicatedness of lovemaking that we find in few novelists:

> He was having difficulties, and Ella knew this was because she did
> not really want him, and so it was her fault, though he was blaming
> himself. (204)

If the dissection of Richard Portmain in "Free Women," or of Paul
Tanner in "The Shadow of the Third," is crushingly precise, then
sincerity demands like examinations of Anna, or her equivalent,
Ella. Thus the beginning of her affair with Paul triggers for Ella
memories of her sexual repulsion for George, her ex-husband (an

equivalent of Willi Rodde–Max Wulf), which she had attempted to cover by applying the "conventional argument" that the marriage failed because he had, by infidelity, broken the "moral code" (181).

Anna sees her sessions with her psychiatrist, Mrs. Marks, or "Mother Sugar" as Anna and Molly call her, as a process of individuation, the freeing up of individual psychic pain by one's recognition that existence consists of aspects of an archetypal "epic story," so that one may separate oneself from the experience, fitting it "like a mosaic into a very old pattern" (471). But Anna, the new woman as she sees herself through Ella, disagrees with Mrs. Marks's reach for therapeutic universalization because she is "convinced that there are whole areas of me made by the kind of experience women haven't had before" (471). While Mother Sugar may claim that there is "a great line of women who have been artists, have been independent, have insisted on sexual freedom, stretching out behind you into the past" (472), Anna, the thinking artist who wishes to separate that in herself which is archetypal from that which is new, cites the contemporary nightmare of nuclear annihilation in contending that her predecessors "didn't look at themselves . . . feel as I do . . ." (472). Though Anna and Molly may speak only ironically of themselves as free women, Anna insists to her analyst that there is "something new in the world . . ." (472). A session with Mrs. Marks may seem successful if, say, a certain man is recognized as emblematic of some recurring archetype—wolf, knight, monk—yet Anna claims to meet people who are "cracked across . . . split," who, while not "whole," are "keeping themselves open for something" (473), presumably the new currents of the age. Meeting Nelson, one of the split, open American males in *The Golden Notebook,* Anna responds to this kind of man who understands "we are on some kind of frontier" (482). While Mrs. Marks claims that Anna is so aristocratic a writer that she writes only for herself, the artist sees herself as one of thousands all over the world who are writing secretly because they are experiencing new ideas, forms of living, and, as a result, are "afraid of what they are thinking" (475). The failure of the Jungian viewpoint in the face of "what is new" is reflected in what Anna sees as the insufficiency of the conventional novel as a means for the new consciousness to include "all of myself in one book" and it is why a new type of novel is necessary for Anna and for Lessing; a new kind of novel that will approximate that gestalt, which is *The Golden Notebook.* To a novelist who, more than anything, is interested in "how our minds are changing"[10] the center of study for the new novel will be, as it is in the *Children of Violence* series, the relationship between the individual conscience and the collective.

If the final sections of the notebooks, particularly that of the Blue Notebook, point to the fusion of previously distinct characters (for example, of Anna and Saul) then they also see an increase of interactivity between political and personal existence. As Molly talks over the phone to Anna in the conversation that will lead to Saul and Anna meeting, she mentions that an old Party member, Tom, paterfamilias to other members, has left the Party in despair after the Soviet crushing of Hungary. He has gone to work for an advertising company—an ultimate capitulation to an age for which even the conservative Mother Sugar finds slight hope, so that, responding to Anna's suggestion that she imagine tentative blades of grass poking through a million years after an H-bomb explosion, the psychiatrist must acknowledge that perhaps "we will have to rely on those blades of grass springing in a million years" (545) as our means of psychic survival. In a dead or dying society individuals must try not to feel.

Saul, however, takes Anna's stand not to sell film rights for "Frontiers of War" for granted because, he feels, committed individuals must make stands, even when the issues seem bad. But Anna is not so certain that the assumption that "people can be expected to be courageous enough to stand up for their individual thinking" (565) is secure. Unlike Saul, she feels that McCarthyism is already taking place in England. The once outspoken hero is now "sycophantic, lying, cynical," not merely because of physical fear, but, in an uncertain age, of "being thought a traitor" (565). So the public events of the western world make up a frontal assault on the heroic consciousness. Dr. Paynter, some new version in the Blue Notebook of Mrs. Marks, responds to Anna's concern for Saul by saying that he has seen the sickness in others—it is "all due to the times we live in" (574). All Saul, the sick hero, can do to assert his faltering independence is to spit out his name and repeat "I" like a machine gun in an attempt to hold together the fragmented personality.

Lessing's attempt to render the nature of a shared system of belief that is yet in conflict with the demands of the individual conscience brings us close to the condition of the epic novel in the mid-twentieth century. It is a time, for Lessing, when "the most epic movement of change ever known in history is taking place."[11] Yet the work that attempts to glimpse that movement must also know people, must render the individual consciousness; the work that reaches towards a kind of unity must examine the fragmentation of its maker.

In the Black Notebook, the rendition of human personality competes with what Anna Wulf refers to, in connection with leftist doctrine, as the question of morality in art. After writing the first section of the Black Notebook, she disdains her rendition of the Gainsborough group by recognizing that it has been nostalgia that has governed her representation of events in Africa. At Mashopi, sexual matters seem to override the political. Yet the omnipresence of the political—the group at Gainsborough who share the *Fiesta*-like weekend at Mashopi are an active, if frustrated, Marxist sub-cell—suggests the point at which *The Golden Notebook* differs from a work, so similar in its multivalent technique, as *The Alexandria Quartet*. For while technique is similar—both novels, for example, juxtapose and interweave, third-person and first-person narratives—with Lessing sex and politics are interactive, whereas in Durrell's work political or social analysis tends to be submerged, despite the political activities of Nessim, Justine, Pursewarden, and Mountolive (such activities serve essentially as a romantic backdrop of intrigue rather than carrying the weight of authentic political philosophy).

Lessing's intention "to write of the intellectual and moral climate" (x) of Britain in the mid-twentieth century comes close to what she sees as the role of the nineteenth-century novel. What differentiates that age, where the novels of Tolstoy and Stendahl were "a statement of faith in man himself,"[12] from the present age is the insecure and uncertain condition of the world in which we now live. The condition of the present age ("one of the great turning points in history")[13] is reflected by the continued tension between the third-person narrative of "Free Women" (or of the completed, published "Frontiers of War") and the first-person narrative complex of the notebooks. This tension is paralleled in microcosm by the relationship between the omniscient stance of Anna's "The Shadow of the Third" in the Yellow Notebook and the intrusive, devaluative first-person Anna who interacts, fuses with, that stance. The strategy is fragmentation, with a dialectic between global reach and the intimacy of the internal at the root of the novel.

In the last section of the Blue Notebook, Anna recognizes that the experience of post-war Communists is that with any cause fought for and achieved "new tyranny arises" (601). This is an example of tensions within the work that reflect Anna's view of the complexity of existence and as such they are external to the form of the novel. But there are other oppositions which are intrinsic to the structure of the novel. In "Free Women" Tommy is the tragic result of the marriage between Richard Portmain and Molly and becomes a blinded, zombie-like character; but in the Blue Notebook he is a disappointingly conventional young Socialist, married to a "sensible little wife," and, in short, is what Molly sees as a representative of the "improbable farce" that is the temper of the time (599). There are, then, apparently deliberate contradictions in the work that detach the reader from the fable.

Mark Spilka has pointed out the similarities between the opening of Lawrence's *Women in Love* and of *The Golden Notebook*.[14] The discussion between Anna and Molly in that opening section of "Free Women" touches upon subjects of men and marriage close to the pioneering conversation of Lawrence's two heroines. Yet the sense of achievement carried by a title like "Free Women," while it may reflect new attitudes towards the condition of women, while it may reflect Anna's point of disagreement with Mother Sugar's claim that her patient's experiences are part of an archetypal pattern instead of being on the edge of the new, is undercut a good deal by events and relationships in the novel as a whole. In "The Shadow of the Third," for example, the alter egos of Anna and Molly, Ella and Julia, sardonically discuss their condition of being "free women" in what Julia terms a "sexual madhouse" (458). Being free hardly works if men themselves are not free, if they still see women in terms of "good women and bad women" (458). "Free" is hardly an appropriate term if men can "get erections with women they don't give a damn about, but we don't have an orgasm unless we love him" (458).

Another term, central to Lessing's pre-Canoptic writing is even more diced with than "free." In the Blue Notebook, "real" life, for the moment used in comparison with the nostalgia of "Frontiers of War," reveals paradox as Jimmy, in fear, survives his war missions, while Paul, unafraid and safe because his connections have enabled him to obtain transfer to India, is killed by accident after the social disaster at Mashopi. Other characters in the Black Notebook reveal complexity. For example, George Hounslow and Willi Rodde are found to have natures that undercut their surface roles—of sensualist and theorist. George is aware of his own "general inadequacy and also of his ugliness," while Willi, of whom George is in awe, is unaware that his assumed role of cell theoretician comingles with his possessive, emotional nature. To render Willi is, for Anna, to admit that no label will fit him. In fact, the Black Notebook seems to suggest the conflict between social theory and "knowing someone." What Anna senses is that the true novel, as opposed to, say, visual recollections, deals with the complexities of things, even if she must use words as inadequate as "nice" and "good" to render personalities.

There is a striking difference between the subjectivity and tentativeness with which the Black Notebook begins and the crisp opening of the Red Notebook which begins "without any hesitation at all . . ." (153). Yet that crisp style is quickly undercut with the infiltration of the objective/political by the personal. The Marxist life is informed with paradox and hypocrisy—from such a slight detail as a Party couple being ambitious for their children to the central fact that the Party is controlled by dead bureaucrats so that any real work is done in spite of them. Michael, the exile, learning that three friends have been hanged in Prague, cannot believe that they were traitors, yet can neither believe that the Party could frame and hang them. He must talk himself away from reason. Anna, too, is touched by the paradoxes of Party life. She notices that everything she writes about the Party is negative, yet she still belongs. She attacks the Party in discussion with members, yet defends it in the company of outsiders with the stock phrases that irritate her when used by other Party members. She also realizes that her only frank discussions about politics are with ex-Party members whose idealism, like hers, is tinged with cynicism. Both Molly and Anna have paradoxical reactions to the death of Stalin. Though they are aware of his tyranny, like Michael they recognize that he has embodied their yearning for a great, beneficent man.

Yet coupled with the pervasive cynicism of the Party machine is a type of individual idealism, which Anna recognizes as a positive force. Compared with the literary set, for example, the Party seems like a worthwhile cause, and, when she sees Molly leaving for that "atmosphere of friendliness, of people working for a common cause" (154) present in Party meetings, she recognizes that same cultural resonance that she had observed as the primary function of the Socialist movement in Africa. She realizes, as the first section of the notebook concludes, that most Party members are not particularly political, that they join either through loneliness or "through a powerful sense of service" (169), there being an intrinsic paradox about the membership of such a political party. That "sense of service" echoes her recollection of Koestler's claim that, in the West, people remained in the Party "on the basis of a private myth" (160). She sees her own myth as the hope that there will be a turn back to "real socialism" (160) in Russia. Both Koestler and Anna's reasons for Party membership suggest an ironical

intermingling of social philosophy and inner personality among
Marxist ranks. As possibly "the first attempt, outside the formal
religions, at a world ethic" (xiv), Marxism, after the revelations of
Stalinist oppression, exists as a type of mythical embodiment for
all the dreamers of an ideal world—the type of dreamers like the
young Martha Quest in the first of Lessing's *Children of Violence*
series who imagines a Utopian city as she peers into the African
landscape. Thus, while Anna is willing to admit that Stalin may be
a mad murderer, she still likes to hear "a tone of simple, friendly
respect for him" (302), for to hear the opposite a dream would be
dead, at least for the present generation. That dream of perfection,
for the Marxist mind so often represented by the image of a benign
Stalin, is at its most ridiculous and pathetic in the short story of
Comrade Ted that Anna reads to her study group. This representative story, so crudely written that it switches unconsciously back
and forth between first-person and third-person as Comrade Ted
chats with and gives advice to the great dictator, reflects, as every-
one in the study group is forced to agree, the fantasy of Socialism.
This produces a mutual recognition of hostility in the group. Parallel to Comrade Ted's story is the dream Anna has of a soft, living,
embroidered mythical fabric which gives off a red glow representing the Soviet bloc. As the dream progresses Anna, off in space,
watches the red glow merge with other color blocks, representing
other parts of the world, to yield an "indescribably beautiful" synthesis of happiness that swells up and explodes (299). The dream
seems to move from the political to the physical, from the public
to the personal. While Comrade Ted switches from third-person as
his fantasy peaks, Anna moves from past to present tense as she
recalls her dream intensifying into a personally felt ecstasy. As she
ponders her dream, Anna realizes that "I don't care a damn about
politics or philosophy or anything else, all I care about is that
Michael should turn in the dark and put his face against my
breasts" (299). For Anna, now, more seems due the individual than
is due the collective, and it is as she lies with Michael that she is
able to say "I am Anna Wulf, this is me, Anna, and I'm happy"
(299).

The Red Notebook may be an attempt at recording Anna's political life, but it is infiltrated by personal consideration. Just so, Anna
may intend to write strictly of her personal life in the Blue Notebook, but public matters filter through. In the second section of
that book the tensions that Anna experiences with Michael are
paralleled by the simultaneous tensions that she experiences in her
public affairs, especially in her dealings with the British Commu-

nist Party. As in the Red Notebook, Anna works for a Party publishing house that reflects a dialectic between fresh young idealists and the fossilized, hypocritical bureaucrats who have control of the Party. The fossils are represented by John Butte, himself of upper-middle-class background, who, though once a fine, rebellious young novelist, is now dead and dry, beaten down by the Party apparatus, and must use Anna as a symbol of his own youthful self, which he must defeat. A crisis is reached during a discussion of the merits of a bad, lifeless book that, however, conforms to current Party myth. Anna realizes that the discussion over whether *For Peace and Happiness* should be published is a charade, that Butte has already made his decision, and she attacks his methods as "a crystallization of the intellectual rottenness of the Party" (348)—the betrayal of the ideals of nineteenth-century humanism. Neither can Anna accept the rationale of Jack—the nominal head of the publishing house, a "good Communist" because, like a character from an old morality play, he has driven out the "false pride" that would lead him to resent his lack of independence under Butte—that Communism must be seen as a process over centuries rather than in terms of final "intellectual collapse" (342). But while Anna's spirit is crushed by Party hypocrisy, deadness, she also recognizes that nowhere outside the Party does she find "certain types of intellectual" who reflect that "high seriousness which existed in international communism years ago . . ." (343). And it is the tragic condition of the Communist intellectual that such a poetic spirit "was killed by the desperate, crazed struggle for survival which we now give the name Stalinism" (343). Jack is able to accept the resultant fragmentation of the personality as a necessary condition in a complex scientific age, but Anna, the humanist, in her personal quest for wholeness, cannot accept this split, feels betrayed by Jack because "humanism stands for the whole person, the whole individual striving to become as conscious as possible about everything in the universe" (360).

While Anna insists to Comrade Jack that their arguments revolve around the integrity of "the individual conscience, the individual sensibility" (350), his response is to question whether the individual conscience can produce that "joyful communal unselfish art" (350) to which the committed Socialist writer aspires. As part of her Party work Anna gives lectures to small groups in which she compares the "group consciousness" of the communal art of the Middle Ages (in line, with Benjamin's storyteller or Foucault's nostalgia for the communal, impersonal authorship of old) with the "driving egotism" of art in the "bourgeois era" where art is but a "shriek of torment" (349). Thus, she lectures, art must return to social responsibility and to brotherhood. But the stammer that she develops during her lectures reflects her own fragmentation between the reach towards a personal art and that towards "commitment." Those poles are mirrored at the one end by dead, hypocritically accepted novels such as *For Peace and Happiness*—Jack agrees that it is merely "communist cloud-cuckoo spit" (346)—and at the other by the internal "psychological impulse" that was the impetus for Anna's own "Frontiers of War" of which she is now ashamed. Though she has come to believe that "flashes of genuine art are all out of deep, suddenly stark, undisguisable private emotion" (349), Anna's writing block stems from her rejection of her own "unhealthy" art while at the same time she is unable to accept the "banality . . . of impersonality" (349), which is the stamp of "healthy" art. The interior "The Shadow of the Third" in the Yellow Notebook contains the same dilemma for Anna's alter ego that we find in the Blue Notebook. The story of a young man's path to suicide seems so much a part of Ella that it is as though it had "already been written somewhere inside herself" (174). Yet she is ashamed of her work because, as with Anna, she recognizes that, in terms of the Socialist stance towards art, its subjectivism is indulgence.

2

The acute perceptions of the details of the days of our lives that we find in "Free Women" come in stark contrast to the deadpan chapter headings of the short novel. The heading of the second section of the novel ("Two visits, some telephone calls and a tragedy") or of the fourth section, which announces that "Anna does not feel herself," are ironic understatements for the vertiginous states, the highly charged renditions of human sensibility, which follow in the narrative of those sections. The ironic relationship between chapter heading or subheading and the dense texture of what follows is not new to the novel. But I suspect that there is another source, outside the history of the novel, though certainly influenced by it, for Lessing's application of this dialectical tactic. Willi Rodde, Anna's lover in the Mashopi sequences of the Black Notebook (she will admit in the Blue Notebook that Willi is really Max Wulf, her "real" first husband), whistles from *The Threepenny Opera* and casually wonders what happened to "a man named Brecht . . . he was very good once" (113). One may make a case for Lessing's comparatively early familiarity with Brechtian strategies: "Free Women" takes place in 1957, a year after the Berliner Ensemble presented the two-weeks-dead playwright's works to a London audience and Brecht's theories of dramaturgy quickly influenced such British playwrights as John Osborne, John Arden, and Lessing herself.

In her interview with Florence Howe, Lessing suggests that what interested her in *The Golden Notebook,* what still interests her, are "the ideas." Thus she sees the work as much more detached than did the critics who either attacked or praised what they saw as its intense contemporary female vision. When Lessing says that "you have to be a little apart . . . from an idea before you can see it"[15] she comes near to a technique that Brecht had used to foster "that great epic theatre which corresponds to the sociological situation" and that would radically transform the theater so that it would "correspond to the whole radical transformation of the mentality of our time."[16] Just as Plato preferred epic poetry because it was less able to distort the real than did tragic drama, so Brecht believed that responsible social drama must avoid the Aristotelian premise that the audience should be made to believe that what they are witnessing is happening here and now. Whereas the popular illusionistic theater invited the audience's absorption into character and into a plot that headed towards emotional fulfillment, Brecht's epic theatre demanded a performance "presented quite coldly, classically and objectively." The primary method of achieving such detachment was the Verfremdungseffekt—the distancing of the audience from the events on stage. To accomplish this distancing, illusionistic theater techniques were undercut—flaps, backdrops, wires, and lights were openly revealed rather than disguised. Banners were hoisted across stage revealing what was to come so that the audience would be freed "from the distraction of suspense."[17] Songs often contributed to the destabilizing of the play's rhythm, with the expression of the music working at cross-purposes with the meaning of the words. Whereas Stanislavskian technique attempted to immerse the actor into the personality of his character, Brecht applauded such performers as Charles Laughton, Peter Lorre, and Helene Weigel for their ability to withhold themselves from the characters they portrayed and thus avoid playing to the audience's hearts. Thus Brecht aimed to foster a theatre of ideas rather than a theatre of dreams.

So, in *The Golden Notebook* the tensions between chapter headings and actual narrative situation, the opposition between inside and outside narrative stance with "Free Women" and the notebooks, and the complex prismatic structure formed by the staggered sequence and interpenetrations of the novel's six primary components (the five sections of "Free Women," the four sections each of the Black, Red, and Yellow, and Blue Notebooks, plus the penultimate sequence which is the inner Golden Notebook) achieve a distancing that closely follows Brecht's struggle to have the theatre appeal "less to the feelings than to reason."[18] The distancing also keeps Lessing's own self at a kind of arm's length from her story until the final inner Golden Notebook when the inner sensibility of the artist fully comes into play, when she is with her characters.

In the final section of the Blue Notebook Anna tries but fails to summon the image of the African patriot Tom Mathlong. She has failed to summon him, she decides, because of his quality of ironic detachment, "something we needed badly at the time," and which is something "certainly a long way from me" (597). But, in fact, that ironic detachment has been Lessing's, if not Anna's, primary technique in the early stages of the novel. It has been a kind of Brechtian alienation that has held off the dissolving of flat characters into each other, and it is a technique which gives way, in the inner Golden Notebook, to a breakdown of divisions, just as there is a dissolving into a character integration from early flat characters in *Briefing for a Descent Into Hell* where an initially integrated sensibility moves away into detached and tragic fragmentation. It is perhaps useful to keep in mind that Brecht was finally to modify his idea of "Epic Theater" in favor of the more flexible, complex "dialectical" theater, which could contain the possibility of "the unexpectedness of logically progressive or zigzag development, the instability of every circumstance, the joke of contradiction. . . ."[19] Lessing's own system of dialectics in *The Golden Notebook* doesn't serve merely to keep us a little apart from an idea so that we may see it; it is, too, a way of rendering the complexities and insecurities of the modern age which prevent the contemporary novelist from enjoying that "faith in man himself" which the nineteenth-century novelist could afford to make.

For Anna, Mother Sugar's remark that the "artist writes out of an incapacity to live" (62) is one more nauseating attempt at compartmentalization; it is a remark that Anna feels her psychiatrist would be ashamed to make anywhere but in the consulting room. The Jungian approach to existence, with its emphasis on recurring patterns, itself seems to simplify matters by neglecting "what is new" (473). Just so, characters in the book are not merely simplified and labeled (Anna, we assume, does this to life in "Free Women"—compare, for example, the characters in the Golden book with characters in the last section of the omniscient novel within *The Golden Notebook*), but tend to simplify, flatten each other and perhaps themselves. The catastrophic events at Mashopi are directly caused by Mrs. Boothby's inability to understand herself or the manners of members of the group and by the group's inability to see the complexities of Mrs. Boothby or of themselves. The hostess, for instance, dismisses her black servant Jackson for what she mistakenly interprets as an affair with Jimmy, whom she cannot accept because he is not a "real man." Mrs. Boothby is unable to accept the behavior of Jimmy, Paul, or George because the assumptions of her culture are different from those of England. At the same time Anna, as she writes the Black Notebook, realizes that the Mrs. Boothby, whom she saw as an "aborigine," and whom she has so depicted in "Frontiers of War," was in reality—bewildered by her daughter, neglected by her drinking husband—a "lonely pathetic figure" (141–42). Thus throughout the novel, Anna the artist and social being becomes concerned with finding, rendering the "real," with presenting character and circumstance as they are and not through the filter of nostalgic sensibility. Indeed, the journey towards the inner Golden Notebook is a movement towards the real thing.

The Black Notebook presents a variety of sexuality, from the homosexuality of the Oxford group and Maryrose's incest to George Hounslow's miscegenous adultery. To Mark Spilka, *The Golden Notebook* "speaks freely and positively of 'real men' and 'real women'"; and, for Spilka, Lessing's "most obvious example of a 'real man' is George Hounslow in the African notebook."[20] Certainly Anna's initial presentation of Hounslow makes a strong case for his candidacy to "real manhood." He is "a real sensualist, not a man who played the role of one, as many do" (124). And he needs women, unlike the typical "affectionate, non-sexual men of our civilization" (124). His quandary seems to be his very sexuality, which is out of place in a sexually lukewarm society:

> When George looked at a woman he was imagining her as she would be when he had fucked her into insensibility. And he was afraid it would show in his eyes. (124)

The black notebook is an attempt to come closer to the real thing, to be less fictive, than the rendition of Anna's experience in *Frontiers of War*. Why, asks Anna of that work, "a story at all. . . . Why not simply, the truth?" (63). But truth is not necessarily simple. The new revelations found in the notebook—supposedly to counter the impetus of yearning for freedom and license behind "Frontiers of War"—are, we find as the first section is closed, themselves couched in fiction. Anna's situating herself in Africa as the tobacco farmer Stevens's wife is not, we will find, true; Willi, whose complicatedness Anna is at pains to delineate, is not real—he is a version of the "real" husband, Max Wulf. As she writes the notebook, Anna realizes that at the time of the book's action she was living in a "subjective highly-colored mist" (137) so that this new version of things is an attempt to achieve objectivity. Yet some time after the report of Mashopi is finished, Anna, in retrospect, must admit that even this new attempt at truth is "full of nostalgia, every word loaded with it, although at the time I wrote it I thought I was being 'objective'" (153). Thus events and characters in the notebooks must be warily accepted as "real" as successive passages achieve new versions of truth and new versions of self-parody.

In later sections of the novel the term "real" is devalued. In the Blue book, the world from which the "unhealthy" novelist, Anna, must separate herself—the banal, fossilized, hypocritical world that the new Communist Party now represents—has no difficulty in pronouncing what is "real." Rose Latimer, the narrow-minded publishing house secretary, sees the "British Worker" and Party officials alike as "marvelous real people" (357). Likewise, in "Free Women," Anna's conventional daughter, Janet, whom Anna hopes will grow up to recognize one of the "few real men left" (404) when she meets one, reacts to Anna's short-lived decision that her homosexual tenants Ivor and Ronnie must leave by demanding to go to "a real school" (409)—a boarding school like that in the story which Ivor has read to her with an intermittently sarcastic, cynical exaggeration. We see notions of the "real" undercut in other Lessing works: in "The Eye of God in Paradise," where two friends naively set out to visit "the real Germany—rather old-fashioned, a bit sentimental, warm, simple, kindly";[21] in *The Summer Before the Dark* where Kate Brown's life of being "really married to a real husband"[22] is ploughed under by a psychic excursion that forms a deeper kind of existence; in a recent Lessing collection carrying a title short story—"The Real Thing" after James—where a received way of life is undercut by an outsider.

Much of the Blue Notebook, the diary entries certainly, deals with Anna's sessions with her psychoanalyst. Anna will claim that it is her fears of universal death and destruction that have caused her to seek out Mrs. Marks and, though she announces that she will never write another novel, Anna also tells her analyst that she is "not here because I am suffering from writer's block" (232). Yet the randomness, the lack of feeling, that she experiences is closely connected to the anti-artistic stance which she projects. Anna's dreams—for instance, that she is a concert pianist who cannot play a note—connect her lack of belief in art with lack of feeling. Art, in her dreams, is "false art, caricature, illustration, parody" (235). She is as suspicious of her art as she is of her dreams which offer a more satisfactory experience than real, waking life. She must disdain her African novel "Frontiers of War" and the reworking of that novel in the Black Notebook because both were written out of "nostalgic pain" (239). Thus "the root of that book was poisoned" (239). The very wish to be an artist seems to be emblematic of a discontent with real situations not recognizable a hundred years ago when people were content with the stations "which it had pleased God to call them to" (236).

Even the depiction of George Hounslow, to which Mark Spilka attaches his standard for the real, seems to be tinged with overly romantic passages. Anna is attracted to his sexuality—"I fled inwardly, but inevitably turned towards" (128)—yet to read that Hounslow's "black eyelashes made tiny rainbows as they trembled on his brown cheek" (133) is to wonder whether this is an exact recollection or whether it is Anna's current sensibility in operation. The initial presentation of Hounslow is undercut by the excessively sentimental postures that he displays as events progress. George's reaction to Willi's undermining of his dilemma as father of a half-caste—"Now he stared off into the sunlight, blinking away tears and then he said: 'I'm going to get my glass filled'" (131)—his "No, my bye-blow is not present" (133), or his remark, as he sees Jackson—"the father of my child" (142)—verge on sentimentality. His fantasy of a future reconciliation with his probable son comes across as forced, as much away from the real as Anna's early parodic synopsis of "Frontiers of War." His last scenes—such as "and George kept leaving us to pay visits to his caravan" (146), or, when, as he is finally confronted by Jackson, he stammers "like an idiot talking" (148) and stumbles from the kitchen—are a falling away from the character we first meet. It is Willi, the whistler of Brecht, who (though he cannot recognize that his claimed objectivity is itself infiltrated by emotions) most distances us from a character such as George and tends to undercut his romanticism when, for example, he suggests that the "tragedy of George" is not Jackson's wife Marie and the predicament that she and her child are in, "but George" (148). At one point, Anna claims that "Frontiers of War," written under "intoxification" after she had seen the caravan containing George and Marie, and the current notebook "have nothing at all in common" (182), but the language that fills the Black Notebook and the later recognition that nostalgia governs her writing, suggest that the intoxification persists.

We see throughout the notebooks a game in which the "real" identities of characters are revealed only for new and more "real" identities to expose them as fiction. For instance, Peter Carey in "Frontiers of War" is really Paul Blackenhurst plus a touch of George Hounslow. But for *The Golden Notebook* this game is not simply something which writers play, as Anna claims, with themselves. It is part of a distancing strategy that operates for Lessing in a way similar to Brecht's alienation methods for attaining an epic theatre. It affords Lessing, I think, a way of examining the relationship between experience and fiction and it offers a way for her to move from the fragmented to the integrated personality, a way for Lessing herself to participate in the true experience of the inner Golden Notebook, when Anna, Ella, Molly, Saul, indeed all the faces from the four notebooks and "Free Women," become the one voice of an inner universal experience.

So, in the Black Notebook we are quickly distanced from intensities of the Mashopi experience. Thus the romanticism of Paul and Anna is undercut by Anna's discovery of the drunken Latimer attacking his wife and by Willi's confrontation with Anna when she returns from her night out. Our last vision of the sexual prototype George Hounslow is of someone who seems "old and sad and unfinished . . . joking to save his life" (151), a description that less shows how the world birches swingers than operates to diminish Anna's initial elevation of him. As much as the parodic synopsis of "Frontiers of War," what follows in the Black notebook reveals the inadequacies of the conventional novel's reach for the texture of experience.

Though it would be myopic to deny that the sincerity of felt, authentic experience permeates the early Black Notebook, one must also accept Lessing's testament that one "could put names to" the notebooks' characters "like those in the old Morality Plays" (viii). Thus George Hounslow might be as much a filtered aspect of personality as is Richard Portmain, the masculine stooge of "Free Women." If we are to find a right "real man," we might find him in the increasingly complex characters of Paul Tanner from the omniscient "The Shadow of the Third" in the Yellow Notebook, Michael from the Blue and Red Notebooks, and Saul Green in the Blue and inner Golden Notebooks—where Saul and Anna merge into one dense personality, operating at one with their author's own consciousness.

Paul is by far the most complex male character in the early stages of *The Golden Notebook,* certainly more "real," in the sense that he has more faces, than Richard or that first blueprint of a "real" man, George Hounslow of the nostalgia-ridden Black Notebook. He is a forerunner of the Americans Saul, in the Golden Notebook, and Milt, in the final pages of "Free Women." Ella senses a duality when, as they are first making love, she opens her eyes to see Paul's "hard, almost ugly look" (193); yet simultaneously she can find love and warmth in the touch of his hand, the tone of his voice. Later in their affair, she may recognize that Paul is telling her that there must be strict limits in their relationship, so that she feels "completely rejected," but at the same time she senses that he's "full of love for her" (200). Thus Paul's "shadow" is that of a "self-hating rake, free, casual, heartless" (207)—he is a prototype for Jack, whose wretched childhood turns him into a hating exploiter of women in *The Four-Gated City.* The Anna-Janet-Michael module of the Blue Notebook is a supposedly more real (less fictional) version of the Yellow Notebook's Ella-Michael-Paul construct. But what is real and what is not real is always open to question in a notebook that paradoxically contains real newspaper headlines. Anna's psychiatrist, Mrs. Marks, says that Anna is a "real woman" (237), yet both Anna and Mrs. Marks herself must laugh at this term.

Saul Green of the Blue and inner Golden is a "psychological chameleon" (539), like the man in the eighteenth story projection of the Yellow Notebook whose mistress must change to meet each emerging personality. Indeed, his sickness is such that he doesn't, at times, realize that it is Anna who is with him. He will use a southern accent thinking he's with a different woman than Anna, and, shocked out of that role, switch to "a rake's voice" (582). He will be the two men—one defending his male liberty, the other pleading the irrelevance of this promiscuity—then become a tender, protective third to whom a "third" Anna responds, and he will seem to her to be five or six different people in any one conversation. He will move up and down to different levels of maturity and must fight against this sickness by continually asserting that he is Saul Green ("I, I, I, I, I,—I") until he is a creature at the limits of himself as his energies are "absorbed in simply holding himself together" (590).

Given the multiplicity of Saul's personality it is understandable that Anna has trouble deciding who is Saul and who is not Saul.

After they first make love she notes that she had forgotten the experience of making love to "a real man" (651). But Saul is less free and positive an example of "real manhood" than George Hounslow, the real man of the initial section of the Black Notebook. As Anna reads Saul's callous journal entries, she has trouble reconciling the man she knew with the diarist who is "totally self-pitying, cold, calculating, emotionless" (571). She is forced to conclude, uneasily, that she herself has had difficulty recognizing the Anna Wulf of her own notebooks. Anna tenuously decides that it is the Saul "who thought, judged, communicated, heard what I said, accepted responsibility" (591)—in short, perhaps the Saul who, he claims, is a product of Anna's Hollywood fantasy of domesticity—"who is the real man" (591) and that the abusive Saul is "not 'him' talking" (592). This decision remains a product of Anna's continuing romantic bent.

As Anna becomes increasingly involved with Saul, so does her personality become increasingly multifarious: thus as Saul's third self shows through, friendly and affectionate, so a third "obedient" Anna responds to that self. And Anna the self-chronicler is acutely aware of the disparity between her intelligent self and the "female creature" who makes, as Saul says, "molasses happiness" (564) out of their "set up"—the creature of longing who is jealous, who sulks and wants to hurt back, who is more frightened at the thought of "not being a good lay" (573) than at not being liked. Indeed, the conviction which was manifested through Ella in "The Shadow of the Third"—that a man's sincerity in making love will determine female response—is undermined. The swirled, caught up Anna longs "to be free of my own ordering, commenting memory" (585), and, recognizing Saul's sickness, the newly complex Anna hovers between jealousy, malice, pity, and protectiveness for her mirror man-figure. If Saul is a more complex version of Paul, then Anna is a new, complicated, more real version of the Anna-Ella of the Yellow Notebook.

If the inner Golden Notebook is the novel's place of decompartmentalization, then one would assume that Saul Green, the sum of all other men, is more a "real" man than George Hounslow in the novel's hierarchies, that Saul contains George's masculinity, his nostalgic sexual immaturity, just as he contains the sexist power of "Free Women's" Richard Portmain and the ambivalence of Paul Tanner whose "real" equivalent is Michael. Saul claims that, thinking he'd be dead by thirty, he has never thought in terms of becoming mature. He attacks his former American friends who have sold out, have informed because of "the wife and kids" (624). He complains that "some kind of guts have gone out of people" (624) and senses that his crack-up is the burden of the effort to hold on to some integrity. To Anna, though, Saul's condition is not quite so simple. She assumes that he will fight his way through the present insanity to become "a very gentle, wise, kind man" who will help people to know they're "crazy in a good cause" (626). It is the state of maturity ("Real people, the phrase is, radiating serenity") reached, Anna claims, only after "a history of emotional crime." "Real people" leave behind "sad bleeding corpses that litter the road to maturity" (626).

At one level of the narrative Saul is a product of Anna's wish, after the initial parody of "Frontiers of War" in the Black Notebook and throughout the attempts at rendering the truth about her day to day existence in the Blue Notebook, to achieve realism. In other words Saul Green is "real" only in the sense that he is a satisfactory product of the efforts of a writer who wishes to render reality. Though Anna renders Saul Green in her own first-person, her achievement of Saul-Anna, her coupling with the new-world figure, represents, in its reach towards wholeness, a kind of omniscience for her, while for Lessing, the propagation of Anna-Saul represents an achieved fusion of her own sensibility with her tale of the tribe.

3

As the short novel "Free Women" begins with Anna saying that "everything's cracking up," so the Black Notebook begins with "broken scribblings and half sentences" and the idea of fragmentation permeates this section dealing with the Gainsborough Hotel group, which has itself been formed by the "self-dividing principle" (67) of a larger Communist "party" and is finally fragmented on the culminating catastrophic weekend at Mashopi. Early in the notebook, Anna differentiates between the old novel that was used by, say, Thomas Mann to make philosophical statements about life and the new journalistic novel that is used to provide information about aspects of society outside the reader's domain of experience. Thus the "novel-report" has become "a function of the fragmented society, the fragmented consciousness" (61)—its very reason for being suggests that humans have become "more and more divided, and more subdivided in themselves" and that the novel is a desperate reaching out toward "wholeness" (61). Mark Spilka sees this passage as Lessing's "unwittingly striking epic notes."[23] I think that he is premature, at this point in the novel, to equate Lessing with Anna. But I think he also fails to recognize Anna's wish to

escape from the new kind of novel, which reflects both society's
and her own fragmentation, and to write the novel which she is
currently incapable of writing because of her own diffusion. Such
a novel would be "powered with an intellectual or moral passion
strong enough to create order, to create a new way of looking at
life" (61). But that new vision will require the rendering of current
fragmentation through the four initial notebooks.

As she walks to the Wests' party, Ella of "The Shadow of the
Third" connects the depressing streets and houses with the letter
in her handbag from the lonely neurotic woman whom Dr. West
refuses to help. If London is a social contrary to the ideal world
of Ella/Anna, her relationship with Paul/Michael represents a contrary to the protagonist's ideals of sexual relationships. It is Paul
who suggests, as their relationship disintegrates, that Ella is an
absolutist who measures "everything against some kind of ideal
that exists in your head" (222). That yearning after alternatives to
the current situation, a variant of the nostalgia that informs the
first section of the Black Notebook, is apparent early in the book
when Ella, on her first drive out with Paul, wants to escape from
the sterile English villages to "where there isn't anything at all."
Her desire for a more authentic present than that available in a
land where houses and homes seem "all in fragments, not one of
them a whole, reflecting a whole life, a whole human being; or, for
that matter, a whole family" (222) is of a piece with Anna's own
reach for the wholeness that will allow her to write the kind of
grand philosophical work that she wishes to write. Each successive
segment of the notebooks seems to be an attempt to begin a new
novel, to encompass more of the real truth of things; and, especially early in the notebooks, each attempt in the quest towards
completion is subjected to a continual undercutting of art and the
artist by the distrust of the writer in her own endeavors towards
simplicity.

Anna's exterior "The Shadow of the Third" is an attempt to
externalize her own pain at the loss of her lover Michael. The
notebook looks "like the manuscript of a novel"—it has a title,
begins "like a novel" and has a detached omniscient perspective.
Yet while it may seem a more overt work of fiction than the previous notebooks, it has a type of authenticity that they lack. Anna
recognizes that while the "form" of the early Black Notebook is
nostalgia, the "form" of "The Shadow of the Third" is pain. But
though "The Shadow of the Third" may be a more satisfactory
version of the truth for Anna than her African notebook, it is still
a frustration of what she knows as real life. The novel is at best

real life recollected, so that the trouble with "The Shadow of the Third" is that "as soon as one has lived through something, it falls into a pattern" (227). Thus Anna's story of Ella and Paul fails to adequately reflect the more real story of Anna and Michael because it is rendered in terms of a recognized end that distorts actual experience. Anna's attitude towards her unfinished novel thus parallels Lessing's attitude towards "Free Women," a reflection of the "dissatisfaction of the writer" with the conventional novel (xiii–xiv). Anna recognizes that no matter how she plans her work she would "still be instinctively isolating and emphasizing the factors that destroyed the affair" (228).

Anna follows the first section of the Black Notebook and begins the Blue Notebook by wondering why she must turn everything that happens to her into fiction. She resolves to begin writing a diary—so that she will tell only the truth. But the diary itself becomes a suspect artifact. As she begins her diary on January 7, 1950, she remembers a diary she began four years before (which apparently was the basis for "Frontiers of War" and the Black Notebook) and finds an entry that describes a night that she spent with Max. She finds the entry and reads it: "I came in last night from work. . . ." The couple decide to make love with the intention of having a baby. But the old diary entry continues without current interruption to say,

> That was the morning Janet was conceived. We married the following week in the registry office. A year later, we separated. . . . But there's Janet . . . I think I shall go to a psychoanalyst. (231–32)

Anna, in her current state of confusion, is unable to keep from fictionalizing even with a diary entry, so that three separate time periods are concentrated in the one entry: Anna remembering a previous night with Max; Anna remembering what had happened a year after that night; and Anna responding to a current phenomenon. Past and present seem interchangeable. The undercutting of assumed or expected versions of reality is perhaps a Brechtian distancing technique, a way of being "apart, a little bit, from an idea before you can see it,"[24] but it is also a reflection of the complexities of modern experience and of the difficulties in reaching a moral stance in the face of those complexities. It might be fashionable to apply deconstructive instruments to "Lessing's" text, but I think that Brechtian dialectical theory wastes less print than Derridean erasure.

Anna's feelings after her lunches with the agents of "the art form of the future" (293) about the television rights to "Frontiers of War" are not of the righteous indignation of the real artist (we assume that Lessing, like Mailer, anticipates Baudrillard by decades in her recognition of hyperreality), but are of self-disgust for going to a meeting which she knew would be insufferable. Her mood turns into "a sort of hysteria" where she knows that she will childishly lash out. As she passes a war-disfigured newsvendor who shouts of "War in Quemoy," the inauthenticity of her own war novel is brought home to her. Thus, when Anna tells Tarbrucke that she would like "Frontiers of War" to be turned into a comedy, she is not merely parodying the shallowness of a cheaper art form, but is recognizing that the agents saw what her book "was really about—nostalgia for death" (287).

At first, Anna's stance toward Tarbrucke is that of the committed novelist dealing with a failed, compromised artist. Thus her joking with him of not wanting "to rush" her second novel because the "second novel is so important, don't you think?" (283) is less a self-directed irony than the separation of herself from an inferior being. But her hysterical reaction to the deformed newsvendor who, along with the newspapers he sells, represents a truth in contrast to both television and literary fabrication, touches off a new depression in Anna so that she decides that the only reason she has gone through with the luncheon is to affirm for herself that she is "right not to write again" (288). She must also admit to herself that the desire to shock Mrs. Wright by telling her that she is a Communist is childish, even though that moment of breaking through the "comfortable surface" may be the only honest moment of her meetings. What does separate Anna from Tarbrucke and Mrs. Wright is the sincerity manifested in the act of writing her journal. There is a movement away from the nostalgia in this second section of the Black Notebook as the realities of the present infiltrate from other notebooks.

In the third section of the Black Notebook, we are told that an American friend of Anna, James Schafter, has submitted a short story to a magazine in lieu of a review of a dozen novels. After the parenthetic note comes what one assumes is Shafter's short story, "Blood on the Banana Leaves." But this piece is obviously a parody, again, of "Frontiers of War" and thus seems to be a product of Anna's mind rather than of a character such as Schafter. In fact, the American's name shifts from Schafter to Schaffer, so we must accept that his short story is a product of Anna's (and/or Lessing's) continuing fictionalizing.

The brief, final entry of the notebook describes a dream that

Anna has had of the filming of a television version of her own description of Mashopi that has been scripted by someone else, but remains true—the director assures her—to her own version of events. The "set" becomes "the real thing" (524) as though the characters had been transported to Africa; even the smell of gum trees ("wine rising off white dust") is as Anna remembers Mashopi. But the cameras are like machine guns and the director's choice of shots, timing, and angles seems to completely change the power-less Anna's "story." The characters, "among whom was Anna, myself, but not as I remembered her" (524), seem different, as do their relationships, and their dialogue is not as she remembers it. The director is hurt when she asks him why he changed her story: "You saw what I saw? They spoke those words didn't they?" (525) he asks her. The film has again undercut the validity of the fiction: Anna concludes "that what I 'remembered' was probably untrue" (525). The director seems to echo the nihilism of the previous two sections, and of the film agents in earlier sections of the Black Notebook, when he tells her that "it doesn't matter what we film, provided we film something" and this apparent admission of the meaninglessness of the artistic process is impetus for Anna to close the notebook. If she were with Mother Sugar she would "name" the dream as a confession of "total sterility" and the two black lines across the page indicate that the notebook is finished.

An extended diary entry in the Blue Notebook purports to de-scribe the events of Anna's day on September 16, 1959. She was too unhappy to write that evening, so the actual entry is apparently written on the following day. On the recorded day itself, Anna realizes that her period has started and she must deal with feelings of "shame and modesty" in order to maintain the integrity to write at this time. She is aware, too, that language itself will distort the importance, or unimportance, of her period relative to the events of her day. She recalls that Joyce's description of a man defecating was shocking despite the apparent intention of robbing words of their power to shock and doubts the validity of "a day's recording" even before she begins to record. Language itself destroys the real thing. The decision to write, in fact, destroys the balance of aware-ness. She wonders, too, if her decision to leave the Party has been precipitated by her earlier decision to record everything.

At the end of the long entry, we are again told that the attempt has not come off, has been crossed out, has been a "failure as usual" (368). Thus a new nine-line entry describes the events of Anna's climactic day. But that entry, neat and orderly, is dated "15th September, 1954"—the day when Anna had decided to record a day in her life, in response to Michael's belittling her imagination—not the actual day of the events, and not the day when Anna apparently wrote the long entry. Anna, the trickster artist, has been at work on her attempt at the real thing. The validity of the diary form, the seeming real thing, is undercut by the confusion of entries. Indeed, the validity of Anna as a writer separate from her creator, Doris Lessing, the deft arranger of Anna's novel and notebooks, is undermined.

The black lines that cancel out succeeding passages in the third section of the Blue Notebook indicate Anna's increasing concern for form and its success or failure at capturing reality. Each black line indicates, apparently, the necessity of a new approach to be taken by the writer towards the real stuff of experience. But though the black lines may indicate a rejection by Anna of her efforts, the outer arranger-describer (Anna or otherwise) has seen fit to include those canceled passages in the total work at hand—they represent Anna's reach towards common ground between life and the novelist's art. The frequency and predictability of the black lines in this section verge on the monotonous so that, when a passage that begins to discuss Anna's sexual relationship with the American playwright Nelson is canceled to be followed by the admission that "the reason why I don't want to write this is because I have to fight to write about sex" (482), the excuse seems contrived within a book so frank about sexual matters.

Anna has had high expectations of the Blue Notebook, for since it was a diary she had thought that it would "be the most truthful of the notebooks . . ." (468). But the black lines record her sense of failure—it is "worse than any" of the other notebooks. The short entries at the beginning of the third section are as much a failure to capture the real stuff of Anna's existence as is the extended account of September 16, 1954 in the previous section of the notebook, which now, like the reread accounts of Mashopi in the Black Notebook, seems dominated by "emotionalism."

The rejected short entries at the beginning of this section give way to an account of Anna's arguments with Mother Sugar (Mrs. Marks) over the relationship between the psychiatric approach to existence and the novelistic approach. While Anna admits that her sessions with Mrs. Marks have left her "less in conflict, less in doubt, less neurotic" (470), she defends neurosis as a condition of being highly conscious and developed (just as Martha Quest is to defend the almost telepathic powers of Lynda and, indeed, herself in the closing chapters of *The Four-Gated City*), for the essence of neurosis, like that of art, "is conflict." To Anna, now, "wholeness" is achieved only by blocking things out, by limiting oneself.

The final section of the Blue Notebook begins in a present tense as Anna is considering whether to rent out the room in her flat after the departure of Ronnie and Ivor (a situation which spills over from "Free Women"). There are no dates to mark the diary-chronicle, though we are given certain information, such as Molly's announcement that Comrade Tom has left the Party "over Hungary," which suggests that the section covers some time from late 1956 to 1957. The outside editor, whose work is apparent in the exclusions of the last sections of the Black and Red Notebooks, has little presence here. We are told that the book resumes without dates, and that it is ended, like the other books, with a double black line, and at one point we are told that Anna begins to include numbered asterisks in her text. There are nineteen such asterisks in this section, just as there are nineteen entries in the last section of the Yellow Notebook, and they point up that the same themes are being covered in both books. While the Yellow Notebook's short story and short novel projections are fiction (Anna has claimed that in this notebook she makes stories out of her experiences—witness Anna-Michael as Ella-Paul) the Blue Notebook is apparently the real thing, the true account of Anna's experiences.

Since the Blue book is real and the Yellow book is a conversion of the real into fiction, we might assume that similar entries would come first in the Blue book and then in the Yellow book. But we become aware that the real has followed fiction. Thus when Saul tells Anna sarcastically that she is a permissive woman, an entry is first made in the Yellow Notebook (the sixth short story entry) and is reported after he says the same thing again in the Blue book. What seems to be the case is that, during the time under consideration, Anna writes both "in this and the Yellow Notebooks" (575). But at one point fiction seems to precede fact: When Anna inspects Saul's diaries she finds an entry about one of his lovers, Mavis from Detroit, who attempts to kill herself. The entry ends with the cold words "Pity. A nice girl," which echo the entry of an American writer in Anna's seventh projection in the Yellow Notebook. Saul's entry frightens Anna because she has already written the Yellow Notebook entry when she discovers Saul's heartless diary. Thus the Yellow Notebook entry has been written from "some other kind of knowledge . . . some awful second sight . . . much too painful to use in ordinary life" (572). It becomes difficult to distinguish between fiction and the real, to assume that the Blue Notebook is any more real than the Yellow book. For example, when Anna decides that Saul is in need of professional help, she phones "Dr. Paynter" for his advice. Yet we have heard no previous mention of this character in the notebooks. Anna's analyst has been Mother Sugar—Mrs. Marks. So there is some concern as to whether this final section of the Blue book gives us the real thing or whether Anna is again making fiction in an attempt to capture the essence of a relationship—which she has wanted to do back in the early stages of the Yellow Notebook and at the end of the first section of the Black Notebook.

As the borders between fiction and reality become blurred, so does the relationship between language and meaning break down. Comrade Ted's narrative in the second section of the Red Notebook could be taken, the study group realizes, either as parody, as irony, or seriously. For Anna, Comrade Ted's wish-fulfillment fantasy is an expression of the fragmentation that results from the disparity between the disintegration of language and the density of experience. And in the pasted-in entries describing the Party study group meeting of November 11, 1952, none of the group is able to directly say how bad the treatise under discussion—ironically enough Stalin's pamphlet on linguistics—really is. As she listens, in the study group, to the gap between what words are supposed to mean and what they mean, as "words lose their meaning suddenly," Anna thinks of novels which deal with the "breakdown of language, like *Finnegans Wake*" (300). For Anna, the disintegration of language reflects the "cracking up" that she speaks of at the beginning of "Free Women": the result of the fact that an "epoch of our society, and of Socialism, was breaking up at that time."[25] At, as Michael says, "a time when it is impossible to know the truth about anything," language itself loses meaning, and perhaps only the small, personal voice of the novelist can reestablish the authenticity of language.

And the message of fragmentation from the Red Notebook bleeds into the Blue. Anna experiences states of vertigo where words are devoid of meaning, becoming incoherent babble to dissolve and be replaced by "spawning images which have nothing to do with the words" (476) that preceded them. Nelson, the at first warm and understanding American expatriate, descends into an hysteria so that his "words lose their meaning" (496), and what makes the Ceylonese De Silva the most intense embodiment of the principle of joy in destruction is that things "don't matter," his malicious acts are meaningless, reflecting "the emptiness of emotion" (502) so that Anna will spend the night with him because it "didn't matter to me" (501). The general breakdown of language

and meaning is also "a breakdown of me, Anna. . . . For words
are form, and if I am at a pitch where shape, form, expression, are
nothing, then I am nothing" (476–77); and the "certain kind of
intelligence" (477) that is Anna's identity in the notebooks appears
to be dissolving.

The fragmentation between word and deed, word and meaning,
which De Silva's personality represents comes close to the theme
of breakdown that permeates the novel and which, indeed, is seen
by Anna, in opposition to Mrs. Marks, as a peculiarly current
condition—indeed, could be for some, Anna feels, a pioneer heroism as the individual allows the cracks, avoids the amputating
wholeness, in hopes of new possibilities. Anna's own quest for a
new kind of wholeness, indeed a new kind of consciousness to be
reflected by a new kind of art, must involve a breaking down in
order to reach an authentic modern, integrated personality.

In the fourth section of "Free Women," Anna's state, in the midst
of the chaos around her, is akin to the nihilistic vertigo she had
seen in Nelson and De Silva (and had felt in herself) in the previous
section of the Blue Notebook. When she discovers that Ronnie has
reentered her household, her reaction (after the great struggle she
has previously made to dismiss him) is to catch herself thinking
"What does it matter?" Indeed, she considers taking Janet and
leaving the house to Ivor and Ronnie—realizing that she is "not
far off lunacy" (507). And Molly, too, reacts to Marion's invasion
of her flat by wondering, "Well why not? What does it matter?"
(510). Anna cannot put a name to the force that Tommy has over
everybody (he seems, for example, to draw everybody into his
own misdirected blind gaze); but when she giggles, she remembers
Tommy's own "bright meaningless giggle" (511).

If the controlling mood of the chapter is hysteria, and if, as in
the Blue Notebook, things lack meaning, then words, too, seem
not to hinge on anything meaningful. Thus, as Marion, terrified
that Anna will drive her from her refuge in Molly's flat, talks of
her political activity with Tommy, Anna "switched off; something
inside her went dead. . . . She stood there, looking at words like
love, friendship, duty, responsibility, and knew them all to be lies.
She felt herself shrug" (514). It is the same response that Anna has
had to Marxist rhetoric in the Red Notebook, to the nihilism of
the Blue Notebook—as though "Free Women" is now infiltrated
by the notebooks' themes. As she tries to talk of African politics
to Marion (who seems to represent Anna's own naive self) Anna's
voice cracks and she is sickened by the sentimentality of her own
words. When she tells Marion that they should not let what Tom

Mathlong stands for "look cheap," she tells herself that "I'm making what he stands for look cheap in every word I say" (516).
Language and meaning are dissociated. The most striking example
of this occurs as the chapter ends when Ivor, in a last ploy to stay as
her boarder, presents Anna with flowers addressed "To the nicest
landlady in the world" (523). Free indirect discourse is used for
one of the few times when we are told that "Meanwhile he stood,
weary with disgust: this money-grubbing woman, well what can
one expect?" (523). It is as if Anna intuitively hears his "real"
words and her angry rejection of him—she strikes him with the
flowers—bears out that some new kind of extra-verbal relationship
between meaning and sensibility is taking place.

But if lunacy seems an ingredient of the times, if language breaks
down, if things seem to lack meaning, something new seems part
of current experience. When Anna speaks, as intermediary, on the
phone with Richard, it is as if words are merely surface signals
of deeper necessary compulsions. When she leaves off talking to
Richard, she tells him that she will do nothing to alleviate the crisis
between the tycoon and his son and wives; but she knows, too,
that a logic outside of the words she uses is at play—that she
will do something. And when Anna begins to talk realpolitik with
Marion, she listens, still interested in what she herself is going to
say—it is the sound of her voice as much as what she says which
conveys her meaning, her state of mind. Thus, when she begins to
talk about the African revolutionary Charles Themba's breakdown,
she realizes that she has been "meaning to talk about Charlie all
the time" (516–17). Some intuitive, averbal mode of understanding
has taken over.

In her interview at Stony Brook, Lessing, discussing *The Golden
Notebook,* mentions that what interests her "is how our minds are
changing."[26] And if there is anything in "Free Women" to dispute
Mother Sugar's claim in the Blue Notebook that all is repetition
of the same patterns, it is Anna noticing that the demonstration in
which the apparently naive Tommy and Marion take part is different from previous protests (old, orderly Communist Party demon-
strations or Labour Party maneuver). This almost spontaneous
demonstration "was fluid, experimental—people were doing things
without knowing why. The stream of young people had flowed
down the street to the headquarters like water" (511).

In the last section of the Blue Notebook, Anna realizes that
Saul may speak two languages—one verbal, one emotional—at the
same time; and his sleeping self "speaks" a different language from
his waking self. In the same way that there is a disparity between

the "real" Saul's language and the cold entries in his diary, his bad
lovemaking is marked when the source is an idea rather than an
emotion. As Saul sleeps, Anna smells, rather than hears, his fear,
and his personality switches are indicated not by a pattern of words
but by a tightening in Anna's stomach. All this, along with the
tension between Anna's "intelligent self" and the longing "creature
inside" her, indicates a continued undermining of words as denomi-
nations of meaning, a primary concern of Anna as far back as the
second section of this notebook, and, before that, in the second
section of the Red Notebook where words "lose their meaning,"
where Anna notices an unbridgeable gap between what words "are
supposed to mean, and what in fact they say" (300).

As Anna reads the newspapers after not reading them for a week,
she experiences "a kind of shifting of the balances of my brain"
(588), recognizing a parallel experience to the occasion a few days
before (we notice that the notebooks are covering closer and closer
time periods as the novel and Anna's writing block come to an
end) when "words like democracy, liberty, freedom" (588) had
faded under pressure of a new kind of understanding. The knowledge is bitter—of the logic of war which controls the present
world—but it is "a new kind of knowing" (589) which words cannot
convey. It is visionary power of a piece with the "game" that Anna
plays. And she recognizes that the very words she is using to
describe it have no way of conveying either the meaning or the
creative process of the knowledge. Just so, when Saul and she
begin to discuss "the fragmentation of Socialist movements everywhere," Anna knows that her vision of the previous night—"that
the truth for our time was war" (591)—undercuts the truth of their
conversation. And the premonition-like entry that Anna has made
in the Yellow Notebook of the American dismissing a girl's suicide
seems part of her new powers as she anticipates the entry that Saul
makes in his diary over the suicide attempt of the girl from Detroit.

At their most cynical, the Anna and Saul of the inner Golden
Notebook use Marxist terms such as "comrade," "masses," and
"correct" in a jeering fashion, reflecting their disillusionment in
previous ideals. As in the other notebooks, words come to be objects of mistrust, stratagems to block out truth. Before she falls
asleep to experience her second dream session in this notebook,
Anna "knows" that she will be visited by the projectionist of the
first dream and "knows" what he will tell her. But there is "no way
of putting this sort of knowledge into words" (633). The artist
Anna, the blocked writer, finds words inadequate to convey her
most powerful experiences, must play with them, hoping "that . . .

even a chance combination will say what I want" (633). Even a
"row of asterisks" might better describe "real experience" (633).
Anything would be better than words. Indeed, Anna concludes that
she cannot express her new knowledge, her anticipation of things
to come, except to say that those "who have been there, in the
place in themselves where words, patterns, order dissolve, will
know what I mean and the others won't" (633–34). Thus the primary struggle of the inner Golden Notebook, and perhaps its triumph, is not merely the achievement of unity from fragmentation,
but the rendering of extra-verbal experience, knowledge, through
what Brecht might have termed a dialectical literary construct.
The barriers of that Brechtian ironic detachment, the apartness,
of "Free Women" and of the diffused notebooks, has been removed
so that characters rush together here into a new complex, whole
personality, into an experience beyond the language of the earlier
sections. Anna-the writer/Saul-the-writer are perched on the edge
between language and knowledge—just as they are on the edge
between the subjective and the universal, between the masculine
and the feminine—and the existential essence of that phenomenon
manifests itself by the integration of previously diffused matter.
Tony Tanner's notion that the American novel is distinguished by
its proximity to the edge of experience perhaps should extend
across the Atlantic to a work such as *The Golden Notebook,* which
in its very techniques reaches the edge of contemporary western
experience.

After meeting with Richard Portmain, in the third part of "Free
Women," Anna is reminded "of her own discordant self" and the
panic she feels intensifies as she rides home on a crowded underground. She begins to wonder about the nature of breakdown:

> If someone cracks up, what does that mean? At what point does a
> person about to fall to pieces say: I'm cracking up? And if I were to
> crack up, what form would it take? (389)

And she must reassert her control by repeating that her name is
Anna and then by using her child's reliance upon her as a reason
to remain stable. Her reverie leads to a vision of the haunting
Tommy leaning over and turning to pages of her own ordering,
mess-avoiding notebooks. It is a scene in which nihilism connects
with a kind of control. As Anna leaves the train and is followed
by an ugly and obscene man, and when she is confronted by Ronnie's spite, the panic comes upon her again. And when the tur-

moiled Marion visits her, Anna must "set her brain on the alert, a small, critical, dry machine" as a barrier from "cracking up" (395).

If we expect that the "Anna [who] does not feel herself" (507) will be dealt with late in the fourth chapter—it is the third phrase in the chapter subheading—we are surprised, for, after three brief sentences, her condition is announced: "She had now understood that she was not in control of what she did." The dissociation which takes place in "The Shadow of the Third" when Ella watches herself making love to the American Maitland is repeated as Anna watches herself talking on the telephone and later sits "crying, watching herself cry" (516) as she talks with Marion. And the vertigo of that *Alice in Wonderland*–like self-detachment is continued in other ways: in Anna's hysterical response to the now blinded Tommy's slightly off-focus stare, in her wondering what she will say as she has begun talking to Marion and "who the person is who will say it?" (514). Her meeting with Tommy and Marion, as she tries to dissuade them from naive political protest and from taking over Molly's flat, drives her to the breaking point as she shares in their hysteria. She has "no control" and her cracked voice reflects her point of breakdown. She has reached that point from which the inner Golden Notebook will depart.

This theme of breakdown that has built throughout the book is also "a way of self-healing, of the inner self's dismissing false dichotomies and divisions . . ." (viii). In the inner Golden Notebook "things have come together, the divisions have broken down, there is a formlessness with the end of fragmentation—and the triumph of the second theme, which is that of unity" (vii). Thus we can assume that the faces, the relatively face card characters of "Free Women" and the notebooks, merge into the two principal personalities, Anna and Saul Green, who indeed "break down . . . into each other, into other people. . ." (vii). That distancing, which is the principal strategy in passages outside of the inner Golden Notebook, is abandoned in the inner section, which is "written by both of them, you can no longer distinguish between what is Saul and what is Anna, and between them and the other people in the book" (vii). That sensibility—"the sunlight, crystallized beside each glass on the white paint in quivering lozenges of crimson and yellow light" (13–14)—which seems alien in the relatively detached earlier sections, becomes fully accommodated in the Golden Notebook, where Lessing is able to fuse with her characters and participate in the novel's push toward unity. Up until the Golden Notebook we are kept at a kind of arm's length from Lessing's self, but in that section the inner sensibility of the artist comes into play, she is with her character.

In the Yellow Notebook, unlike Maitland, the naive, self-assured American, Ella's life cannot "be described by simple succession of statements: my parents were so and so. . . . I do such and such work" (321). Her life reflects that complexity that differentiates the modern novel from the more simple, linear, social novel of, say, George Eliot. And Ella's writing is itself nonprogrammatic—she cannot say "I shall write a novel." She must be, like the mature, in-tune Martha Quest, in "a kind of open readiness" as though the "story was already written, in invisible ink . . ." (314). And the nature of Ella's art is at one with the surrealistic technique of Anna's own narrative, where Ella, as though in Wonderland, detaches "herself from Ella" and stands "to one side, watching and marvelling" (323). After the embarrassment of Maitland's sexual ineptitude, "Ella became herself, one person, both of them thinking as one" (324). Part of Ella steps out into the omniscient sphere of the author Anna and Anna steps back with Ella into the inside role of Ella. It is as though the nonlinear nature of Lessing's narrative allows her, in a way different in technique, but approximate in effect to Mailer's fused narrative discussed in the next chapter, to enter into and weave away from the consciousness, the shared experience, of her characters. Though Lessing has insisted that *The Golden Notebook* should not be read as "The Confessions of Doris Lessing,"[27] it is difficult not to slip into the assumption that Doris participates in Anna as much as Anna participates in Ella. Saul may naively tell Anna that she is the two women who will become the Anna and Molly of "Free Women," but, like Saul who is a fusion of all other male voices in the book (in fact, fuses with Anna who is all female voices), she is a complex of voices in which the ostensibly outside author/editor participates.

In Anna's own outer "The Shadow of the Third," Ella's father, stoically accepting his lot, attacks the modern desire for happiness, which he sees as being inspired by Communist doctrine. Ella's reply is that her kind has been prepared "to experiment with ourselves, to try and be different kinds of people. But you simply submitted to something" (466). And this defense of her generation is the impetus for another projected fiction: "A man and woman— yes. . . . Both cracking up because of a deliberate attempt to transcend their own limits. And out of the chaos a new kind of strength" (467). Thus Ella's artistry offers the key to her own recovery. Indeed, her story seems the germ for the inner Golden

Notebook—so it is the key towards Anna's own recovery. Art offers its own path to breakdown and resultant recovery.

Though Anna may insist that she "must keep them separate" (537), it is clear that the divisions by notebook are beginning to break down as the sweep towards the inner Golden Notebook is paralleled by an increasing interest in American social and sexual matters. Americans Cy Maitland from "The Shadow of the Third," the writer James Schafter/Schaffer from the third section of the Black Notebook, Nelson, the hysterical expatriate playwright from the third section of the Blue Notebook, all anticipate the American male's presence in the inner Golden Notebook. The increased frequency of American males builds up to the Yellow Notebook's final entry, the Kerouacian "The Romantic School of Tough Writing," where Anna's bitterness towards the modern man and his sexual problems—his neurotic preference for male company, the interchangeability of sex and violence, the stereotyping of "round-ball butt" (541) feminine sexuality—is angrily parodied through the elegiac adolescence of Mike "the winged-with-words" (540) writer. That the narrator's name is Mike seems to suggest that part of Anna's anger is directed back at her affair with Michael—that the American is symbolic of the male self-image, but the American also perhaps represents that dangerous new order of experience that the voice of the novel seeks to achieve.

The parodic nature of the Yellow Notebook's final entry seems in contrast to the frank examinations of sexual complexities and failures in the previous eighteen fragments of this section. It is as though the barriers break down and Anna's rage at male inner-directedness is given full play at the expense of objectivity. But the parody surely does not confine itself to the man-boy mentality of Kerouac (or Saul); it also reflects Anna's dissatisfaction with her own investigations into the nature of sexual relationships, so that the parody turns upon itself. So also, the ironic title "The Man Who is Free of Women" of the eighteenth fragment—a projection of a short novel about an emotionally immature, dependent male, suggests the irony implicit in the title of the short novel "Free Women" within *The Golden Notebook*. The women in that work, free as they might try to be and may indeed be by conventional standards, feel anything but free, are prisoners to their need of men. Anna terminates the Yellow Notebook because she has fallen into parody. Yet the devaluation implied in that descent is two-sided. Like the Red Notebook and the Black Notebook, the work self-destructs; yet the breakdown of Anna's plans allows for the dismissal of dichotomies, divisions, in her writing and makes way for the raw, but unified narrative of the inner Golden Notebook.

The fourth short story projection from the Yellow Notebook is fulfilled in the Blue Notebook as Anna begins to share in the anxiety and physical pain of Saul's sickness. Recognizing her symptoms as part of his madness, seeing that he needs an adversarial relationship as much as a loving one, she concludes that he must go, but the effort to detach herself is close to impossible. She recognizes that they are both "inside a cocoon of madness" (582), and her own sensibility, as she deals with Saul's mad tyranny, descends to the point where common surroundings, objects take on phantasmagoric qualities so that the "floor between me and the bed was bulging and heaving" and "walls seemed to bulge inwards, then float out and away into space" (599). As she tries to deal with Saul's crack-up, Anna finds herself dropping deeper into chaos—and that descent seems to allow the fulfilled play of individual sensibility which, in the early chapters of the novel, was glimpsed only rarely. Thus those out of place "quivering lozenges of crimson and yellow light" in the first chapter of "Free Women" would fit with the Blue Notebook's accommodation of "the stuff of the red curtain, and the feel of it . . . dead and slippery, slimy . . . dead stuff, to hang like dead skin, or a lifeless corpse at my window" (542).

As Saul's intense neurosis begins to infiltrate Anna's own personality, she, too, becomes physically and emotionally ill. But her decision that Saul "must go" is not easy to fulfill. Indeed her effort to detach herself fails to the point that she wishes to be free of her "own ordering, commenting memory" (585)—that part of herself that is able to write the notebooks. The interior female creature exerts her power to the extent that the intelligent Anna must realize that "I could no longer separate myself from Saul" (587)—she has "gone right inside his craziness" wanting to be the "all-mother" figure that he needs. Just as Saul fuses all his personalities into one fight "for survival," so Anna's personality becomes fused into Saul's as his language becomes hers. She describes his erection in his terms ("his prick was big") and it is she who first dreams of, enters into, the Algerian freedom fighter who will become the opening figure in Saul's novel. The descent into madness also allows Anna to accommodate the characters from her past, from her previous, fragmented notebooks. Thus, letting the characters from Mashopi dissolve into her, she is able to slip "back into myself" and dream "an ordinary dream" of "the smell of sweet spilt wine" in Mashopi and know that she has "been delivered from disintegration because I could dream it" (600).

After Anna has tried, but failed, to summon the ironically detached Tom Mathlong, has reached instead the insane Charlie Thembla, she sets out her four notebooks but puts back all but the Blue. Saul asks her why she keeps four notebooks and she says that it has "been necessary to split myself up" (598). But from now on, she says, she will use only the one book. Still, she is unable to pick up the pen to write in the book and, after telephoning Molly, has her surrealistic flight into the third world. In a dream that she has shortly after this hallucinatory journey, she and Saul go through every "man-woman role imaginable" (603) (a fulfillment of the projections in the last section of the Yellow Notebook) and when she wakes she begins to write another novel and she admits for the first time that she has a writer's block. He, in turn, admits his jealousy over the success of "Frontiers of War." That dream that Anna has of their going through roles together represents their ultimate fusion (at least as far as this notebook is concerned) so that they "break down" into each other and "into other people" (vii). And this healing process makes way for Anna's purchase of the Golden Notebook (originally ordered at the stationer's by an American) which, true to Anna's new extra-verbal way of knowing, is pleasant to touch and to look at. Her refusal to give the book to Saul breaks the sadomasochistic cycle of their relationship and allows her to end the fourth notebook by deciding to begin again by putting "all of myself in one book" (607), thus setting out on a fulfillment of the primary gesture of the novel as a whole. That action is made possible by Anna's merger with Saul, but ironically demands, too, a rejection by her of Saul's sickness, of the child who cries for possession of the book, who writes its first words, which are a schoolboy's curse—itself a signal that this new book is not quite Anna's alone. And the process of devaluation which has led to the rejection, the ending, of the four notebooks, leads to the creation of a new, integrated narrative that will fulfill the need of Anna to capture the totality of experience.

The penultimate section of the novel, the inner Golden Notebook, like the final section of the Blue Notebook before it, sees Anna swinging from a "pure happiness" when Saul and she are content in their lovemaking to a terror that comes upon her when his madness infects her own personality. The intense pleasure that she can feel in her benign interludes with Saul gives way to a war nightmare, which culminates in a "blackout" where she experiences a vision of annihilation as a "small ugly container of death

exploded, soft, soft, it exploded into the waiting silence . . . while
I screamed, soundless, no one hearing . . ." (629), so that states
of chaos and order correspond with states of happiness and terror
in their movement towards a vortex of human experience. Close
to waking from this dream of annihilation, Anna continues her
connections between Saul and a tiger of which she'd dreamed. She
decides to write a play "about Anna and Saul and the tiger" (616),
but the controlling presence tells her to put aside the play, to "stop
playing with bricks," not to make up stories about life but to "look
at it straight"—which is what both Anna, the author of the notebook, and the outside creator of the novel as a whole have been
striving for in their passage towards this inner notebook. The controlling presence in Anna's dream becomes a projectionist—becomes "He," a male, becomes the menacing, breaking down Saul—
who insists that Anna go back and look again at scenes from her
life that she has covered in other notebooks. As the projectionist
questions the validity of the emphasis that Anna, the authoress,
has placed upon the scenes from her life, she experiences nausea
at the strain of trying "to expand one's limits beyond what has
been possible" (519). The projectionist lets out a jeering laugh as
a flash indicates that the film is "Directed by Anna Wulf" and she
tries to disclaim that the scenes are hers. But faced with these
scenes Anna is faced also with the task of recreating order out of
"the chaos" and is unable to distinguish between invention and
experience. She realizes that her invention has all been false; it is
"a whirl, an orderless dance" (620).

As Saul becomes the projectionist, the film changes genre, becoming an early Russian or German "realistic" film, and scenes to
which Anna the artist has given emphasis slip past, whereas other
scenes from her life slow down. As versions of her life fuse, Anna
projects another short story or novel on the order of the projections in the last part of the Yellow Notebook. She sees a character
like herself trying to free herself from "her capacity for surrendering herself to a man" (636). She wonders how Ella, her alter ego
from the earlier sections of the Yellow notebook's "The Shadow of
the Third," would adapt to such a story, begins to imagine Ella
with Saul, but realizes that her imagination is again distancing her,
and Ella, from reality. And Ella, in the very middle of a renunciation of the imagination, steps from fiction into the real, takes her
place in the inner Golden Notebook's reality, merges into the
novel's "all of myself." Indeed, Ella's real presence in the inner
Golden Notebook and the reemergence of other characters, situations, from the notebooks, signals a new beginning to the novel.

This beginning emerges as the characters fuse into a single male-female sensibility after the breakdown of the novel's structures is fully realized in this notebook through the multiple images of annihilation in Anna's dream.

When she experiences the dream film of Mashopi, Anna recognizes that "the terrible falsity of nostalgia had gone out of it" (616). The film is emotionless, speeded up—only the image of butterflies turning into atomic explosion breaks from flat experience. As Anna is perfunctorily shown scenes from her life, as she sees character after character, she understands that she must still "work on" her past, that the real truth of experience is still to be attained. Thus when the projectionist challenges her to "do June Boothby," the daughter of the proprietors of the Mashopi Hotel, the result, to the projectionist's delight, is "the style of the most insipid coy woman's magazine" (620)—a parody of Anna's own presentation of June Boothby in the first section of the Black Notebook. This devaluation of rendered experience reflects Anna's general descent into chaos, to the omnipresent image of annihilation, and reaches its most intense stage as the projectionist forces scenes upon the dreaming Anna that contradict her rendition of things: we see Mrs. Boothby in her kitchen listening to cruel voices and laughter; we see Willi Rodde hurt by Anna's flirtation with Paul Blackenhurst; and Paul Tanner, the Michael version of "The Shadow of the Third," is given different emphasis as he is seen coming home to his wife in the morning. But the process gives way to a new beginning, as dialectic opposition of versions of reality merge into a synthesis of character: Anna dreams Paul Tanner and the real lover Michael becoming one and the film enters a new experience, "a fusion," as "scenes, people, faces, movements, glances" (635) come together. Anna is becoming "all of myself." Anna and Ella become one, characters dissolve into each other's experience, divisions break down, so that the dream film becomes a series of moments: a soldier on a hillside like the character Anna will give Saul; a woman "awake in darkness, saying, No, I won't kill myself, I won't, I won't" (635)—the step towards a new unified sensibility forged from Anna's crack-up. Likewise, Anna projects Saul as he goes upstairs to pack his suitcase as a "strong, broad-shouldered man when he had worked through his illness into health" (641).

If the strategy of the earlier notebooks has been compartmentalization, of being "apart, a little bit," then the form of the inner Golden Notebook is of breaking down into synthesis. The *Play with a Tiger* that Anna projects as she comes out of her initial dream sequence parallels a play of the same title by Lessing where an English woman and American male emerge from a variety of other quite stock male and female characters to melt down into a single persona in the final act. Just so, in the inner Golden Notebook, Saul and Anna become "so close we could have become each other . . ." (621). As they each accommodate other personalities from the notebooks and from "Free Women," divisions break down, as Lessing says, into a triumph of fusion (vii). Just as Saul and Anna give each other themes, first sentences, for each other's novels, break each other's writing blocks, so they share authorship of this inner notebook. They are fellow creatures on the edge of experience. Their mutual rite of passage is to work through the variety of stock sexual roles prepared for them in the last chapter of the Yellow Notebook—and their lowest descent to the abasing roles of begging, cradling female and cradled male, provoking a "mutual shame and humiliation" (641), allows them each a new beginning. Now Saul's rake's stance, the masculine role first played by Paul Tanner, provokes in Anna not anger but a feeling as if they are siblings, that they would "always be flesh of one flesh, and think each other's thoughts" (641). They are playing out a mid-twentieth-century version of the fortunate fall from Eden.

Both Saul and Anna have kept themselves from writing by their wish to be revolutionaries rather than writers, to be on the true edge of experience, and the gift they give each other is of a new edge that lies between subjective artist and "real" social dynamo: Saul sets Anna to write of the complex personality of woman and Anna sets Saul to tell of a new relativistic revolutionary hero. Their art is no longer the subjective twentieth-century art that Anna has complained of, stammered because of, in her lectures, but is a new kind of communal art—they are, as Saul says, "part of the team . . . who'll go on fighting . . ." (642). Writing is now a shared endeavor—so that when Saul picks up a book he might recognize it as a task he need not do within the communal cause, so that the pioneer social-sexual ground of the inner Golden Notebook is the eclectic product of Anna, Saul, and their kind. The devaluative path of the notebooks gives way to a new state where breakdown becomes assertion of new voice, where a new way of looking at experience is reached. The separate voices of the fragmented Anna give way to an integrated voice of Anna/Saul, just as Mark and Martha become "interchangeable selves" in *The Four-Gated City,* the component of *Children of Violence* that achieves in its post-holocaust epilogue the teenage Martha Quest's vision of unity.

At least half of the "real" inner Golden Notebook is not made available in the existent text. That is the full text of Saul's short, and apparently quite successful, novel about the Algerian revolutionary and his encounter with the French soldier who is his jailer. It is another rite of fusion as the Algerian, whose feelings are never those that are expected of him, and the Frenchman, whose thoughts and emotions conform to pigeonholes, blend into a single committed personality. But the outside editor of the notebooks chooses only to present a summary of this section of the Golden Notebook. Somehow, a personality outside that of Saul and Anna is at work even in the inner notebook, so that if the narrative voice of this notebook includes Saul and Anna, it also includes another presence—the omniscient presence of the novel. The dialectic of the subjective and the omniscient has given way to a presence that accommodates both outside and inside personality, author and narrative voice. If the inner Golden Notebook represents that point where Anna Wulf, the artist, is able to include "all of myself in one book," it is also the point where Doris Lessing is able to fully participate in the consciousness of her character, to realize through the novel the totality of the mid-twentieth-century experience. Thus I think that Irving Howe misreads the shape of *The Golden Notebook* when he suggests that Lessing "fails to keep a sufficient distance from her heroine, so that Anna's hysteria comes dangerously close to taking over the narrative."[28] To say that the "enormous intensity" achieved "through surrendering herself to Anna's suffering" results in "a loss of critical objectivity she had maintained in earlier pages"[29] is a failure to recognize that the very gesture of *The Golden Notebook* is to merge the author's own "small, personal voice" with that of her character. Sincerity now demands a narrative voice that participates in the confused path of the representative mid-century man/woman.

4

In the second section of "Free Women" Anna is working on the notebooks when Tommy enters her flat. He reads out loud different passages from different notebooks—for example, from a March 1956 entry in the Blue Notebook, which will be merely summarized briefly, rather than quoted verbatim, in the third installment of the notebooks. Tommy demands of Anna why she must keep four notebooks instead of just one, which would admit chaos. The question suggests that this section of "Free Women," apparently taking place in the summer of 1957, predates the inner Golden Notebook—the fifth notebook—which will be Anna's attempt to contain "the mess," the chaos of her life, and which will represent an escape from the cowardice of compartmentalization and an advancement of artistic development and sincerity from both the other notebooks and from the omniscient, relatively detached, self-contained "Free Women." Anna says that she must use four notebooks rather than one because one notebook would be a scramble, a mess. Accusing her of insincerity, Tommy wonders why it shouldn't be a mess and why, in a particular section of the Blue Notebook, Anna employs different kinds of handwriting and why she brackets off certain sections. An entry in which she describes a dream (curiously it is not an entry presented in those portions of the notebooks included in *The Golden Notebook*)—

> I could see myself lying on the pavement. I was two people. Blood and brains were scattered everywhere. I knelt down and began licking up the blood and the brains (272)

—is set off in brackets, while a description of an everyday shopping expedition is left unbracketed. Thus Tommy is able to claim that Anna is afraid of chaos: her notebooks are a stratagem to hide the truth, so that "everything is divided up and split off" (274)—compartmentalization is a kind of cowardice. Indeed, that "we must not divide things off, we must not compartmentalize" (x) is a lesson that Anna, the reader, and perhaps Lessing herself, must realize through the course of *The Golden Notebook*.

In the last chapter of "Free Women" Anna is no longer "all of myself in one book" but is once more the face characters who make up "Free Women" and the four notebooks. There is a new kind of ironic detachment as the novel closes—Molly and Anna laugh, in turn, at Molly's new compromising marriage, at Anna's new work, at Tommy's adjustment to his father's capitalism. Tommy, says Anna, "is in tune with our times" (665) so that the new way of knowing things from the inner Golden Notebook has been forgotten. The short novel has returned to the ironical nature of its title, has become "a comment about the conventional novel" (xiv) and its inadequacies in light of the mass of material that makes up Anna's experiences. Indeed, there is a fairy-tale-like detachment to the book's last chapter. In the first paragraph Janet moves from "a little girl" to an independent "thirteen-year-old" (647)—and Tommy's sudden transformation to where he's "already installed, and taking things over" (664) at his father's tycoonery, seems to totally neglect the tragic figure of previous chapters of "Free Women." He seems to have leaped over from the pages of the notebooks where he had remained the conventional son without traumatic experience. This final chapter pales beside the sincerity of the inner Golden Notebook, is inadequate to save the unifying process that has led up to the penultimate section from diffusion. The narrative voice is more closely aligned to that of the outside editor who comments upon, arranges, and cuts from the five notebooks, than to the Anna who struggles to "get all of myself into one book."

Considering the continued activity of the outside auditor/editor of the notebooks, I would suggest that the claims of Betsy Draine and Anne Mulkeen that Anna Wulf is the sole authorial voice in the "macrofiction" *The Golden Notebook,* and of John Carey that, by assigning "Free Women" to Anna, Lessing "filters herself out of the novel entirely . . . ,"[30] neglect the fact that Anna's authorial stances are continually undercut by Lessing's turns of the novel and thus that Lessing is the prime mover behind the revealing mask of Anna—just as Ella is a thin, but welcome and necessary, mask for a fictitious novelist who is struggling to begin again.

The achievement of an accommodation with the mess, the rendition of the real thing, required a very different kind of work than Lessing had written before *The Golden Notebook.* It was published between her fourth and final novels in the *Children of Violence* series. An early Lessing novel, such as *The Grass is Singing,* has a movement towards a vortex of intensity as does *The Golden Notebook.* But the movement towards that penultimate state of intensity is far smoother and the state itself less all-encompassing than in the later work. And what happens to character and form in *The Golden Notebook* allows Martha Quest's final accomplishment of wholeness in the visionary, apocalyptic epilogue of *The Four-Gated City.* It is not difficult to recognize in the fragmented Anna's dissatisfaction with the nostalgic "Frontiers of War," Lessing's own dissatisfaction with the smooth-flowing path towards the heart of romanticism which is the structure of *The Grass is Singing.* And it is not hard to see the Mashopi affair of the Black Notebook in Lessing's renunciation of the parallel incident of *Landlocked* where Martha Quest rejects Anton Hesse and accepts Thomas Stern as her lover. But for Martha to achieve her quest in a real contemporary experience, the romanticism of these characters, their one-dimensionality, must be replaced through new women, new men. Lessing must go beyond Thomas Stern/George Hounslow into Saul Green, just as she must discover twentieth-century complexities of narrative while she attempts to examine an age of tremendous upheaval.

If the vortex of *The Grass is Singing,* or of "Frontiers of War," is nostalgia, a romantic death wish, the inner Golden Notebook involves something else. The journey through psychic dissolution fuses Saul-Anna and all characters and the tension between Anna the notebook writer and the outside auditor (who arranges, edits, describes for us the notebooks) breaks down. So also, our differentiations between Anna, Anna who is Ella, Lessing, and all other voices (including that of "Free Women") melt into the raw stuff of the inner notebook.

3

A Physician Half-Blind:
Implosion and Public Address in *Why Are We In Vietnam?*

1

WHY ARE WE IN VIETNAM? PROVIDES THE CLEAREST EXAMPLE of the interplay of the first-and third-person narrative voice reflecting interaction of personal and public concerns. For Norman Mailer it represents the culmination of an accommodation of the personal voice—from the early outside sensibility which dominated *The Naked and the Dead* through the first-person, but still relatively outside narrative sensibilities of *Barbary Shore* and *The Deer Park,* and beyond the more personal sensibility that dominates *An American Dream.* The nonfiction work *Armies of the Night* provided inner and outer voices in less complex configurations than in the novel that preceded it. But, after *Why Are We In Vietnam?* the intense, cathartic inner sensibility gives way to the more distant voices and sensibilities of *The Executioner's Song* and *Ancient Evenings.*

Reflecting its two voices, there are two simultaneous narrative situations throughout Mailer's fifth novel (neglecting *A Transit to Narcissus,* the early, journeyman effort). The initial given occasion is that of a young disc jockey to America broadcasting his genius over the airwaves to his national audience. But this speaker—apparently Ronald Jethroe—ultimately reveals a firmer narrative situation: he is at the family dinner table in Dallas, tripping on LSD. The latter situation implies that the narrative is an inner stream of consciousness while the former suggests the outward relationship of the artist with his readership, however self-parodied that relationship may be by the author/speaker.

From the opening lines of Intro Beep 1 on through the whole novel, D.J.'s inner discourse carries the traditional informality of the American novel ("Call me Ishmael," etc.) to a new reach of effrontery. By Intro Beep 2, D.J. is speaking to "muzzfuckers . . . , footlings . . . , hot shit artists, those who give head, and general drug addicts of the world. . . ."[1] If D.J. is some approximation of an artist, he, as opposed to the audience, is free, heroic, in tune with the circuits of the national gestalt. In one sense, this rough trade with the audience serves as a kind of shock treatment to a blind, sick nation. Thus there is a continual metaphor in the novel of electricity—motifs of electronic circuits, radioactivity, and magnetic fields—operating as therapeutic awakening for the American public. Yet such affront does not merely impress the work's moral public stance upon the reader, does not merely serve to reawaken its national audience's dormant conscience. It reveals also the speaker's own intrinsic arrogance: the relationship of speaker to reader is one of master/genius signalling passive pigeons who must turn and "wheel on a bird whistle" (162) for the controlling narrator.

With the abrasiveness of the disc jockey towards his audience, his receivers, comes an admission of confusion. The apparent random connections of the novel's opening passages, the forced wit, the fact that the novel's introduction is merely a "Beep," the plea by the speaker for his audience of "young America" to "hold tight" (7), represents not only a parody of contemporary media, but the self-denigration of a frantic authorial voice as it attempts to deal with issues of the day. D.J. may set himself up as a prophet, but at the same time the order to his audience is to "glom onto the confusion of my brain" (24). As the narrative begins, the audience is situated "out there in all that implosion land" (8)—both America the fosterer of the nuclear bomb and America the victim of its own electronically enhanced, inner-directed, locked-in mindset. And while D.J. may seem, at first appearance, to be reaching outward in an explosion of abusive wit, we soon find that his narrative may itself be an inner stream of consciousness, a reverie "recollecting" a possibly fabricated past, so that the long meditation on the Alaska hunting trip is perhaps induced by a reaction to the dinner plate before him. What at first seems a unified prophetic voice is revealed as the imploded vision of an audience, which may be D.J. auditing his own dubious memory.

The occasion of a nighttime broadcast across a nation's airwaves allows for a complex of voices which, as Tony Tanner contends, constitutes the "multiple voice of American Dream Life."[2] D.J. himself insists upon a panoramic identity containing multiple vectors of the American gestalt. For example, in Intro Beep 2 he will contend that he is, perhaps, "a crippled Harlem genius" (57) rather than a white Texas teenager. His scatological account of the American mind reaches out beyond a Dallas family as his mother Hallie traces her family from "Norloins" to Arkansas and as his father's family, the Jethroes—a catalogue of Texas types—reaches back to Boston ("Upper Clam City"), where also Hallie's psychiatrist, Rothenberg, was educated. The multiple plays which D.J., via Hallie, makes upon Rothenberg's name reflect the complexity of identity in America. D.J.'s friend, Tex Hyde, seems to represent the underside of Texas as opposed to the relatively genteel Dallas of the Jethroes. His parentage is an emblem of "the kink which resides in the heart of the Lone Star" (166). Gottfried and Jane McCabe Hyde, along with Rusty and Hallie Jethroe, are the coordinates that define the genius of young America—D.J. and Tex, whose journey into the Endicott Range represents a rejection of the culture which has formed them.

D.J.'s broadcast is permeated with echoes of vatic voices from the Old Testament. We are told early to "listen to my words" (8), a sly reference from Ecclesiastes like the later confession that D.J. has "wasted his adolescence in company mansions and has eaten off their expense accounts all his days" (50). But by Intro Beep 5 D.J. claims that his narrative is two years old, that he is now sitting in his parents' mansion in Dallas, at a formal dinner with his family, along with Tex, and the dinner guest, "the ex–American Ambassador from Bringthatpore" (74). By the end of the book, D.J. has jettisoned the ambassador and claims that the dinner is in honor of Tex and himself on the eve of their departure for Vietnam. He is on LSD—an extension of Stephen Rojak's nightmare narrative in *An American Dream,* although D.J.'s nightmare has the intensified surrealism of William Burroughs's novels so that the acid trip becomes a primary equivalent for the nature of the American presence in Vietnam. The narrator's arrogance implies the very adolescence of war as a literary subject, a commentary by Mailer himself upon the implicit juvenile sensibility driving *The Naked and the Dead.* Now the novel is not of men at war, although the war is implied throughout by the primary narrative of the hunt. The account of the journey or quest that is made into northernmost territory becomes distorted by the phantasmagoric movements of the drug experience and this vertiginous state carries also a metaphor of the embattled writer in mid-twentieth century. D.J. becomes a metaphorical equivalent of the tormented Saul Green of *The Golden Notebook.* The revelation that the novel's broadcasting, prophetic voice is fantasy becomes emblematic of inner-

directedness, implosion. Of course, the metaphor turns again if
one considers that the nuclear bomb, an implosive device, is a
public concern—so that the interaction of inner and outer impulse
reaches a vertigo rivaled only by that of *Gravity's Rainbow.*

The novel's initial narrative occasion carries its own dense set
of correspondences for cultural conditions, so that the reference
of the speaker to himself as "Geiger and his counter" paves the
way, as the novel opens, for the electronic/magnetic imagery that
permeates the work. This metaphoric medium, besides operating
as the vatic narrator's shock therapy for "young America," enables
the narrative to shift both temporally and spatially. In addition, it
situates the narrative within the technological wasteland that is
contemporary western culture. Thus the hunting trip in Alaska
provides an illustration of how human technological endeavor de-
forms all natural being, so that D.J. will declare that Alaska's "psy-
chomagnetic field was a mosaic, a fragmented vase" (114). The
"grizzers" that Rusty Jethroe wishes to hunt "have now gone ape"
(114) from the intrusions of hunters' helicopters. Indeed, D.J.'s
narrative assault upon his reader/listener/self corresponds to the
technological infiltration of Alaska.

Electronic fields of force become a primary way for D.J. to
describe what he considers to be the overloaded circuits of contemporary America. Two such corporate flunkies as "Medium Assholes" Pete and Bill are "vacuum tubes, man, ideal diodes" and
Pete, having been awarded a bear at his boss's expense, is afraid
that his receivership to Rusty is lost, so that "the filament just
burned out on Pete's tube" (120). The Arctic Circle itself is a super
power circuit, everything "tuned into the same place," so that, just
as D.J. is a receiver for all the currents of contemporary American
culture, the Brooks Range itself is a receiver for the totality of all
of the United States.

In Intro Beep 9, as D.J. and Tex push further into the Brooks
Range, D.J. sees (now, at least, in his act of recollection) the two
boys as pioneers who are approaching the vortex of American
experience, so that "all the messages of North America go up to
the Brooks Range" (172). There is, D.J. claims, a "magnetic-electro
fief" that belongs to the world of sleep, and that contains the totality of one's experience. For example, a surgeon's "M.E.F." consists
of all the diseased organs upon which he operates so that the dream
world of the "M.E.F." contains all that the conscious being seeks
to discard. The closer that D.J. and Tex, along with the narrative
itself, come to the center of the northern magnetic-electro field
the closer they will bring us to the true American personality. Thus

the electronic metaphor will build in intensity in "Chap Ten" to where the boys witness electricity "charging the joint by night, those ice ass pinnacles of the Brooks Range are vibrating to the modulations of the waves" (174). That struggle to reach the full revelation of the magnetic-electro metaphoric payoff, like the struggle between inner and outer narrative occasions, reveals, as Tony Tanner puts it, "what it is like to be a vexed and struggling consciousness in contemporary America."[3]

The guide Luke Fellinka "sends out a wave every time he has a thought, . . . you can feel that one bear out in those woods sending out its message—don't come near mother-fuck—that message transmitted from the bear to Big Luke and relayed to us; you can tune in on the madness in the air" (54). Big Luke is one with the circuit of Alaska, the "nervous system running through the earth and air of this whole state of Alaska" (54). Thus D.J. returns to the initial premise of Intro Beep 1, that the medium is the message, and the Brooks Range is the primary receiver for America's M.E.F. D.J. and Tex receive the message of madness from the bear ("don't bullshit buster"). But D.J. excludes his father from the circuit: "Rusty, of course, reads this not" (54) because the corporation man puts his faith in modern man and machine; has fallen from the natural world. The narrator of the early "Chaps" claims to be a contemporary American prophet who "suffers from one great American virtue, . . . or disease": he "sees right through shit" (49). And that which he claims to see through is the nature of corporate America. For though D.J. transports us to a hunt in the Brooks Range, his concern remains to delineate representatives of the modern corporate temper.

Rusty Jethroe is all Texas willpower. Yet his nickname "Rusty" suggests that he may be like all Dallas men of whom Hallie's psychiatrist could write if he "wasn't afraid of drilling a little career-and-cancer piss right into the heart of Texas" (12). Rusty's company has inserted "Combined" into its earlier title—Central Consolidated Chemical and Plastic—so that it will not have the same initials as the Soviet Communist Party. Thus D.J. accomplishes a series of puns upon the initials of this "bunch of tight assholes," culminating in his explanation of Rusty's assignment of "FourC-ing the cancer market" (30). Rusty markets a plastic filter, "Pure Pores," which, while it "traps all the nicotine," also "causes cancer of the lip" (31) so that the technology of the corporate leviathan exists merely for its own perpetuation, with moral consideration a problem to be circumnavigated by Bernaisian deception.

Because Al Percy Cunningham, Rusty's counterpart in another

division of 4C and P, is forced to remain in Dallas on emergency
assignment, Rusty must replace him with two of his own flunkies:
"Medium Asshole Pete," Assistant Procurement Manager, and
"Medium Asshole Bill," a personnel director, for Pure Pores.
Though "corporate pricks . . . may be dumb and benighted . . . ,
they are not all that dumb," for they can "pick up what you're
trying to slip by them . . ." (50–51). If Rusty is to boast of his
exploits in the Brooks Range, yeomen like M.A.'s Pete and Bill
can only verify the authentic, because "they cannot strain" their
voices past their "own natural elasticity" (52). Thus the "corporate
powers . . . cooking in Rusty's veins" must produce a major kill—
a honey-grizzly bear—or his flunkies will be unable to support his
boasting with an appropriate "choir of Texas ass-purring" (52–53).
For Rusty to return with merely a caribou, as Luke Fellinka
wishes, would expose him to corporate ridicule. He will have failed
to reach the heights of those big American hunters whom D.J. lists:
Roger Blough, Gary Cooper, John Glenn, J. Edgar Hoover, Robert
McNamara, Arnold Palmer, Charles Wilson. Athletics, business
and showbiz, politics, and technology all mix into current
America's governing gestalt.

The hunt itself is a corporate enterprise for "the minions of the
Great Plastic Asshole" (46). Rusty and Al Percy have planned their
trip eighteen months in advance and D.J. projects an intense competition between his father and "kid Tendonex" to see who can
"light a light of love" (47) in the eye of Big Luke. But Cunningham
stays in Dallas because Tendonex, his subdivision of C.C.C.C. &
P., is competing with the Fiberglass Corporation of America for a
"contract to put a plastic Univar valve and plug into the bottom of
the collapsible built-in space suit chemical toilet in the Gemini"
program (47). As corporate America is burlesqued in the intense
competition to build such an absurd plastic product, the space
program itself is undercut as D.J. leaves the Gemini mission's "Roman Numeral Unstated" (47). When Rusty recalls joking to Cunningham that he'd better "load up on Pure Pores" while the "big
sweat is on" (48), we are reminded how Rusty's own cancer-causing
branch of the company is itself a product of corporate madness.

The first three "Chaps" of *Why Are We In Vietnam?* deal with
the problems of the United States as typified by corporate Dallas
society. Chap Four takes us into "the essential animal insanity of
things" (70), which D.J. claims to witness after the first kill of the
hunt in Alaska and which parallels the state of American
corporate-military civilization. The next Chap brakes the narrative
of the hunt by concentrating, through an epic cataloging of arma-

ments, on the folly of acculturated corporate man. For M.A. Pete, "who don't know enough about hunting to go out and shoot at Texas cactus" (80), the sudden invitation to go to Brooks Range means a "two-to-five-year expediting of his . . . ascent of the corporation ladder . . ." (80). But when he learns that the "Savage 110 bolt action with Weaver K-4 scope" (81) that his father has loaned him for the hunt will only stop game "if the shot is *well placed*" (81), he purchases from—shades of Jack Ruby and the recent American tragedy of the Kennedy assassination—"a third-string Dallas Mafia type" (81) a "banged-up, African rhinoceros-hippo-elephant . . . double-barreled .600-.577 custom, only-one-of-its-kind-ever built Jeffrey Nitro Express carrying a 900-grain bullet for Shot #1, a 750-grain for Shot #2, and a recoil guaranteed to knock a grand piano on its ass" (82). When Pete fires at a caribou that he notices by accident, the recoil 'canted his vertebrae 3 degrees 21 minutes right then and there . . ." (90). Thus Pete has been swindled of a thousand dollars because the barrels of the Nitro Express are so "crooked they could shoot each other" (83)—and this expense must be added to the four thousand-odd dollars which the trip, and possible corporate elevation, has already cost him, and for which he has had to sell his second car and his Dreyfus Liquid Assets. Of course he cannot touch, for fear of offending his superiors, his "Pure Pore debentures," nor dare he go "further into installment debt" (83). He is a pathetic figure without the courage to escape the swallow of the corporate leviathan.

Rusty's reaction to Pete's "Nitro Express" is both one of envy that his "flunky" has a bigger gun than even he owns and of fear that, with a group member possessing such an absurd weapon, Luke will no longer take the trip seriously. The "rusty" hero's method of overcoming a threat of condescension is to attack Luke at what Rusty thinks may be the hunter's weakest point: the possibility that Luke, who carries two guns, "has lost more nerve than Ollie" (84), who carries only one. Thus he associates Pete's overkill with Luke's two rifles by defending British mass-obliteration, rather than pinpoint, bombing of German cities in World War Two, and suggests that the best way to fight a man is "to destroy him half to death . . ." (85). As Tex points out, this connection is hardly perfect (meat tastes better when the animal is killed by only moderate firepower rather than by blitz); but Rusty, who has "put in years being a first-line Ranger Commando in 4C and P" (84), alludes to a primary metaphoric theme of the novel as he couples war with hunting. The corporate man must use instances of aggression to approach the stature of the "natural man" Big Luke Fellinka.

Chap Four, continuing the argument between Rusty and Luke over the possibility of hunting bear in the Brooks Range, has its first scene in a "super deluxe motel bar of a dark chocolate-red velvet interior" (59) in Fairbanks. D.J. explains that the interior is an imitation "English Pump Room," imported, absurdly, from Hawaii. He claims to have forgotten the name of the motel, though it could be "Alaska Cavalier" or "Fairbanks Frontier Arms" (63). Such grandiose names are an attempt to compensate for Fairbanks being "near as flat-ass as Dallas" (63). Thus the initial locale of Chap Four situates us midway between the corporate setting of the early sections of the novel and the wilderness of the later sections, balancing us between the worlds of Rusty and what, up to now, we have assumed to be the pioneer stance of Big Luke. It readies us, too, for the infiltration of corporate America into the wilderness, revealed later in this Chap and, more fully, as the hunt develops.

The dialectic between Rusty and Luke, who is backed up by Kenny Easterly, "the olive oil in the operation," continues through the first half of Chap Four, with Rusty insisting that he is on a "guaranteed bear trophy hunt" (62). What the other side must reveal is that the wilderness of the Brooks Range has been infiltrated by the representatives and techniques of the corporate/technological society. The absurdly titled Moe Henry and Obungekat Safari Group has attracted lesser "counter-type safari groups like Hunting, Ltd., and the Sam Sting Safari" (65) who cater to less wealthy clientele excited by *"greed . . . and a terror of being cheated"* (64). Rusty's insistence on hunting bear culminates in Easterly claiming that the rival groups "maim game all over the damn place and then let them suffer" (64)—sins that will shortly be carried out by Rusty's party. For now, Luke's territory has been invaded by rival groups and three grizzlies have been wounded and are still alive. Thus the "wild game is changing its philosophy" (65). Ollie asserts that with airplanes overhead "animal no wild no more, now crazy." Though Rusty announces that he is uninterested in debating "the merits and vices of technological infiltration" (65), Luke counters that the crazed, wounded bears have attained "in certain ways the intelligence of man" (66)—recognizing their new enemy, they too have taken on destructive, insane natures.

The helicopter, a recent addition to Luke's hunting apparatus, is a new ingredient of obscenity for the hunt. It is given a fitting scatological/authoritarian tag—"Hail the Cop Turd" (100)—for it is an instrument of oppression with which Rusty and his fellows are quick to comply. Thus it is described in obscene images— "vibrated above like one giant overgrown Hog! its carburetor farting . . ." (101)—as it controls a goat hunt—"pushing the Rules and Regs of Cop Turd hunting" (102)—by cutting off the movements of the herd. Lest this all seems nothing more than symbolic hyperbole, Ted Kerasote's recent *Bloodties* discusses just such helicopter-driven hunting in Siberia.[4]

Like the herd, D.J. has been hypnotized by the helicopter when he makes his first kill. Since he has acted as conductor for technological will and as agent for the acquisitive money/machine world, he cannot remain at one with the surrounding wilderness: "he was only part of them, the asshole sulfur smell of money-oil clinging to the helicopter" (100). Again, corporate commerce and aggression is linked—as Freud insisted—to preoccupation with the scatological, the retentive. Always, D.J.'s visions of the natural are infiltrated by the inherited values of Dallas. Thus a panoramic description— "top of a mountain, edge of a bull moose pond, across a canyon from Dall ram, near a feeding ground for grizzer" (100)—is interrupted by information about the results of the helicopter's ability to bring the hunters to such places. As Chap Six begins, D.J. gives his audience a Reichian warning: "you deaden a mystery and your liver goes to shit" (94). Indeed, the conquest of Alaska by the technology of corporate Dallas, the interference of the natural order of things, carries an implied parallel with America's imposition of its will, via the helicopter, upon the impulse toward a comparatively natural order of things in southeast Asia.

Chap Four, where the hunt begins, climaxes with Tex Hyde's shooting of a wolf and Ollie's ritualistic burial of its head. The following Intro Beep makes for a transition from that first kill to a caribou that Rusty's lackey, Pete, "has just wounded . . . with a horror of a gun and cartridge" (75). Chap Five leads us up to the tracking of the caribou as the young genius of a narrator sets his sights upon the artillery of the hunters and upon the personalities of M.A. Pete and M.A. Bill. It hardly advances us in time from the previous Chap, but it does expand the presentation of the hunt's gestalt. The technological "rundown on the guns" (77) begins with those of Big Luke who was "agent for Unerth for a while" (78) and thus carries one of their guns. Passing quickly through the artillery of D.J., Tex and Ollie, we reach Rusty who "travels like a big-ass hunter" so that his first gun, an Apache, "looked like it was vomiting big equipment out of its guts" (79). Three of Rusty's guns are described in detail, but the list seems endless and wears itself out:

> Gun #4 is Ruger . . .
> Gun #5 . . .
> Forget it. (80)

D.J.'s abrupt termination of the catalogue increases devaluation of
the weapons and what follows—a description of Pete's artillery—
leads into surreal absurdity matching the condition of acculturated
corporate man.

After encountering Rusty's disapproval—"I haven't heard of a
double Jeff Nite Express since they used it to kill a Swiss dragon
who was terrorizing some Tyrolean village in 1921" (82)—Pete is
ready to put the engine aside in favor of his daddy's Savage 110.
But M.A. Bill, who "like most ballistics nuts was as near-sighted
as an old hound with silver rim lenses" (88), warns Pete that the
factory-made ammunition for the Savage is unreliable. Bill's knowledge has been gained at the ballistics department of the FBI, where
he has spent his two weeks' summer vacation as a special student
along with "the head of the Ghana Police Department, and the
Mozambique Police Department and native fuzz from Spokane,
Walla Walla, Greensboro" (86): the misguided corporate drive is
again connected with domestic oppression and American-directed
foreign oppression. While Bill's assessment of ballistics is merely
"academic" (88), the fears in Pete causes the cowardly hunter to
spend a sleepless night with "visions of a grizzly bearing down on
him with a wild cry like a negro washerwoman gone ape with a
butcher knife . . ." (88). Thus, next day, he will maim and kill with
the Nitro Express.

D.J. has already revealed that Tex's shooting of the wolf has
been less smooth than he let on in the relatively pastoral narrative
of Chap Four. Indeed, he now claims that "the whole fucking kill
was unaesthetic" (79). Thus Tex's first bullet "went right through
the wolf's two legs, breaking only one" (79). Yet this hint of obscenity is topped by Pete's horrendous wounding of the caribou
after the long cataloging of artillery. Images become Burroughs-
like when D.J. reports Pete's .600 900-grain blast through the caribou as "a hole to put your arm in, all your arm, up to the shoulder
if you are not squeamish" (97). The reader is forced to participate
in the perversion of the narrative as a culminating image describes
the caribou's trail—"silver dollars up to florins" (94)—using a
monetary term, a tool of acquisition, to describe drops of the animal's blood. The notion that, later, Pete "could claim (and believe)"
that the deer's horribly shot-up face represents the scars of a "big
buck caribou fighter" (98) goes beyond D.J.'s definition that comedy is "the unsound actions of the cowardly" (81) into a state of
corporate self-accommodation which matches the abhorrence of
the killing itself. A poignant description of the wounded caribou's flight

but now the caribou trail was rising up to timberline again, and in the
distance, up along a thousand yards, was what looked to be the caribou
. . . (95)

is punctuated by Fellinka's remark that Pete has "hit him an outside rump shot," a sordid interjection which is compounded by
D.J.'s punning: "'Say,' said Pete, trying shift the rump of the subject . . ." (95).

Luke's "message" to the Texans is a meal from the destroyed
animal: "one blood pudding of a cocktail vibrated into total promiscuity" (98). It is a message directed in tainted human terms at the
disconnected culture of technological mainland America. What
was once an American realist/naturalist tradition spills into the
surreal so that the hunters, having forgotten Kenny Easterly's ad-
monition at the beginning of the hunt about greed, line up in the
culminating scene of Chap Six for a photograph with their trophies.
The "five shit-eating grins" (105) are frozen in the necessary surrealism of the occasional photograph's dislocation as symbols of
technological alienation from being.

Images of contemporary American culture break down sustained
natural imagery so that a tension builds up between images of the
wilderness and of the technological society that invades it. Thus
the first sentence of Chap Seven reveals D.J.'s ironic interplay
between "velvet guided tours" and "unspoiled wilderness" (113).
The "military fix" that Luke effects for his hunting party as it
awaits bear, his creation of a concentrated firing position for fear
of losing a client, is in opposition to the setting of "the bank of
mud-lick where berries grow" or "one alpine meadow . . . and
patches of buffalo berry and blueberry" (116). Human endeavor
continually adulterates the wilderness. A male bear's dignified dying is undercut as the party slings stones to test whether it is dead,
and the female bear has "her belly half demolished by the Nitro
Express" of the "Procurement Manager Pure Pores Pete" (119).

If the technological monstrosities of weaponry and transporta-
tion move to obliterate the natural world, elegiac images of that
natural world provide the main opposition to the surrealistic pursuit by the corporate hunters. The narrator must confess that it
was night before he was relaxed enough to remember the "red
dying eyes" (100) of his first kill. The movements of the just shot
mountain goat are initially described as "a step dance like an old
Negro heel-and-toe tap man falling down stairs or flying up them
. . ." (99). Through his gun's scope D.J. has seen "almond oval and
butter love for eyes, a little black sweet pursed mouth, all quivering

now, two nostrils cunning as an old Negro witch . . ." (104). The idyllic movement and aspect of the animal victim is twice connected to a repressed segment of American society, which is also, Mailer is prone to claim, the closest to raw existence. Such imagery has already been used to describe the movements of M.A. Pete's badly wounded caribou—"each step a pure phrase of the blues" (97)—so that the natural movement of the dying animal is aligned with the spontaneous art of African-American music, reviving the existential references to Edison and Miles Davis at the book's beginning. The goat is at one with the wilderness; even its horns are "coils . . . around the nerve which turn the herbs . . ."(104).

Following the compromise between Rusty and Luke in Fairbanks over how they will kill the bear, the party moves by seaplane closer to the wilderness to Dolly Ding Bat Lake where "the smell of the pine forest could make you a religious nut . . ." (67). There is a tension between the reverence of physical response to the natural and what is perhaps a current invention of D.J.—his parodic name for the lake. Not until he begins to describe the group's journey northward by packhorse does the narrative achieve full intensity, relatively free of devaluative parody or self-parody: "the trees get more individual, they have a continuing life story now with the wind" (67). This poetic intensity builds as the group reaches its destination in the mountain range—"water presenting itself to the teeth like moonlight on snow" (68). When Tex kills his wolf, D.J. offers an elegiac response: "for an instant the hills clapped together. Down at timberline trees shifted, air moved in the wave which follows a breaking glass . . ." (68). Whether or not D.J. is appropriating a neutral landscape to reflect his own sensibility, the natural world is that element which is juxtaposed to human intrusion.

By Chap Eight, Rusty and D.J. have broken from the group and are off on their "free" through the Brooks wilderness where all things seem to draw together in a continuous circuit under the pull of Magnetic North. Geological phenomena are described in terms of corresponding animal phenomena, so that, if bear is now on D.J.'s mind, the "soft hump of mountains" becomes "sleeping bears, big haunches of hibernation" (120). Father and son, caught up in sustained ecological encounter, are amazed to discover a landscape of flora in the Arctic Circle as the rich spectacle of "a canyon and a long field of tundra turning red and yellow already and a pioneer tree in the middle of it" (130) appears. This lushness reaches a peak of intensity as Rusty and D.J. pass into a superpastoral bower:

an aisle of forest scents, herbs offering their high priest of here, here is the secret lore and the cold fires of the temple, and the leaf mold, wet molderings, some kind of forest good-bye weeded in from the messages of the wind, sending back to the peasant, back to the farm, then moss, new greenings. . . .(140)

In such surroundings, or with such current idyllic invention by D.J., the narrative sweeps forward, escapes the backup of authorial, self-parodic presence, self-attention, which permeates the Intro Beeps. In such imagined surroundings a redeveloping love of father and son is able to situate itself within the natural lore of the frontier that existed in the American novel in more secure times. We learn how to start a fire in the rain by using "dry punk, that dry perfumy sort of rot stuff in a tree, and that's your tinder and your paper all in one" (131) and that a rifleman "is in trouble . . . when he steps from sunlight into shadow . . ." (132). This romanticism of the frontier is recollected by Rusty from childhood and D.J.'s version of him changes from the earlier image of "high-grade corporate asshole."

After Rusty, in Chap Eight, has unnecessarily shot a dying bear, there is little description of the hunt, as a backup dominates Chap Nine. A brief return to a continuing narrative constitutes an attempt to return to the ideal state within a natural bower shared by Rusty and D.J. before their splintering encounter with the bear. Thus, as Tex and D.J. trek through the cold early dawn towards the Endicott Range, we are told of "the early fall nip cold of the August night, breathing in the hint of the chill of the frozen stream and the icy vise of the magnetic north . . ." (158). Though without the lush floral description of Chap Eight, the wilderness offers some promise of a new beginning for the narrator. By Chap Ten, Tex, a new leader for D.J. replacing Rusty, has the idea to establish a "purification ceremony" (175) by abandoning all weapons "except the knife," so that they will forgo technology in favor of the old frontier bravery. D.J., jealous as he was when Tex made the first kill of the hunt, insists that no binoculars, sleeping bags, or compass be brought further. Thus the pair "own clean fear now, cause they going to live off the land" (176). The narrative, halted at the point where Rusty shoots the dying bear, picks up with D.J.'s recollected feelings. D.J. and Tex, alone in the wilderness, retreat to "go back a little on their new found principles" (177), to pick up non-killing gear, including the binoculars, which will allow for D.J.'s graphic description of the landscape. But their ensuing encounter with the wilderness is an overwhelming experience free of the "mixed shit" (178) which has stayed in them since the hunt began.

Given the tensions between inner and outer voices and the tension within those voices as the pull of the hunt competes with an elegiac reaction toward animal/botanical victims of that hunt, it is not surprising that indeterminacy pervades this novel more, even, than in Mailer's other novels. For example, while the "yeahs" which D.J. uses align his voices with those of the Old Testament (the prophet warning his people to change course before that impending doom by plagues visited upon themselves), "yeah" is also used to mark D.J.'s enthusiastic recollection of juvenile enthusiasms during the hunt. When D.J. denies that he is a disk jockey and makes varying claims that he is at dinner in Dallas "composing in his head" (150) and when he thrice repeats that he is really "a genius of a crippled spade up in Harlem" (133), he expands the American panorama of the work, but adds to the confusion of narrative identity.

Contemplating his ability to confuse his audience as to his identity, the speaker has announced that "there is no security in this consciousness" (134). This condition is a good distance away from the clarity that such a conservative moralist as Wayne Booth or such a rigid classifier as Tillyard might demand. Indeed, it is a distance away from the more secure stances of *The Naked and the Dead* and of the later novel *The Executioner's Song*. But it represents a vital component of the novel's simultaneous processes of self-analysis and social prognosis.

The hunt becomes a means by which the vatic voice of the narrative may track down a national identity. But unlike the sure footing of Podhoretz's nonfiction work *Why We Were In Vietnam,* D.J.'s quest offers little escape from the vertigo of narrative uncertainty. Mailer's preface to the most recent paperback edition of the novel claims that the Alaskan trip was initially conceived as a way to locate two teenage murderers (D.J. and Tex) in the dunes of Provincetown, Massachusetts—as though Vietnam were hardly an omnipresent issue. Only as the boys returned to Dallas from Alaska, Mailer claims, did he realize that their story was over. Yet this tale of a tale would seem to minimize the peculiarities of narrative mode and occasion in *Why Are We In Vietnam?,* and it hardly does justice to the sense of incompletion at the novel's end. The inside broadcast is abruptly terminated with a "Vietnam, hot damn" (208) almost arbitrarily closing the novel, just as *An American Dream* seems to end within an unfinished quality of a nightmare. This sense of incompletion that permeates so much of Mailer's work is explained in a poem included in *Cannibals and Christians,* "The Executioner's Song," which mixes sexual and literary imagery to suggest that the speaker cannot execute a fine finished poem (or a satisfying orgasm) because he is "bad at endings"—his seed shoots too "frantic a flare."[5] If he were cold and efficient, an executioner, the speaker would be able to control, dominate, the muse who owns the realm of poetry; but he lacks that cold efficiency.

Though the "True Life novel" *The Executioner's Song* marks a return to a more omniscient stance for Mailer, it exhibits, I think, the same preoccupation with incompletion and indeterminacy as the poem. The use of free indirect speech allows Mailer to continually enter the minds of most of his characters, but one character is never fully comprehended, pinned down, executed by the author's trick of trade. Gary Gilmore, the convicted killer and existential antihero, warns a relative early in the novel, "don't pick my brain,"[6] and though free indirect speech may allow us to travel along with the minds of all other major characters in the book— Gilmore's cousin Brenda, his lover Nicole Baker, the entrepreneur Larry Schiller—the mystery of *The Executioner's Song,* Gary Gilmore, cut apart as he is by an autopsy scalpel, remains ultimately undefinable by the novelist as executioner. Though the lengthy sections of Gilmore's prison letters to Nicole do reveal much of what perhaps Gary himself wishes to be revealed, the work's ending sees the author/executioner reestablishing his character's mysteries. Just before the murderer is eventually put to death by firing squad, several witnesses have differing interpretations of Gilmore's final state of mind. And, just as he is to die, Gilmore surprises Father Meersman, a well-meaning Catholic priest, by saying to him "dominus vobiscum." The priest is shocked into replying, "Et cum spirito tuo," so that the normal priest-congregation roles are reversed, and Gary finally sneers, "There'll always be a Meersman."[7] Yet at a moving memorial service, Meersman conveniently forgets that last line, telling his audience that Gilmore's last words were, "Dominus Vobiscum. May the Lord be with you. . . ."[8] Thus the complex personality of Gilmore evades the ordering hand of the executioner. Just so, the abrupt ending of *Why Are We In Vietnam?* represents a continuation of the dilemma which the author has set out to address through the disordered mind of D.J., denying us the security of a finite understanding of our nation's condition, just as it denies us any security in our narrator's identity or in our own identity as audience. While Jameson claims that the unclean ending of the novel is an indication that the artist has been unable "to do his job" of conveying "the historic socio-economic causes of

American violence,"[9] I would suggest that all of Mailer's novels render in their endings the inescapable mystery of things (even the "To be continued" of *Harlot's Ghost*) and that, as Lionel Trilling proposes, the artist escapes dogmatic entrapment.

Given the insecurities contained within indeterminacy of the novel's narrative voice, *Why Are We In Vietnam?* remains tenuous in its purchase on epic status. Certainly the novel contains machinery that seems to point it toward epic candidacy. For example, our introduction to Rusty Jethroe, the corporate hero, moves into an epic catalogue of his work and extracurricular activities as "executive, and/or director, and/or special advisor and/or consultant and/or troubleshooter and/or organizer and/or associate of, and/or paid employee for the 4C and P, the CIA. . ." (32). But epic machinery is reduced to the format of the corporate manual. The catalogue becomes increasingly the product of D.J.'s own dark comic invention as we are told that Rusty is a member of "the Dallas Citizens Council for Infighting and Inflicting Symphonic Music" and of "the Warren Commission Boosters" (32). Rusty is heroic now within the confines of corporate requirements.

Just as there is an epic catalogue of Rusty's credentials, of the hunters' artillery, of the sins committed by rival safari groups and as there is in Rusty's epic boast of past hunting exploits, so we are given a series—"it wasn't just because . . ., it wasn't cause . . . , or it wasn't even . . .—no . . ." (46)—of the assets of an heroic alternative to Rusty, Big Luke, who, D.J. stresses, "was a man!" (47). But by Chap Four the dialectic between "the high-grade asshole" of Chap Two and the "man" of Chap Three has virtually collapsed. D.J. and Tex speculate that the guide's brushes with danger have weakened his "Arnold Toynbee coefficient" so that he is now less "interested in challenge than response . . ." (60). "Despite the big man death guts charisma," Big Luke is now possibly more performer than authentic frontiersman in the tradition of the nineteenth-century American novel. His use of helicopters adds to the defoliation of natural experience. Epic possibilities seem continually undercut so that we verge upon the mock epic. Thus the hunt ends with a sardonic Texas version of standard understated epic closure—"And they figured the bear in his natural state had stood nine hundred pounds and more counting the claws" (148)—and thus in the final Chap, the "killer brothers" who "each bit a drop of blood from his finger and touched them across and sat, blood to blood, while the lights pulsated" (204) are in danger of becoming over-romanticized comic frontiersmen.

Why Are We In Vietnam? is divided into only eleven "Intro

Beeps" and eleven "Chaps" so that the epic proximity that would be fulfilled by an extra Beep/Chap pairing is denied as the novel perches precariously between epic and mock epic, a genre which Mark Spilka sees as the shaping tradition of the modern novel.[10] The frantic opening of the novel, mixing literary references with modern electro-technical images on obscene, punning turns of wit, seems to deny the possibility of epic control and that lack is continually reinforced by narrative indeterminacy. D.J. is an intensified version of Mickey Lovett of *Barbary Shore,* who will one moment present a disconnected first-person self—a mind-wounded amnesiac—yet will assume, too, the trappings of a prophet—"Now, in the time I write, when others besides myself must continue a name, a story, and the papers they carry";[11] who is conscious author, fabricator of "the little object."[12] So D.J.'s frantic pleas for an audience, the cacophonous static of his signal, modify the epic reach of his frequency.

As the caw of the moose in the novel's final stages becomes the sound of the "sharp wounded heart of things," it speaks "beneath all else to Ranald Jethroe Jellicoe Jethroe and his friend Gottfried (Son of Gutsy) 'Texas' Hyde" (197). What epic depth is approached by the elegized moose is destroyed by the mock-epic elongation of the boys' names, as Ronald repeats his mother's early nasal pronunciation of his first name (I assume that Solotaroff is mistaken in proposing that "Ranald" is the true spelling of the name). Thus D.J., like the epic actor in Brecht's theatre of alienation (and like the ironic narrative voices of *The Golden Notebook*), is at once caught up in, yet detached from, the resonance of his narrative, forcing the reader to straddle his ironic stances. If our conventional epic expectations are denied us by the form of D.J.'s narrative, its schizophrenic existentialism catches the condition of a civilization experiencing a new kind of tragedy of immense proportion. And if the electronic broadcast that is the given narrative medium offers seduction, the undercutting of that medium by literary intrusions or identity crises demands detachment. Thus the mock-epic impulse of the novel commands the critical faculties of the reader at the same time that the artist, with his intrusive, arrogant narrative posture, devalues the currency of his invention.

Tillyard insists that the epic must achieve "tragic intensity" in its attempt to present "what it is like to be alive at a certain time."[13] Perhaps the subject—announced by its title—of such a confused and confusing work as *Why Are We In Vietnam?* reaches full tragic intensity precisely as it lacks the pretense of "serene security" that Tillyard also demands. Indeed, the fragmentation of Mailer's novel strikingly mirrors the texture of what we have come to recognize as a contemporary American tragedy. For Tillyard, the epic writer "must seem to know everything before his mission to speak for a multitude can be ratified."[14] Thus insecurity of the twentieth century would eliminate the epic kind. Yet he also asserts that "what most makes the epic kind is a communal or choric quality. The epic writer must express the feelings of a large group of people living in or near his own time."[15] It is precisely the inner and outer dualities of Mailer's elliptical Vietnam novel, reflected in the variations of its narrative voice, which makes this a representative work for its nation and age.

2

Just as D.J.'s current schizophrenic condition provides a dialectical of narrative occasion as he fantasizes that he is speaking to a nationwide audience rather than meditating to himself, so the elegiac treatment of the natural world gives way to duality as the narrative progresses. The high peak of descriptive intensity in Chap Eight when Rusty and D.J. enter their super-pastoral bower is followed by a passage which describes a bear's charge. This duality will become D.J.'s rationale for behavior and feelings in the final events of the hunt when menace is no longer the technological butchery of the Americanized hunt, but stems from the natural world itself. After the bear of the narrative's penultimate sequence leaves the scene, the boys climb down from their tree feeling "sweet as caribou" (193)—one of which has just been killed by the bear, not because of hunger, but because of greedy savagery. Thus D.J. and Tex, finally able to sleep after wakeful distress at the helicopterized hunt, witness the duality of the natural world.

Their first encounter during this section where they are without weapons is when Tex, the controlling force in the relationship, sights a white wolf running the beauty of the snowline: "he's just running along the ridge, and taking a bound now and then, and his big white fur goes up in the air and separates just as lithe and quick ass from the snow" (180). But the description becomes sinister as D.J. focuses on the wolf's head—reminiscent of the head of Ollie's ritual—which stands out against the snow:

> . . . mouth, nose, and eyes, black outline black as paint, two green-gold eyes, black stub of a nose, air so clear you can see the shine in the cavity of the black nostrils, and then the mouth, black outlines, red gums, red as cut-open flesh, and white teeth, fangs. (180–181)

The fortunately retrieved binoculars allow a new satanic presence into the hitherto idyllic trek. It is not long before "Animal murder is near" (181). The wolf has picked up human scent and D.J. supposes that electronic waves are emanating between beast and boys. This phenomenon gives way to a battle between the wolf and an eagle whose murderous tactics D.J. remembers from Rusty's lecture during the trek of Chap Eight.

Attempting to escape the pursuing "Cop Turds," D.J. and Tex discover and enter a "forested Bowl" beneath the snow line and they sight a "pale pink fox go springing through the snow to pin a field mouse . . ." (185–86). Thus a pattern of duality is established in the account of this final trek through the wilderness. Either D.J. is remembering this duality to justify his actions and feelings, or the LSD has taken a negative turn as it governs D.J.'s invention. The duality builds into the climactic encounter with the final bear. Initially in this episode there are brilliantly comic descriptions of the bear eating and scratching, sustaining the empathy that D.J. has had for the previous bear victimized by Rusty's frantic overkill. The new bear has discovered berries, despite previous claims about the year's blight:

> . . . so he grabs with a paw and hooks in about two hundred buffalo berries at a pop, and swallows, and lets blue juice and red juice run out of the sides of his black wet leather mouth, and then raises one paw in the air and wipes said mouth on his shoulder as if imitating a weight lifter sniffing his own armpit. . . . (188)

This comic-positive description of the bear continues as it digs for roots and scratches its behind on a tree. All nature seems to exist in harmony as mice appear, a sparrow settles on the bear, and a slight wind springs up. But this peace is broken when a "convention of antlers"—caribou—crosses the scene and the bear suddenly wheels after them and is able to kill a stumbling calf. The already satiated bear is content just to urinate and defecate beside the dead animal and D.J., jolted out of his entrancement at nature, wishes for a rifle so that he might compare this murderous bear to the placid dying bear of Chap Eight. Thus, while the initial dialectic of the Chap is between the beauty of the wilderness and the Cop-Turd that hunts the two boys, the dialectic shifts when he witnesses "Griz #2" (193) murder the caribou calf and "her death goes out over the ridge and slips into the bowl . . . and this afternoon takes a turn . . . everything is altered . . ." (192). The turn is to a dialectic of nature, a fragmentation intensifying with the return of the

dead calf's mother as D.J.'s sensibility infiltrates this visitation and
he speculates that the odor of death is connected by the mother
with "the scent of conception not ten months ago" (193). Yet this
is not, as D.J. claims, "the last thing they saw that day," for D.J.,
"the pure American entrepreneur," launches into the high poetic
as he notices the colors of the day change from "snow gold and
yellow to . . . coral bright as the underside of the horn of the Dall
ram" (194)—and magically two rams appear in D.J.'s narrative.

In fact, the "odor of death" that D.J.'s highly charged sensibility
encounters after the bear's kill is partially lifted by the sight and
sound of a flight of cranes, with "high cawing and wing beat clear
up to the fanning and vibrating of reeds some high long-gone sound
such as summer coming to the very end" (194). The animal murder,
and D.J.'s meditation upon it, are further tempered by the appearance of a group of rams at a salt pond and finally by the arrival of
a bull moose at sunset. If the cranes are the last animals "they saw
that day" (194) the rams and the moose are an additional therapeutic invention/fantasy overcoming the remembrance/fantasy by
the acidified D.J. of the bear's brutality. This incremental description adds to the elegiac note of the Chap. But the downside of
nature seems to return that night as the "lights" of the North now
tell the boys that God is "no man . . . but a beast . . . of a giant
jaw and cavernous mouth with a full cave's breath and fangs, and
secret call: come to me" (202). The beast that is God has his light
show (via D.J.'s dubious recollection) command them to "fulfill my
will, go forth and kill . . ." (204) so that this newly found malevolent
nature, rather than the corporate/technological/military fix of contemporary American society, seems to be propelling the boys toward their mission in Vietnam.

D.J. claims that he is able to see "right through shit" (49) and
seems privy to information not expected of a first-person narrator.
Thus he is able to take on the penetrative powers—a first-person
omniscient stance—enjoyed by Serge O'Shaughnessy as he enters
the consciousness of Charlie Eitel in *The Deer Park*. For example,
D.J. is able to assume knowledge of how M.A. Pete has acquired
the two guns that he has brought along on the hunting trip and he
is able to enter the surrealistic perspective of the cowardly Pete
setting sights on the caribou. Omniscience becomes at times a kind
of cloak to allow D.J.'s own fantasies full operating power as they
project themselves onto, for example, Hallie, Rusty, and Tex. It
will also help the first-person speaker of the present to detach
himself from his past character (or present fantasy of the past)
when ultimate disclosures are to be made.

The early shooting of the caribou by M.A. Pete achieves a simul-
taneity of spectacular rhetoric and the ludicrous. First there is a
burlesqued epic posture as Pete, the mock-hero, sights the animal:
"And standing around, looking at the dead wolf, he looked up, and
he, the medium asshole, was the first to see a caribou two hundred
yards away through the thin trees . . ." (89). And the absurd, cowardly savagery of Pete is extended as the narrative follows the
shooting of the caribou film-like through the nervous eyes of the
hunter himself, a narrative viewpoint more akin to omniscience
than to first-person:

> and in the accurate fevered inaccuracy of being awake all night . . .
> the cross-hairs on the scope ran a figure eight around the horns which
> then plummeted down around the hooves, flew up past the tail into the
> air, about, and back over the caribou's flanks to a view, all abrupt,
> honest, naked, and hairy of the buck's testicles, magnified 4X . . . and
> then past caribou's deer nuts in a blur as if M.A. Pete was in a movie
> traveling the curves so it was a blur, and around came the sights again
> to the back of the hocks and up and RUMBA! (89)

Thus the penultimate moment of the Chap is achieved by rendering
the pathetic vertigo of the corporate "yes-man," out of place in
the wilderness, against the natural flow of the "honest, naked"
animal's movement. The surreal style by which Pete's condition is
presented matches the act which he commits. While such stylistic
achievement allows the outside author, Mailer, to distance himself
from objects of satire, for the currently recollecting Ronald Jethroe
the achievement of this finely wrought style is a buffer to the obscenity of the hunt.

When Pete butchers his caribou, D.J. is able to produce pathetic
fallacy as the trees are "cowardly spectators, man" (95); yet the
next killing will be his. When he shoots the third victim of the
hunt, a goat, his response is as strong as the self-retribution that
overwhelmed the ancient mariner: "Wham! the pain of his exploding heart shot like an arrow into D.J.'s heart, the animals had gotten
him . . ." (99). Ronald must speak of himself in third-person. Another way for D.J. to detach himself from the obscenity of the hunt
and from other problems is by some kind of aesthetic or structural
evasion. For example, though he will apologize in Intro Beep 5 for
his hang-up on numbers during a description in the previous Chap
of the group's artillery, he will conveniently slip back into that
hang-up during ensuing kills. The digression on the Saskatchewan
whore Ruby Lil, who cannot bring to ejaculation an "auditor from
Manitoba" (115), is offered as a meditation by Big Luke on his

failure of will due to fear of losing a client for the first time. But it is revealed to be D.J.'s own invention, just as Hallie Jethroe's session with Dr. Rothenberg in Chap One is admitted to be the speaker's own "stream-of-conch" (23) projection. D.J. admits that his fantasy about Ruby Lil and the auditor is not "Big Luke's thought" but that of "D.J. on the edge of masturbating in the Alaskan night. . ." (116). But he will not admit that the narrative fantasy is a present one; it must be relegated, for present evasion, into the past.

Such a manipulation is similar to the way by which D.J. shuttles between self-reference in first-and third-person. Thus Chap Ten ends with D.J. suddenly stepping outside of himself and speaking of "Ranald Jethroe Jellicoe Jethroe and his friend Gottfried (Son of Gutsy) 'Texas' Hyde" (197). This outside movement continues through Chap Eleven which begins by concentrating on the movements and feelings of Tex so that we seem, indeed, outside of our initial speaker. Yet D.J. has continuously referred to himself in the third-person stance of "D.J." rather than as "I," and though Chap Eleven seems more outside than previous Chaps, an occasional "you bet" or "yeah" still signals his enthusiastic presence. Again, it is possible that parts of the narrative are products of current invention (that is, fantasy stirred up under LSD while sitting at the dinner table in Dallas) rather than accurate remembrance. Thus the movement into third-person in Chap Eleven could be less evidence of Mailer's taking over, as Poirier puts it,[16] than it is an attempt by the current D.J. to retrieve himself from his past (a separation which tends to break down once more in the Terminal Intro: Beep and Out). The announcement that the two boys "hung there each of them on the knife of the divide in all conflict of lust to own the other yet in fear of being killed by the other" (203) might be the product of current suppressed fantasy, rather than an objective report of the past by outside author. A description such as "a corona of red and electric green wash and glow colors rippling like a piece of silk and spikes of light radiating up like searchlights, diamond spikes from the crown of the corona" (201) and so on is perhaps the acid-induced hallucination of the current D.J. embellishing the past as much as it is an outside authorial voice defining the exact lighting of a special Alaskan night. Separation of past and present, as well as of character and author, becomes suspect, becomes the signal of repression, as current fantasy seems more at work than the ordered remembrance of a separated past.

Intro Beeps operate both to devaluate narrative and to evade the continuation of narrative. For example, Intro Beep 8 interrupts the account of the father and son "free" to bring us back into a diatribe within the time zone of present dinner in Dallas. Intro Beep 9 promises that the narrative is not yet over, that the climax of the Alaskan adventure is still to come. Yet the following Chap hardly advances the narrative. We learn that D.J. and Tex have decided to leave the rest of the party (just as Rusty and D.J. have split in the previous Chap) in the early morning following the day when Rusty loads what he claims is his bear onto the helicopter. But it's some time into Chap Nine before this new escape is mentioned; instead D.J. opens the Chap with speculations about social life in Dallas. Even when we enter into the Alaskan narrative again, there is an increase in digressional commentary halting the account of the boys' journey so that the narrative once more backs up. And when D.J. begins to build a description of the landscape through which he and Tex embark on their "bona fide tear" (162) the reader is instructed, even though he may be "ready for the next adventure," to "hold your piss." First, we must examine the antecedents of that "consummate bundle of high contradictions" (162) which is D.J.'s alter ego, Tex Hyde. Only as Chap Nine closes are we allowed to "carry on up to the mountains" (167); but even then the extravagantly impulsive D.J. will order us to have patience before he is ready to resume his composition. Intro Beep 10, in fact, will launch an anti-academic tirade against the reader: "shit ecologist big university librarian groper" (169)—so that by Chap Ten D.J. will admit that he has been hanging "on the edge of a stall" (174). Yet Chap Ten also begins with a digression as D.J., continuing his speculations upon electrical phenomena, launches into obscene connections after explaining to his "creep technician" reader the "superconductivity of metals at absolutely low temperatures" (173). Soon, however, he must admit that his comic improvisation is merely evasion, that he has allowed the narrative to backup because he is "hung up on a moment of the profoundest personal disclosure" (174).

In Intro Beep 9 D.J. tells us that frustration can make "you more telepathic because it makes you more electric" (152). But too much frustration, he observes, will cause stasis. Thus, stalling at the opening of Chap Ten, the young wizard of the airwaves hears the static of his own voice—"Fuck this noise!" (174)—before attempting to resume his narrative. If the disclosure that D.J. says he will soon make involves Tex, himself a substitute for the failed father, then the emphasis on the power of the "cold bare electric land of the North" (196) operates as a buffer to personal disclosure. D.J. claims that the electricity of the Arctic Circle, and its role as receiver for the Magnetic-Electro Fief of the dream world of America, is what controls all things—including the desires of the boys up in the Brooks Range. Thus D.J. seeks to explain his relationship with Tex by describing the forces of the North upon them rather than by examining the relationship as a product of that failed relationship between father and son described most fully in the Rusty/D.J. episode of Chap Eight, but which permeates the entire narrative. Thus D.J.'s connective, associative metaphors of the electric power of the far North operate not simply as examples of creative and therefore authorial non-implosion, but as means to prolong D.J.'s evasion of a true understanding of his own nature. Two years after the events in Alaska, D.J. remains uncertain about the implications of the events that he describes regarding Rusty and Tex, so that concentration upon electronic imagery, and narrative stances which set up the speaker as a disk jockey ranting over the airwaves rather than as an inner-directed fantasist are perhaps convenient modes of evasion.

D.J.'s early plea to "Let go of my dong, Shakespeare" sets up parallels with the dual inner and outer stance of that masterpiece, which both mirrors Shakespeare's age and, as Hegel suggests, provides an investigation of the individual's soul. *Why Are We In Vietnam?*, like *Hamlet* initially situated in the nighttime world of the dream, reaches both outward to the American corporate and political world and inward into the soul of D.J. who seems as troubled by both social conditions and family relations in Dallas as Hamlet is in Elsinore. If D.J. continually adopts modes of evasion to escape plucking out the heart of his own mystery, he also exhibits as much confusion as the Prince of Denmark about both what he does and who he is. Thus, in the early stages of the hunt he may be reverent toward his surroundings and toward hunted animals, yet he is also caught up in competition with Tex. He identifies with the wolf that Tex shoots to the extent that the animal seems to reflect his own concerns—"a wolf silence like he had to come to some conclusions about the problems of life and occupation, near relatives, in-laws, phratries" (68)—yet he is "half-sick watching what Tex had done . . . since he had had private plans to show Tex what real shooting might be" (69). Thus D.J. seems at once in opposition to his father's venture yet unable to escape sharing in like aggressive enthusiasms. The self-styled genius cannot escape his own adolescence, and the enthusiasm seems to remain, two years after the event, in the present moment of recollection.

His schizophrenic condition contains the hunter who must be purveyor of the obscene so that, describing the next hunting episode, as the helicopter, "pushing the rules and regs" (102), controls a herd's movements, D.J. is still proud to boast that "I got the first shot" (103). Like Huck Finn, he is still able to respond to the natural world; yet he is also the imploded child of corporate Dallas. Throughout the text the elegiac force will collide with human intrusion as D.J.'s two sides fight for supremacy.

The session in Chap One between Hallie Jethroe and her psychiatrist centers on her concern over her son whom the doctor has interviewed and found to be "a humdinger of latent homosexual highly over-heterosexual with onanistic narcissistic and sodomistic overtones, a choir task force of libidinal cross-hybrided vectors" (14). The session seems to take place in the present—that is, after the hunt that will be described later in D.J.'s narrative. In the next Intro Beep D.J. will reveal that the session is his own invention, a way to speak about both himself and his mother—but he doesn't reveal whether or not Rothenberg's interview with him has been an invention. D.J. suggests that his mother's psychiatrist must spend his days "listening to Dallas matrons complain about the sexual habits of their husbands" (12) and he seems to begin to talk about his father when he begins, "Well, like every one of those bastards"; but he interrupts himself to resume in general terms:

> "well every one of those bastards has the sexual peculiarities of red-blooded men which is to say that one of them can't come unless he's squinting down a gunsight, and the other won't produce unless his wife sticks a pistol up his ass." (12)

For the time being, he is able to avoid a direct attack upon his father. But by the second Chap D.J. is asking why he has "such a total rejection of . . . his rich secure environmental scene" (34). Because Rusty is "the highest grade of asshole made in America" (37), D.J. sees that his future is one of suffocation within the corporate-oriented family. Thus D.J., who in his initial Intro Beep has demanded that old genius step aside for a new voice, quickly settles on a recurring theme of society and of literature—parentage and its role in the development of character.

The primary concern of Intro Beep 3 is an incident that took place when D.J. was thirteen—five years before he offers up the current narrative. Rusty, playing tackle football with his son, tries to demonstrate how his son "could not run around him" (39). But, so the current D.J. claims, the thirteen-year-old with the "presumptive hip dip half-back's butt about as big as Scarlett O'Hara's waist" (39) evades his father until—as D.J. now claims—feeling sorry for his dad, he allows himself to be tackled. In frustration, Rusty hits his son hard, bites him on his behind, then tackles him "over and over again" (40) for ten minutes. The early adolescent's reaction to his father's ensuing sermon on being "a nut about competition" (41) is to hit him hard on the head with a pick-axe handle, for which, after negotiations with Hallie, D.J. is banished to a military school. To connect this decision with D.J.'s imminent departure for Vietnam is to realize the major role that Rusty has played in his son's life.

The emblematic incident of five years ago rings through other sections of the book—for example, Rusty makes fun of his colleague at CCCC & P by saying that Al Percy Cunningham "wanted to haul off and split your dad with an axe" (148) and D.J.'s account of the acquisition of an arsenal by M.A. Pete seems an associative conjecture for he allows that Pete's relationship with his "deadly daddy" (80) is hardly better than his own with Rusty. Pete's father, "beginning to breathe thin" (81), gives his hitherto neglected son the Savage. This sets up the obscenity of the hunt in Chap Six when the blasted rump of the caribou Pete shoots—"blood on the cotton white ass" (93)—points back to the bitten behind of young Ronald in "Intro Beep 3." Just as D. J. closes Chap Six by suggesting that the "blasts of rage and gouts of fear" (107) following Rusty's initial botched attempt at a grizzly are caused by his inability to own Hallie "in the flesh of her brain" (107), so he explains the football incident as Rusty's frustration at his fear of biting Hallie's rump.

The football incident is so difficult for D.J. to confess that he prays for the fox-trot—evasion by style—and will also excuse his father's action by saying that they were caused by "an excess of love" (42) for the son himself. Yet such an apology hardly jibes with the emphasis on Rusty's aggression permeating narrative and intro beeps. D.J., alienated from his father as was that earlier Texas-born military figure, the MacArthur-like Cummings of *The Naked and the Dead* (who was also banished to military school for sharing too much in his mother's sensibility), comes close to the role of orphan, which is the status of two previous Mailer first-person narrative heroes—Lovett of *Barbary Shore* and O'Shaughnessy of *The Deer Park*.

D.J. now sees sex in terms of war. The middle-aged Rusty is "like the charge of the Light Brigade, not so light" (40), while his enemy is Hallie, "one with all those . . . Cossacks and Turks up in the hills who want to pick each zippy point of meat-nip and therefore know where to cut on down on the Light Brigade and cut off a piece of that charge for themselves" (40). D.J.'s personality has become the product of the warfare, which he sees as the basis of his parents' marriage and which carries over into his own sexual perspective. For example, he takes delight in telling "Dallas debutantes and just plain common fucks" that "cascades of hot piss" thrown from paper cups at Mexican bull fights smell "like your sweet little home-cooking crotch before you git up in the morning to swab it down" (43). This misogyny is repeated during the "stall" of Chap Ten when D.J., who will address his audience as "dear poontang" (167), discusses Dallas "tooth and cunt hostesses," including Hallie, who are available "closet fucks" (155).

Perhaps such antagonism is an alertness to the danger of his own super-identification with his mother. He is quick to disassociate himself from the "Nazi-type Texas-style state trooper wolf bugger faggots and little languid queer types from Norlins" (42)—we have learned in Chap One that Hallie claims to be a New Orleans Montesquiou—at military school; yet he will also confess that he is not a George Hamilton lookalike, as he has allowed his mother to claim in Chap One, but "a manly clear-featured version in normal features of his mother . . ." (41). Like Cummings, Ronald must overcompensate for identification with his mother, the initial subject, after himself, of his discourse.

The brief Intro Beep 8 brings us away from the father and son "free" that begins as Chap Seven ends and back into the current moment of D.J.'s inner narrative construction at formal dinner in Dallas. He contemplates his mother's "tits popping big tasty hostess heavens" (125) and imagines her lusting after his "best friend, blood brother" Tex—and he again summons electronic imagery to assert kinship with his Vietnam-bound companion and his "X-ed out" (126) relationship with Rusty, so that the enthusiasm that the conclusion of Chap Seven and the better part of Chap Eight discloses for the wilderness escape of father and son is moderated by this non-narrative assessment of things. D.J. senses that love (that which he believes he shares with Tex and which he at least subconsciously feels for Hallie) is dialectic—a giving and taking; but Rusty, caught up in corporate rigidity, is unable to participate in that mutuality. Thus D.J., former hunter and soldier-to-be, separates himself from his father's single-mindedness by sympathizing with the dead female bear of Chap Seven, which is "unknowing of its killer as the poor town fuck must be unknown of the parental origins of her latest . . . embryo in her womb" (126).

Chap Eight, with father and son off away from the hunting party and with Rusty "shedding his corporate layers" (127), seems to offer a new possibility for their failed relationship. The language that D.J. assigns Rusty seems interchangeable with his own, as though the two are subsumed into a mutual gestalt where language ceases to be self-parodic. Now Rusty is able to recall a past from which he has been estranged by his career with Pure Pores. He is able to speak of his "grandmammy, your great-grandmother Eula Spicer Jethroe" (130) and to recall the "East Texas depression years" (131) of his childhood when his father had no work and when hunting was a necessity, a natural activity compared to the current technologically-driven hunt. Rusty achieves a level of purgation on this trek, seems to surrender temporarily his need for control, becomes an individual whose life has been caught up in the socio-economic system—a sympathetic character within the traditions of American naturalism. The idyllic setting reestablishes the broken bonds of father and son. There is a new, fond, rather than abusive, intimacy as D.J. speaks of "Rust" (127) and is carried off into a Huck Finn runaway narrative as he recreates their escape from Luke and the helicopters. A new hip enthusiasm—"listen to the mood man" (128)—describes a juvenile camaraderie where father and son are "tight as combat buddies" (128), as though the imminent trip to Vietnam with Tex is an attempt to retrieve the ideal relationship of Chap Eight. Barriers are broken as Rusty reveals his lifelong fascination with flora (has the relationship between them been so distant that D.J. never knew this, or are we to understand the revelations as a writer/broadcaster's improvisation?) and this new natural intimacy is a working dialectic of love, rather than the failed, broken circuits of father-son love which D.J., at dinner in Dallas, has spoken or thought of in Intro Beep 8. Then D.J. spoke of the failed dialectic because "corporation is DC, direct current, diehard charge, no dialectics man, just one-way street" (126). So the natural forces that father and son confront offer some hope of repair, some redemption from the broken circuits of corporate families. D.J. is "riding high on circuits of love" (134) and Rusty can sense his son's mood and choose not to kill the old caribou that stands before them. But the narrative twists again so that the love between father and son which has built up after the aggressiveness of previous Chaps and Beeps is again shattered as, aware of the presence of a bear, D.J. "is hip to the hole of his center which is slippery desire to turn his gun and blast a shot into Rusty's fat fuck face" (137). Now, well after the revelation of Rusty's biting D.J., we are informed that Rusty beat his five-year-old son— "spoiled little beautiful" (137)—perhaps for disturbing, by screaming, a lovemaking session with Hallie who saved her son as she

did when he hit Rusty with a hammer. Now D.J.—apparently recall-
ing or inventing this incident in his drugged state—wonders, in
Reichian fashion, whether his existence has not been shattered by
such emasculation. Again, he is counterpart to Cummings, of *The
Naked and the Dead,* whose mother's empathy and father's harsh-
ness seem to cause his later fascistic and sexually diathetic
character.

Father and son are finally wrenched apart when Rusty cannot
resist "being a camera-conscious flash-bulb poking American—to
heist the stone and bap the side" (145). Thus he devalues the experience of the hunt, destroying the bear's ease into death by
shooting it once more and then failing to contradict D.J.'s awarding
of the bear to him. D.J. claims that this represents the "final end
of love for one son for one father" (147). Yet his mannered recollection of the idyllic stages of the "free," and his concomitant need
to seek Tex as father-substitute, suggest that the father-son relationship remains more ambivalent than the eighteen-year-old Ronald might wish to claim.

The boys' "bona fide tear" into the "real peaks" (162) of Endicott
Range is prompted by D.J.'s continuing anger after Rusty's claiming of the bear. Thus D.J. claims that on the night following father
and son's return to Luke's party he cannot sleep for fear that he
will "beat in Rusty's head" (157)—a return to the thirteen-year-
old's feelings of patricide. Thus the new trek that begins in Chap
Nine represents a rejection of the competitive, neglectful father
and the attempt to substitute Tex in his place. But the father-son
relationship remains uncertain. As the boys watch a wolf and eagle
fight, D.J. remembers what Rusty has told him of the eagle in the
previous episode, and he remembers, too, Rusty's lesson on how
to start a fire from rotten punk. Yet his parenthetic admission—
"which punk D.J. had not forgot was from the lore of his father of
whom he could not think" (196)—is muddled: the D.J. who inwardly narrates his tale recalls remembering yet refusing to remember his father. He is, and/or was, in a state of confusion toward
the relationship, and the confusion seeps through into his relationship with Tex. No wonder that D.J. seeks to overrun his "profoundest personal disclosure" (174) with electromagnetic imagery, as
though the force of the north is the controlling factor of behavior
rather the individual psyche.

The charged state of the boys in Chap Ten (after the somewhat
evasive concentration on Tex's parentage in Chap Nine) in D.J.'s
version of the way things were, is manifested in sexual banter,
which D.J. is careful to stress does not mean that they "ding ding

ring a ling on . . . queer street with each other" (179)—the ribaldry
is merely an expression of "Texas tenderness" (179) for each other.
Thus, after witnessing an encounter between a fox and a squirrel,
they will, in exhilaration, "mill it up, each taking ten good lumps
to the gut" (186). It seems good, clean fun. But, as Poirier has
noted, the journey into the "ice ass pinnacles of the Brooks Range"
(174) carries a symbolism paralleling that of Dante's *Inferno* where
the ultimate point of degradation is that ice palace beneath the
devil's tail.[17] D.J. himself excuses the "foul talk" (180) that has
accumulated during the trip through Alaska and he quickly
chooses to describe the duality of the purifying but menacing encounter with the wilderness in dominating heterosexual terms. The
experience is like "the best piece of cock you ever mustered up
into a cunt which is all fuck for you" (184); and the danger and
mystery is "a beautiful castrating cunt . . . between murder and
love" (184).

The "profoundest personal disclosure" (174) after the initial
"stall" of Chap Ten is not reached until the middle of Chap Eleven.
D.J. has announced that the reader should not think that the two
boys are on "queer street," but the desire of the boys for each
other is what D.J. feels compelled to describe in the penultimate
section of the narrative. The absence of an Intro Beep to Chap
Eleven might well be explained by D.J.'s need to connect the principal fact of Chap Ten—their witnessing of the caribou calf's killing by "Griz #2" (193)—to the feelings that he claims he suddenly
has for Tex during the night and that he assumes Tex has for him.
Thus D.J. seems to connect the apparently mutual onset of homosexual feelings with their new mutual realization of the duality of
nature, of god; and thus the young soldier is able to justify his
entry into combat as an extension of the hunt.

D.J.'s ability to enter the minds of others (as he has done so fully
with his mother and father in the initial stages of the broadcast),
allows him also to enter into the mind and feelings of his friend
Tex—to project onto Tex feelings similar to his own. Still, D.J.
seems to be the initiator of sexual activity: when the boys wake
up three hours after falling asleep near the salt pond, it is D.J. who
is "hugging ice to ice" (199) against Tex. And the most "personal
disclosure" of the novel comes when D.J., witnessing the beast
that is god, "raised his hand to put it square on Tex's cock and
squeeze" (202). But there is a possibility that D.J.'s desire for Tex
has been a recurring condition, rather than a momentary product
of the electric charges of the north. Thus D.J. has "never put a
hand on Tex for secret fear that Tex was strong enough to turn

him around and brand him up his ass" (202) and thus D.J. is weakened by temptation "at the root of his balls" (203) so that "he always swelled to be muscle hard around Tex" (203).

D.J. has gone out of his way to interpret the incidents between the two adolescents as the result of their new understanding of the dual nature of existence following revelations in Chap Ten when the boys are close to, part of, the wilderness. Yet the incident is checked when the posited mutual desire of the boys to bugger each other is opposed by the fear of the new-made bitch who had been buggered. Thus they become "killer-brothers" (204) ready to fulfill the will of the beast-god. Yet it would be well to consider what other aspects of the narrative have led to this penultimate stage of D.J.'s confessional/improvisation. Certainly his admission that Hallie's "sweet ass was his sweet ass" (202) identifies him with his mother—his connection with her has been so vital that he opens his narrative by projecting himself into her consciousness. And the second Chap, plus Intro Beep 3 and later accounts of the hunt itself, suggest the importance of the shattered Rusty-Ronald relationship. D.J.'s insistence that the wilderness itself has unleashed the eventually suppressed feelings of the two boys for each other operates as a kind of evasion of the truth that his own feelings are the product of his domestic environment. The implosive form of D.J.'s inner-directed narrative suggests that he has failed to come to terms with the principal key to his condition even as he attempts to deal with the implications of the boys' imminent journey to Vietnam. His electrical cosmology is as muddled as that of Blake's little black boy.

To Poirier, keying on the penultimate scenes between the two boys, "this whole book is about buggery"[18]—including, I assume, the speaker's buggery of his audience. Yet perhaps that diathetic gesture, unlike that of *Deliverance,* is contained within a wider gesture of the novel: that implosive compulsion which, in one form or another, dominates a nation's being even as it seeks to ultimately control the narrative form of this novel. Thus *Why Are We In Vietnam?* becomes an extension of that "minority within," which Mailer had brought forth just before the novel's publication in his Vietnam Day speech at Berkeley on 25 May 1965.

That speech begins by focusing on the discrepancies in Lyndon Johnson's public manner: he cannot control his sounds and gestures. The emblematic sensory notation makes way for an examination of the President's "totalitarian prose"[19]—itself an equivalent for the way Johnson's assault on Vietnam has been motivated by his desire to suppress the civil rights movement (the suppression of a nation's minority within). Since all arguments for America's oppression of Vietnam are, Mailer goes on, illogical, the answer to the mystery of our presence must be found within Lyndon Johnson himself. To Mailer, Johnson is an alienated being because, just as his face continually reveals contradictory poses, he has no notion of his own identity. He must compulsively seek action in fruitless conquest "to define the most rudimentary borders of identity."[20] Johnson's need to achieve a single identity, to abbreviate his self, is manifested by his need to abbreviate both his own name and those of his family—an obsession emblematic of a national insanity so that abbreviation is a preoccupation in the Dallas, USA of *Why Are We In Vietnam?*

Toward the end of Intro Beep 1, D.J. muses that there is a continual "tape recorder in heaven for each one of us" (9), recording every sound, indeed every thought, we have, so that the initial narrative stance of a broadcasting voice is set off against the possibility that D.J., contemplating death in his inner space station, speaks not to "you out there in all that implosion land" (8) but to his solitary self. Rather than an outwardly directed "stream-of-conch" (23)—the conch signifying a power of control through sound signal as in *Lord of the Flies*—which might represent the artist as moral amplifier, D.J. conjectures that the narrative might be a "tape recording of my brain in the deep of its mysterious unwindings" (24), thus offering the reader an inside trip into the secret compartments of a contemporary individual mind. If the proposition that the narrative is a "private tape being made for the private ear of the Lord" (174) is valid, then the "grassed out auditor," his punching bag for insults, is as much D.J. himself as God as it is the radio audience that D.J. initially proposes that he addresses or the reader to whom he refers at the close of Intro Beep 2.

After his rendition in Chap One of the dialogue between Dr. Rothenberg and Hallie, D.J. admonishes the reader to "color it rainbow" (22). But this is not completely a confession of fabrication, for D.J. adds that Hallie "don't talk that way, she just thinks that way" (22). Though this is an admittance by D.J. that he projects thought into Hallie's mind, it also suggests that she is a similar being who suppresses her minorities within, so that this book's obscenity functions partly to bring to the surface the suppressive components of American consciousness which distort the complex texture of personality into national aggression.

3

We have seen that throughout the Alaskan sections of *Why Are We In Vietnam?* the elegiac force of the setting collides with forces of human intrusion. D.J. may let his feelings for Tex and his future excursion to Vietnam be explained away by the call to fulfill the will of brute nature, but the negativity of anti-pastoral posture stems from previous images of corporate America—that "strange disease" that the "physician half-blind, not so far from drunk" speaks of in the introduction to Part 1 of *Cannibals and Christians*.[21] Thus the impetus which builds in the narrative through natural/animal description is devalued by images of D.J.'s own culture. On the trail of Pete's wounded caribou, the sun is described as "shining right in the blood with a thousand lights, or so it would look if you had your nose right there on the bloodied leaves close enough to that wet to think that you were looking at neon signs" (94–95). Such hallucinative imagery by the Vietnam-bound late adolescent devalues any reverence that has been set up to describe the power of landscape, the grace of the wounded animals. A hyperactive imagination can describe the dignity of the "bleeding jagged gored red ass" (96) caribou as it climbs towards the woods where it has chosen to die: "and the caribou makes those rocks with lunges and grunt and like then a whimper you could almost hear through the binocs" (96–97). But then the helicopter frenzies the animal and D.J. must describe its new movement in terms of human acquisitiveness: "frantic as a prospector climbing a mountain to get to a hill of gold" (97).

Thus D.J.'s metaphors assault the natural world. The dead female bear gives off an odor "of cigarette breath on the mouth of a bitch who smokes forty cigs a day" (121) and Rusty's need to kill a bear must also be described in terms that defoliate natural experience as "the odor of evergreens might just as well be poppers for his inflamed brain" (123). Nature is deformed by blasted human sensibility. Of course, the "exploding psychic ecology" (114) resulting from the technological invasion of the wilderness is very much a product of D.J.'s own present exploded psychic ecology. Each image that moderates the plot and infiltrates animate and inanimate stems from D.J.'s current connections as he sits at dinner, contemplating not only the past but the people about him and the meat on his plate before him.

Within the strong elegiac strain of Chap Ten, as the boys move

northward weaponless, there is an easing of the devaluative process that has permeated previous sections of the narrative; yet the
undercutting still exists as the hunt ends. The epic metaphor that
the wilderness "rings back" at the boys "like a stone on a shield"
is "blocked" in favor of a reference to "a finger wet on the rim of
the best piece of glass on Park Avenue, New York" (177), so that
contemporary American culture continues to obstruct the narrative's attempt to achieve classical epic reach. The tenseness of the
boys as they watch the last bear from atop a tree is devalued by a
comparison of their breathless state to "airline hostesses serving
Frank Sinatra African rock tail frozen ass lobster" (189). Not only
is contemporary culture minimized, but the authenticity of the
boys' experience and the currency of the narrative endeavor itself
are shattered.

The work draws attention to itself as literary artifact so that
the Intro Beeps, despite the connective wit of D.J.'s drug-induced
speculations, function as interruptive and decreative, rather than
spontaneous and organic, modes. While D.J. may laud, in Intro
Beep 1, the organic genius of Edison's inventive mode, the Intro
Beeps themselves are interference signals belonging to the "pro-
grammed out" (8), Electrolux world of modern decreation. But a
decreative impulse is present also in the Chaps. In Chap Four D.J.
intrudes on his account of the hunt to note that the episode he
describes takes place "early September in Alaska, two years (to
remind you) before the period of D.J.'s consciousness running
through his head" (60). Thus, he tells us, the form of his presentation is "more narrative" (60) because it is a product of memory,
whereas present consciousness is "chaos and void" (61). That act
of making a distinction between past and present consciousness
draws attention to the interactivity of the two fields of time and—
as the sudden jumps from past into present in *Barbary Shore* serve
to show that Lovett's narrative is the very novel he has been trying
to write, is the black object he has been reaching to grasp—D.J.'s
self-intrusions tend to relegate him to a role of a character in his
writer's fiction: that is the "writer's writer" (28) who will be "maro-
oned on the balmy tropical isle of Anal Referent Metaphor" (150).
"Chap" is an abbreviated term from basic fiction and undercuts
D.J.'s initial stance that he is speaking over the airwaves, as though
the narrator is reduced to the guise of metaphor for the condition
of the author himself. And the multiple literary references and
allusions, concentrated in the opening sections but continuing
throughout the book, serve not only to provide evidence that D.J.
is well-read for his age, but to maintain awareness that, outside of

the narrative possibilities of radio broadcast or inner stream of consciousness, a literary endeavor takes place. Thus awareness of the discourse as a literary fabrication opposes the spontaneity of the young genius' mental connections. As Sillitoe's adolescent runner or retired machine gunner fuse writing with running or gunnery, so in D.J.'s account of the journey into and beyond the Brooks Range, hunting and storytelling become one and the same. Chap Six recalls the hunt's first killing (Tex's wolf), as D.J. comments that it "was the beginning of the hunt. Not so bad" (70)—the hunting two years ago wasn't bad, but D.J.'s ability to tell the story hasn't been bad either. The hunt itself risks reduction to literary metaphor.

In Chap Eight D.J. interrupts his account of the father-son "free" by suggesting that he could be "a crippled spade up in Harlem" (133). This present intrusion again takes us away from the narrative power of an oral broadcast into an awareness that this piece is a literary artifact as D.J. confounds the attempt "to read him right" (133), so that our awareness of authorial presence infiltrates the transaction between speaker and audience. D.J. retrieves the narrative by imagining himself zooming like Superman back from his digression of the present moment into the setting of the bear hunt, but he cannot long refrain from inserting parenthetic admonishments to the reader—"thank you, Mr. Philosopher, just show me the hemorrhoids of the Academy, and on that rock" (139); or, "which congregate is the established plural for bruises, look it up, turd pedant" (144)—which destroy our willing belief in the Huck Finn/Yoknapatawpha adventures of father and son. D.J. may try to render the trauma of receiving the bear's charge by concluding that "if the center of things is insane, it is insane with force" (143), but he cannot resist adding a devaluative pun ("But bearable"), which takes us out of narrative excitement into the realm of literary trickster.

Again, in Chap Ten the overt literary reference destroys the authenticity of reported experience. When D.J. attempts to describe the oncoming trinity of "Mountain Peak M.E.F." (186), awe, and dread that will be represented by the forthcoming bear, he is compelled to remind his audience that this is all "emotion recollected in tranquility back at the Dallas ass manse, RTPY—Remembrance Things Past, Yeah" (186–87). This parenthetic dual reference to techniques of Wordsworth and Proust seems to destroy the attempt to render the very tension of reported experience.

When the comic cowardice of M.A. Pete is introduced, the

speaker abandons the role of disc jockey and announces the presence of the literary artist:

> Comedy is the unsound actions of the cowardly under stress, just as
> tragedy is the equal time study of the brave under heroic but enigmatic,
> reverberating, resonant conditions of loss—yes, professor, you may
> keep the change, for D.J. is, mean to say, *has* got more than a finger
> into the cunt of genius, Madam Muse. (81)

Perhaps this speaker is none other than Norman Mailer who com-
pounds the obscenity of his fictive hunt with baroque detail. To
comment that the imaginative connection between deadening a
mystery and bad liver is "pretty literary for adolescent out hunting
with Paw" (94) is to undercut the theater of narrative as radio
ramble by the self-conscious reference to the literariness of the
discourse; and to claim that D.J. has "his purchase on the big
thing—genius" (94) is to enter the realm of Mailerian self-parody.
Whereas the compound literary references of *Barbary Shore* tend
to place that existential/allegorical novel within a tradition of the
committed artist/political theoretician/prophet, the self-awareness
of *Why Are We In Vietnam?* as a literary product tends to question
the literary endeavor in the face of actual contemporary
experience.

In *The Golden Notebook* our assumptions of narrative authenticity are continually undercut by new versions of "the real." Though
the literary nature of *Why Are We In Vietnam?* is less pronounced
than in the Lessing work, the authenticity of D.J. as character
immediately comes into question within the context of literary
references. Should we, having Shakespeare, Joyce, Stevenson,
Melville, and Twain thrown out at us, accept D.J. as, what he claims
to be, a disc jockey, or as, say, Dr. Jekyll, or as Don Juan? Though
narrative authenticity is undercut in a way distinct from how it is
done in *The Golden Notebook,* the effect is the same: the reader
is forced into awareness that he is involved in a fabricated enterprise in which the author's hand, or psyche, is ever present. To
presume that behind the fictive narrator is the author is to see both
aggressiveness in the arrogant expletives towards the readership
and a pathetic kind of self-parody in the situating of the novel's
voice in the mind of a "late adolescent" (11) disc jockey. In the
theatre of the physician half-blind, moral frailty enables him to
deliver a frantic specific to his tribe only in terms of a "wandering
troubadour brought right up to date" (8)—surely a tentative, under-

mined verification of the writer's authority to address in moral terms "young America" (7).

Our uncertainty about the locus of the narrative voice—

the simple would state that Intro Beep 1 is a stream-of-conch written by me, and consequently commented upon by my mother up tight with her libido drained psychoanalyst. But now you know Chap One—is made up by me (23)

—undercuts the vatic posture of the "disc jockey to the world" (24). The metaphor for the amplified voice of the committed artist gives way to the possibility that what we, in fact, immediately receive is Ronald Jethroe's imploded inner circuits and it is devalued by the admittance of the writer into his own invention. A wedge is driven between audience and fable as if a Brechtian alienation device were in operation. If an electronic medium offers seduction, the undercutting of that medium by authorial intrusion demands analysis.

The first book of *Armies of the Night,* the work that followed *Why Are We In Vietnam?,* ends with Mailer writing that same first book immediately after the march on the Pentagon. The history of the march "insisted on becoming a history of himself over four days" and thus will be titled "History as a Novel."[22]

The beginning of Book Two, "The Novel as History," justifies Book One's preoccupation with the writer as principal character. Unlike the mass media which "created a forest of inaccuracy,"[23] the artist constructs a tower out of his own personality so that the reader, wishing for some vision beyond the forest, is offered, through intimacy with "the master builder of the tower . . . some advantage for correcting the error of the instruments and the imbalance of his tower."[24] The omniscient speaker, whose only principal character has been himself in Book One, tells us in parenthesis that the good novel is a "personification of a vision which will enable one to comprehend other visions better"[25]—the vision can be microscopic and telescopic, interior and outward. The artist's account of a significant national event has demanded close self-analysis before the apparent counter gesture of historical observation can be legitimately undertaken. If *Armies of the Night* presents a basic division of fields of vision in Book One and Book Two, the juggle of interior and exterior voices in *Why Are We In Vietnam?* commands a more complex, perhaps more shaky, platform from which to examine a nation's greed, aggression, technological and psycho-social implosion, and genius. As D.J. broadcasts his own and public madness across the airwaves, so Mailer's social analysis of a nation in a new kind of aggression demands the presentation of his own frenzied personality. Just as Rojak's nightmare adventures in *An American Dream* seem to represent a personal confessional at the same time that they are metaphorical visions of a nation, so distinctions between the author, Norman Mailer, and his narrative voice, D.J., become increasingly blurred. For example, D.J.'s projected self-analysis, via his invention of Rothenberg's account of a session with him, comes close to being Mailer's own confessional self-analysis, as the zigzag between the frantic plea for an audience and the arrogant attack on that audience become Mailer's self-delineations.

The traditional author-character-reader framework is most undermined when D.J. ends Intro Beep 2 with: "Nonetheless, if you are really reading this and I am really writing it (which I don't know—it's a wise man who knows *he* is the one who is doing the writer's writing)" (28). Suddenly the disc jockey, or the inward fantasist, has become the writer of this narrative, hardly distinguishable from the writer who is his inventor. Mailer admits himself into the personality of the "eighteen plus years old" genius who "is in fact writing this" (28). The claim that "you're contending with a genius" (22) partly acknowledges an inventive, cultured voice rendered, here, by narrative spontaneity, yet it also reveals D.J.'s own brand of arrogance and, too, becomes Mailer's recognition of the aggression in his public and private personalities. The "late adolescent" (118) refers both to D.J.'s age and to Mailer's own continuing contentions with forces of arrested development. Self-analytical authorial intrusion becomes a mannerism in contrast to the muted presences of free indirect speech in the later *The Executioner's Song* or the distancing from self through time of *Ancient Evenings*.

The "fearsome trip" (28) upon which D.J. promises to take his readers will be an inner journey, via language and style, into Mailer's own psyche as well as an exterior trip upon which D.J. will conduct us in the novel's Alaskan fable. Perhaps Solotaroff is correct in his claim that *Why Are We In Vietnam?* "is a much better novel" than *An American Dream,* but I am not sure that this is because Mailer offers us "a narrator whose sensibilities differ enough from his own to enable the preservation of one constant, if complex focus."[26] What is likely, indeed, is that the ruminations over whether D.J.'s narrative is broadcast (oral), written, or an "expiring consciousness" (26) like that of Proust's Marcel, shakes our normal assumptions over author-character-audience relation-

3: A PHYSICIAN HALF-BLIND 105

ships into a disarray which—like Lessing's continual undercutting of the "real"—admits intense interaction between Normal Mailer and his self-caricature. For Poirier to suggest that "Mailer momentarily takes over the narrative from D.J."[27] in Chap Eleven is to neglect both the speaker's own distancing efforts and the author's own presence throughout the work; it is Mailer's memory, too, that "is the seed of narrative" (74). If, indeed, Mailer is one with the character "who is doing the writer's writing," then we are told a good deal more about him than the "very little" that Poirier detects in Mailer's "self-reporting."[28]

It might be a cheap kind of conjecture to create a regular circuit between the Barney Mailer-Norman Mailer, Cummings-Hearn, Rojack-Barney Kelly, Rusty-D.J. relationships (in his introduction to the later paperback edition of *Why Are We In Vietnam?* Mailer emphasizes the coincidence of Barney Oswald Kelly's middle, rather than first, name); but I do not think it improbable that this novel represents a climactic point in the "self-analysis" that Mailer mentions often in the commentary sections of *Advertisements for Myself.* D.J.'s "stream-of-conch"—especially in light of the analysis concerning him that is topic of Chap One—is a stream of analysis where the formal role of character and the personal role of actor blend in transcendence of traditional assumptions of narrative voice.

For the two boys, the final Chaps of the novel are a dialectic between the scatological weight of the "toilet plunger holes" (175) of the hunt and their attempts at purgation when they free themselves from the adults in the party. This particular dialectic parallels the overall dialectic of the work where the contrary to the narrative's formal gesture of implosion is the purgative function of spontaneous narrative style: the "way you make it is in the distractions" (8) and D.J. quotes a McLuhanesque version of Edison's haphazard discovery of the phonograph in the midst of an attempt to increase the speed of the Atlantic Cable. D.J. quickly connects Edison's associative, spontaneous methodology to the music of Miles Davis—"and that's how Miles Davis was born" (8). The connection principally recognizes the way by which Davis's brand of jazz makes him a kindred spirit to the inventor and to the inventiveness of D.J./Mailer. Part of the metaphoric circuit that D.J. builds around the charged atmosphere approaching magnetic North involves retention, implosion, distortion; but the circuit also offers the contrary to that stasis: the associativeness and inventiveness that D.J. invokes as the novel begins. This is, D.J. will claim, the secret to his genius—he is "pure American entrepreneur . . .

so his mind will always follow a lead" (194). While D.J.'s trip may represent a freaked-out abrogation of moral responsibility, LSD also represents, as Mailer told Oriana Fallaci in 1969, an attempt to recover self from technological dominion, so that the dual trip (within D.J.'s mind and outward into the Alaskan north) represents "a desperate search, as if all these young people felt at the same time the need to explore as soon as possible their own minds so as to avoid a catastrophe."[29]

The schisms in the book's voices are reflected in the dialectic between the inventive spontaneity of the narrative's progression and the counter-text, which is aware of itself as literary product of some kind of neurotic compulsion, some cultural receiver, so that the final gesture of the novel is the threat of defeat for the narrative momentum of the Chaps by the abrupt Terminal Intro: Beep and Out. It is the heroic struggle of D.J., "Grand Synthesizer of the Modern Void" (152), to escape the constraints of the Intro Beeps and "unloose my stasis" (153), achieving the perpetual flow of his fantasy narrative.

We are told in the Terminal Intro: Beep and Out that D.J.'s initial narrative stance (and metaphor for a prophetic voice of America), that he is a disc jockey broadcasting over the airwaves from "Big D in Tex" (9), is fantasy, which becomes emblematic of inner directedness, implosion (of course, the metaphor turns again if one considers that the nuclear bomb, an implosive device, is a public concern). At the same time, a kind of authenticity is established as D.J. struggles against repressive forces to reveal himself, to look into his own "eye of the real." Too, the active improvisation of D.J.'s wit, a confessional self-parody of Mailer himself as it may be, offers some stylistic promise of deliverance from "implosionland." Indeed, one might postulate *Why Are We In Vietnam?* as Mailer's most extended effort of existential theatre, via tape recorder; a work that tries to short-circuit the distances of print and reach back to oral/dramatic traditions. That "profoundest personal disclosure" (174) which we will edge toward in the final Chaps via the improvisational binoculars of D.J./Mailer, becomes an extended piece of spontaneous poetry, a kind of purgative act of the individual—civic theater in which the actor, releasing his minorities within, attempts to purge the arrogance of the American self. It is a culmination in personal disclosure by an artist whose long-term self-analysis becomes a major undercurrent in *Advertisements for Myself* and fulfills the improvisational forays that Mailer was to make in his critically neglected poetry and film.

Though Mailer's second published novel, *Barbary Shore,* might well be termed an existential novel, it is so only in an allegorical sense, so that the form of the novel hardly matches its philosophical source. In contrast, the financial necessities that forced Mailer to write *An American Dream* in installments (like Victorian serial novels) also forced him into a kind of existential method of composition, which fostered something akin to existential style. As with *Why Are We In Vietnam?* the backward narrative reach of the speaker is in dialectic with the existential surge of moment to moment connections. It was Mailer's involvement with film and theatre, I think, which opened up the possibility of the radical improvisational nature of *Why Are We In Vietnam?*. Whereas "professional acting consists of getting into situations where the actor knows precisely just how everything in the plot is going to turn out,"[30] his involvement in the early 'sixties with the theater world offered another kind of acting without the prefabricated tyranny of script and direction: the existential performance where the actor is "forced, as in life, to speak where the moment lead(s)."[31] Thus, Mailer's first movie, *Wild 90* (1967), "was a full-length film for which not a line of dialogue was written"[32] and thus his third film, *Maidstone* (1968), was an "advanced course in existentialism. Nobody knew what was going to happen."[33] If Lessing's experience with theater opened up for her the possibilities of Brechtian dialectical technique that would slyly admit her own personality into the experience of Anna Wulf, then Mailer's involvement in the theater and movie worlds opened up the possibility of an improvisational narrative where he could be fellow traveler with his principal characters within the unsteady alliance of confession and fiction.

In an interview soon after the publication of *Why Are We In Vietnam?*, Mailer suggested that "everything I write is a card out of the same deck."[34] As Zukofsky claimed that a poet writes one great book all his life, so Mailer saw that "I've been working on one book most of my writing life."[35] But he qualified his writer-as-gambler metaphor by suggesting that his one great book began "with *Barbary Shore*, certainly with and since *The Deer Park*."[36] Nine years earlier Mailer had claimed that many readers had difficulty realizing that "I started out as one kind of writer, and I've been evolving into another kind of writer."[37] In Mailer's first published novel, *The Naked and the Dead*, the wide field that the work covers in omniscient narrative tends to necessitate a compartmentalization of personality (like the early sections of *The Golden Notebook*) as character is diffused over a wide range. Though Mailer is able to achieve a kind of choric oneness through the description of a shared sensibility of his platoon, the multiplicity of characters is seldom able to accommodate certain sensibilities which were to become vital to Mailer's literary personality. In this first, vast novel there is still the danger of taking on a Dreiserian "their legs had lost almost all puissance."[38] The affectation of "puissance" detaches the writer from the sensibilities of his characters. Of course, characters such as Cummings and Hearn do achieve considerable depth, but, as individuals, neither achieves that vast complexity that Mailer would investigate in his own personality. His next work, *Barbary Shore,* would be "the first existential novel in America,"[39] with a first-person narrator who is an orphan, a war-wounded amnesiac writing his first novel as events take place. Indeed, the little black object that he inherits as a committed leftist is *Barbary Shore* itself. If so, the work might be existential in theory, but it is allegorical in technique—rather after Sartre's fiction. Lannie, for example, is the other writer in the novel, but, unlike Lovett's, hers is a sensibility which runs wild, as though she were a vortex of all that personal voice straining to be unleashed in *The Naked and the Dead.* Confusing fiction with fact, she has given in to the other side, will not be a fit heroic candidate for McLeod's little object.

In *The Deer Park,* Mailer found a speaker able to accommodate other presences within his own, so that this next orphan, Serge O'Shaughnessy, is able to transmit Charles Eitel's interior self into the latter parts of his own narrative. But it was not until *An American Dream* that Mailer was able to achieve an existential narrative technique that could embrace those "two rivers of American life— one visible, one subterranean"[40] that a writer must simultaneously navigate. Thus Rojak seems to both be and become as the narrative moves and creates itself, seems to exist and create in concert with the personality of the authorial presence itself. And *Why Are We In Vietnam?* takes this interaction of character and creator to its furthest outpost. Thus that early cry of Intro Beep 1—"let go of my dong, Shakespeare"—represents a necessary breaking away from earlier traditions as the new concerns of the novel necessitate new technique.

Despite its small palette of characters, so out of touch with classic conceptions of the epic, and with the narrative very much confined to the sensibility of one principal, antiheroic speaker, *Why Are We In Vietnam?* achieves an existential, romantic epic statement of a pervasive natural condition. Inner investigation fuses with outer occasion in a formula applying Sartrean combinations of Marxist political approach, psychoanalytical technique, and existential style to the novel.

Our sense of incompletion in *Why Are We In Vietnam?* is a reflection of the continuing, and perhaps unresolved, dialectic between inner investigation and public pronouncement accompanied by double narrative modes of drug-induced reverie and public broadcast. Philip Roth claims that the contemporary novelist has voluntarily withdrawn "from some of the grander social political phenomena of our times."[41] But while personality might seem to command most attention in the early sections of the novel (Chap One offers a psychiatric session discussing individual traits and patterns) our concern with individual personality is wedded to the outer world by D.J.'s fantastic narrative of the hunt and by his analysis of the corporate/technological scene. If D.J. seems captured in recollections of things past, the form of his novel, its associative inventiveness, works at cross-purposes to the locked-in fixation with the past. Thus part of the metaphoric circuit that D.J. builds from electricity involves retention and implosion; yet the circuit involves also the contrary to that stasis of suppressed minority within: the existential freestyle that D.J. early connects with Edison and Miles Davis. While Jameson condescends to the "Free Speech Movement quality of the narrator's language,"[42] I'd suggest that it would be well to consider the novel's style as an existential response to American cultural implosion.

In a sense, then, D.J.'s narrative offers escape from his own schizophrenic condition and from the imploded American psyche. The unresolved duality of this work's inner and outer directions are reflected in Mailer's next work, *The Armies of the Night,* which again seeks to achieve historical authenticity by the interaction of individual sensibility and historical moment. This civic act of theater represents a rite of passage for author, character, and audience in its recognition of the shared condition of writer and society. Thus Mailer, like William Wordsworth and Walt Whitman, nineteenth-century practitioners of the romantic epic where the poet's life is representative of his age, establishes the interconnectedness of personal and social lives.

4

Hard Times for Innocence:
Utilitarianism and Sensibility in *Gravity's Rainbow*

1

In *PIECES AND PONTIFICATIONS*, NORMAN MAILER DISMISSES PYN-chon's work with the admission that he couldn't "get through the bananas in *Gravity's Rainbow*."[1] That a surreal set-piece such as the banana sequence is so close to the beginning of Pynchon's masterpiece indicates the difficulties that attend the attempt to reach some purchase upon the work's totality. His narrative parallels the complexity, in its structures and narrative sequencing, as that early-century epic *USA;* but its stylistic spectrum has greater range than that achieved by Dos Passos. Thus an abundance of criticism has been produced that strives to provide keys toward decoding the increasing visitation of surrealistic episode upon the narrative of *Gravity's Rainbow* and the complexity of the work is further reflected by the variety of critical approach. Thus, among the finer critical approaches, we see such differing interpretations as: Hellman, following the lead of Robert Scholes's *The Fabulators,* classifying *Gravity's Rainbow* as the "big book of fabulist writing";[2] Speer Morgan suggesting that the work is a species of Menippean satire; Marcus Smith and Khachig Tololyan viewing the work as an update of the Puritan jeremiad; Mendelson considering the work to be encyclopedic; Lance Ozier finding mathematical imagery as key to understanding heroism and transcendence in the work's offering of ways to achieve salvation in a fallen universe.

My approach to this work attaches Pynchon to those contemporaries—Fowles, Lessing and Mailer—discussed in this study of the epic novel. It is not difficult to detect similar pressures on the

110

narrative in both *Gravity's Rainbow* and in the works of those writers. In order to reach an understanding of the epic nature of this novel, one means of entry would be to consider the dialectical structure of the narrative through initial comparison to an earlier work that operates on a more basic dialectic between utilitarian and natural forces—Dickens's *Hard Times.*

In the early going of *Gravity's Rainbow,* Jessica Swanlake—lover of the almost equally bizarrely-named Roger Mexico—meditates on Mr. Pointsman, a Pavlovian vivisectionist whose hands, betraying a "scientist-neutrality," could "as well torture people as dogs and never feel their pain. . . . "[3] That Jessica has just shared an erotic scene with Roger (an unwilling colleague of Pointsman) in a relatively pastoral setting away from the war indicates the scheme of Pynchon's third novel. Just as Dickens will oppose Gradgrind's deadening classroom instructions with a seminal imagery that describes Gradgrind himself in the first chapter of *Hard Times,* just as Sissy Jupe's inarticulate horse sense competes with Bitzer's horse facts in the second chapter, so a series of initially opposing vectors informs Pynchon's contemporary epic. If *Hard Times* exists on a dialectic between utilitarianism and natural fancy, *Gravity's Rainbow* maintains a dialectic between a scientific/ military/industrial/economic conglomerate and a sensibility that achieves a language capable of rendering, as a prime example, the intense love of Roger and Jessica:

> He and she lie and breathe mouth-up. His soft cock drools down around his thigh, the downhill one, closest to Jessica. The night room heaves a sigh, yes Heaves, a Sigh—old-fashioned comical room, oh me I'm hopeless. . . . (122)

If Pointsman contemplates Pavlov's fascination with "ideas of the opposite" (48), the whole book turns on an interplay between nominally opposite states of being—between the world of art that is *Gravity's Rainbow* and the world of death and inhumanity that the work of art discloses.

The love affair between Roger and Jessica is the most intense example of the sensibility in opposition to the enterprise of World War II and its aftermath around which the primary narrative texture of *Gravity's Rainbow* revolves, although there are other intense, close to supernatural, affairs—Katje Borgesius and Tyrone Slothrop or Geli Tripping and Tchitcherine. In their abandoned country house, in an area evacuated because of apparent danger of German rockets, Roger and Jessica share a bower of bliss—

"They are in love. Fuck the war" (41). In opposition to other war-fragmented aggressors and victims, they have "merged into a joint creature unaware of itself" (38). Close to nature, the innocence of their love reaches a condition of Joycean lyricism:

> One night in the dark quilt-and-cold refuge of their bed, drowsing to and fro himself, he licked Jessica to sleep. When she felt his first warm breaths touch her labia, she shivered and cried like a cat. Two or three notes, it seemed, that sounded together, hoarse, haunted, blowing with snowflakes remembered from around nightfall. Trees outside sifting the wind, out of her sight the lorries forever rushing down the streets and roads, behind houses, across canals or river, beyond the simple park. Oh and the dogs and cats who went padding in the fine snow. . . . (122)

But while they may be in opposition to the war, they cannot be separate from it. Thus, when we first see them together in their pastoral setting, on the night when Jessica meditates on Points-man's neutrality, a nearby rocket strike will interrupt their bower and terminate our close witness to their condition. The last image of Book One is of Roger projecting his loss of Jessica at the end of the war to the more establishment and stable Jeremy (Beaver). Roger foresees that she will become a "domestic bureaucrat, a junior partner" (177). If Roger's relationship with Jessica represents love, dreams, senses, and spirit, he will lose her to Jeremy, who stands for standard work, war, and government. Their relationship fails because Jessica, a modern Eve, is infected by the war. At war's end, Pointsman, the Pavlovian, sees that Roger/Jessica represents a threat to the status quo of his own bureaucracy and he plots to have her transferred to Germany, "out of his own way" (277). Pointsman achieves the separation so that, when Jessica reaches "the Zone," she is lost from the creature that was Roger/Jessica. When Roger chases her to Cuxhaven (where she is domestically established with Jeremy) he realizes that she is no longer a creature outside of the war—though it has nominally ended—and only fearful of the rockets. He sees that both she and Jeremy, a figure in the missile establishment, are now "on the firing end" (629). She has opted for "security" (629) and Roger's only possible response in this new version of *War and Peace* (with considerably less possibility of Christian redemption) is to escape along with the narrative into surrealistic episode.

Initially, the clearest opposition to the lovers' bower is Roger's workplace. "The White Visitation," formerly the Hospital of Saint Veronica of the True Image for Colonic and Respiratory Diseases, which has been replaced by an institutionalized kind of insanity—

the department of Psychological Intelligence Schemes for Expediting Surrender (Pisces)—runs the gamut from psychics to vivisectionists and seems to experiment not just on animals but (though Jessica only innocently muses on such a possibility) on humans. The World War I Commander Pudding, placed in nominal charge of the unit, finds:

> a disused hospital for the mad, a few token lunatics, an enormous pack of stolen dogs, cliques of spiritualists, vaudeville entertainers . . . Skinnerites, lobotomy enthusiasts . . . all exiled by the outbreak of war from pet schemes and manias damned, had the peace prolonged itself, to differing degrees of failure. (77)

The war has saved such establishment perverts as Pointsman and, as the war winds down, he rises to power in PISCES by exploiting Pudding's need to receive pain and humiliation in the form of that property of the war, Katje. Pudding's obsession with degradation at the hands of a mistress of death—in opposition to the natural biology of Roger/Jessica—is the need "for something real, something pure" (232): a ritualistic meeting with his bride of trench warfare. Such perversion in Blightie is connected, through Katje, to Captain Weissmann (white man)—or Blicero (death) as he is also known—the mad soldier/scientific bureaucrat of German rocket experimentation who uses Katje and a military underling, Gottfried, in a series of sadistic postures. The earlier relationship between Blicero/Weissmann and the Herero, Enzian, is also a perversion compared to the natural animal Roger/Jessica. If that natural love can exist only beyond the world of rocket and war, Enzian recognizes, when he is brought to Europe, that love to such a man as Weissmann/Blicero "had to do with masculine technologies, with contracts, with winning and losing" (324). Such perversions of the natural order permeate *Gravity's Rainbow*—from a scene on the *Anubis,* a ship of decadent fools, when Margherita Erdmann, a former German movie star, begins an orgy by stage-beating her nymphet daughter for refusing to sing a Shirley Temple song, to a less sexual example of Katje's seventeenth-century ancestor annihilating the dodo in a frenzy of Christian mania.

As we see by a series of limericks early in Book Three (305-7), the rocket—a link to pre-war, wartime, and post-war sequences in the book—is a primary emblem of twentieth-century perversion of the natural order. Enzian, Weissmann's lover, has become possessed of finding the ultimate rocket of annihilation during "a wet dream where he coupled with a slender white rocket" (297). That rocket of destruction at the book's conclusion becomes a death vehicle for Weissmann's plaything, Gottfreid; and it becomes an ultimate sexual partner in a filmic end-scene where "Weissmann's head ought to be teeming with last images of creamy buttocks . . ." (757). This final achievement of our age's neurosis, the 00000 rocket, contains Imipolex—"the material of the future" (488) in which Erdmann is dressed for a filmed orgy scene and which has been implanted in the infant Tyrone Slothrop to condition his adult erections. Thus the novel, swept along in the neurosis of the war-time establishment and the perverse insanity of technology, will gradually fall victim to tired catalogues of sexual folly conditioned by the shadow of the rocket.

The war dominates the novel's primary settings in England and Germany to the extent that even an absurd candy-eating sequence takes on a military posture as pieces of English candy become increasingly surreal, becoming sweet bombs, guns, and bazookas. While the still innocent Jessica Swanlake may speculate in reverie of a world without war and killing, or while a Christmas service may occasion a long, Dylanesque meditation on the absurdity of the war enterprise, it infiltrates everything. Early in the narrative, American bombers (rather like the bomber that flies over *Daniel Martin*'s innocent Oxford picnic) fly over London as "the slum-makers of war" (17). Thus even the "Home Front," from which the creature of love Roger/Jessica has escaped, is a "lie, designed, not too subtly, to draw them apart, to subvert love in favor of work, abstraction, required pain, bitter death" (41).

While over half of *Gravity's Rainbow* takes place after the end of World War II, it is a peace very little different from war—Points-man's despair as he foresees the success of allied manoeuvres (like Mother Courage's fear that "peace has broken out") is soon miti-gated as the war bureaucracy continues unabated in its domination of individual worth. An early example of the insane intensity of war is Pudding, whose "greatest triumph" was to conquer at Ypres "a bight of no man's land some 40 yards at its deepest, with a wastage of only 70% of his unit" (77). His weekly briefings at "The White Visitation" are rambling stream of consciousness reminis-cences about the Great War mixed with absurdly fiendish recipes and snatches of barracks room songs that match the insanity of current operations. While Jessica eventually believes that there is a distinction between war and peace—if only that war is an excuse for an affair with Roger while peace is a signal for domestic duty with Jeremy—and while Slothrop, the continuing victim, will claim that "they can't shoot you in peacetime" (309), the true message is that, just as there are no good sides and bad sides in war (for examples, British air-raids on German rocket sites have primarily killed "foreign workers"—that is, concentration camp victims), the "real War is always there" (645). Thus as we shall see in other examples, the dialectic of war and peace tends to dissolve after initially clear demarcations.

At "The White Visitation," funded by American money and following what we are told is Eisenhower's "strategy of truth" (74), is Operation Black Wing—a piece of propaganda to demoralize the German people by sending over radio messages and "smuggled" film stories that play upon German racial fears by depicting southwest Africans as actually inside Germany itself. The project actually has an American, Tyrone Slothrop, who is "willing to go under light narcosis to help illuminate racial problems in his own country" (75). In fact, Slothrop is hardly a "willing" subject—he has been taken over in Pointsman's move from experimentation on animals to experimentation on humans. The drug-induced reverie of Harvard undergraduate experiences in Roxbury, with subconscious racial fears and attractions (for example, Slothrop dreams of being sexually assaulted in a Roseland Ballroom bathroom), begins a series of surrealistic sequences dealing with Slothrop, who is to become the book's primary "character," a kind of innocent American lost in Europe. By Book Two, under the sinister direction of Pointsman, Slothrop will have lost all means of identity and will be forced to take on a series of disguises. Thus he begins a dual quest: to find out the origins of the "secret" thing that happened to him in infancy and to find a "way to get back" (623)—presumably to an America of innocence. In fact, Slothrop's quests are paralleled by a series of other quests, which serve as epic components—with the super-rocket of destruction becoming the final quest within the novel. Slothrop's journey has been a reversal of his ancestor's voyage to Massachusetts as a mess cook with Winthrop and accounts of Slothrop's ancestry sweep us between an American past and the present of post-World War II Europe and America. Finally, Slothrop as American hero will fall victim to *Gravity's Rainbow's* primary gesture of entropy—we are told that he has "scattered all over the Zone" (712)—as though the American character itself has failed.

From an apparently futuristic perspective—perhaps somewhere in the narrative time zone of the book's futuristic opening sequence of hopeless annihilation, yet reported in its final devaluative stages—we are told that Slothrop (we assume that this is Tyrone Slothrop, though it may be that his character has bled into that of his truly early American ancestor) was finally one of "those early Americans" who "were a fascinating combination of crude poet and psychic cripple . . ." (738); but apart from certain acts of sexual excess, he is very much a version of the American Adam in contrast to the severity of fascism attached to the American industrial war machine. Indeed, while *Gravity's Rainbow* clearly has global scope in its consideration of twentieth-century conditions, the American temper has a special concern in the narrative—from Slothrop's ancestor, or his Operation Black Wing drug-induced fantasy about the perverse plainsman Crutchfield/Crouchfield, to the final scenes in contemporary Los Angeles. Indeed, there is a dialectic between American innocence (with Lieutenant Slothrop at his most sacrificial) and an American fascism that has a direct link to German fascism through the arrangements between the Bostonian tycoon Lyle Bland and the materials scientist Lazlo Jamf for conditioning the young infant Tyrone. It is the American war machine that supports the insanity of "The White Visitation" and controls at least part of the surrealistic post-war "Zone" in a defeated Germany. If the non-ordained seventeenth-century heretic William Slothrop—dismissed from Massachusetts because he preached for the non-elect—is a "fork in the road America never took" (556), the road taken has been one that can develop a Major Duane Marvy, the most intense figure of American brutality. We shall see, however, that like other dialectical schemes—for example the shifting nature of black-white motifs (from the early Black Wing dreams of Slothrop, which seem an update of *Love and Death in the American Novel,* to the Weissmann-Enzian relationships, to the white and black versions of the ultimate rocket of destruction)—the initially clear-cut dialectic of American innocence and American fascism will dissolve. To understand the way in which the novel eventually displays simultaneous private and public impulses, I will examine in the next two sections of this chapter the nature of the two initially separate prime forces of *Gravity's Rainbow* and then attempt to show how that dialectic is undercut to reveal the personality of the author and his mirror, the reader.

2

At one pole of the macrodialectic that informs *Gravity's Rainbow* is a fascistic establishment bureaucracy and international cartel— the equivalent of the Bounderby, the pre-catastrophe Gradgrind group and their industrial/parliamentary kind—whose individual manifestations range from the American Major Marvy, to post-war

German police who take to violence in the same way that police before the war broke up anti-Nazi rallies, to the decadent "screaming Fascist cargo" (491) of the *Anubis*. It exists most in *Gravity's Rainbow* under that buzzword of the establishment enemy in contemporary literature—"they." It is no wonder that Roger Mexico's grotesqueries at a dinner party, after he has lost Jessica to the establishment Jeremy, are directed at "they." We first run into "they" as the "firm" that controls the British secret service agent Pirate Prentice. Pirate is eventually assigned to a Sartrean hell—along with fellow firm member Sir Stephen Dodson-Truck and the hapless Katje—again run by the imprecisely defined "they." This enemy appears, formally dressed and driving to and fro in limousines early in the novel when rockets fall on London. "They" control the adventures of such victims as Slothrop and Katje, operating like the house system for the wheel at the Casino Hermann Goering in Book Two—indeed, like an omniscient author as opposed to one participating in the consciousness of character. Just as "they" control the adventures of Slothrop, so the Russian agent Tchitcherine is watched by a Soviet equivalent and the Yalta presence of Roosevelt is "a being They assembled as They would dismantle . . . (374). The Potsdam Conference is overseen and protected by "their" presence and the perverse film existence of Greta Erdmann is controlled by a group defined beyond "they" only as "I don't know" (394).

Weissmann, a German secret service equivalent of Pirate and Tchitcherine, is perhaps the most palpable representative of, if not the higher echelons certainly the operatives, "they." He is "a brand-new military type, part salesman, part scientist. . . . They were athletic, brainless men without vision, without imagination" (401). Pökler, the technician, is trapped into working on the rocket-bomb because his radical wife and his daughter have been sent to a concentration camp—Ozier suggests that Leni is a primary example of heroism in her resistance to Fascism. Pökler comes to recognize that "they" have known all along of the presence of Leni and Ilse in a camp—in fact, we learn that the two have been in Camp Dora next to the rocket works to which Pökler is assigned. The complement to Dora is Zwölfkinder, the perverse kind of Disneyland where Pökler is allowed to go on annual leave with successive versions of his daughter. It is a "corporate state" run by the Nazi establishment to render an "official version of innocence" (419).

Weissmann's equivalent from the world of behavioral sciences and from the allied side is Mr. Pointsman who, leaving a meeting,

will raise an arm in "almost a Fascist salute" (48), whose experimental dogs are given Russian names (even a brainwashed octopus
is named Grigori) and who, along with his fellow scientists at "The
White Visitation," treats Pavlov's later writing—"The Book"—as
though it were the ultimate holy word. Pointsman, able to control
Commander Pudding by staging fantasy fulfillments via Katje,
takes over the bureaucracy of "the White Visitation" after the ar-
mistice. Thus Pointsman is left in charge of "the System" (228),
thinking in such terms as "fiscal '46" (228) as he lives in "the
solitude of a Führer" (272).

The quintessence of "they" is the rocket/missile program that
becomes the object of post-war enterprise as characters like
Slothrop, Mexico, Enzian, Tchitcherine—who speaks of a
"Rocket-cartel" (566)—come to recognize. The cartel is multinational, as though it were a puppeteer operating marionette nations
in warfare. Thus, a network exists of IG Farben, ICI, and Shell
that is able to manipulate conditions so that Shell in Holland can
contribute to the war effort against a London that also houses a
branch of Shell. A corporation like Shell has "no real country, no
side in any war, no specific face or heritage" (243).

Through experimentation on the infant Tyrone Slothrop, we see
that an institution like Harvard is part of this invisible conglomerate, that it exists for reasons other than education—that being "just
a sort of front" (193). The "Super-cartel" (284), as we are shown
through instances of pre-war manipulation, is responsible for the
shifting world economy and if a relationship between a Lyle Bland
and a Lazlo Jamf will reveal the intercontinental reach of this
power, then a surrealistic episode between Bland, the freemasons,
and the mafia connects all elements of society within the cartel's
matrix. This "System" is a cancerous feeder upon the natural order
as it exists to remove "from the rest of the World the vast quantities
of energy to keep its own desperate fraction showing a profit" (412).
It is the power of "they" that is able to overcome its opposite
impulse—the love between Roger and Jessica—to the point where
Jessica surrenders to the safety of the war-purveyor Jeremy and
to where Roger, after his rebellious upsetting of an establishment
dinner party, is forced "to live, on Their terms" (713) when the
choice is between merely a kind of life and their threat of death.

"They" are obsessed with the idea of control—Pointsman emphasizes to his colleagues that "WE MUST NEVER LOSE
CONTROL" (144) as he discusses their experimentation on Lieutenant Slothrop. "Control" is a term that ranges in use from economic and rocket manipulation, to spiritual intercession. At the

Casino Hermann Goering—aptly named for its decadence—
Slothrop feels as if he's "under some control . . . the same as a
fixed roulette wheel" (209) and Pointsman, with Katje as his stimulus for controlling Commander Pudding, Octopus Grigori, and
Slothrop, becomes in his madness "a control that is out of control"
(277). We are even presented a dead spirit, Roland Feldspath, who
is a "long-co-opted expert on control" and whose mission in death
is to "show them what he knows about Control" (238).

The system manipulates by deceptions as large as the theatre of
war itself. The "true war," we are told, is a "celebration of markets"
(105). Death and destruction are merely "spectacle," useful as "di-
version from the real movements of war" (105). The mysterious
"Firm" that controls Pirate Prentice and "the White Visitation"
seems to control all affairs in wartime Britain. From it comes
Pointsman's authority to experiment on animals and then on humans. As Pointsman and colleagues like Porkeyvitch, a former
colleague of Pavlov, are preoccupied with cause and effect, so
Pointsman recognizes that Roger Mexico, statistician and lover,
"threatens the idea of cause and effect itself" (56). The dogs upon
whom Pointsman and colleagues perform their conditioning experi-
ments become a metaphoric equivalent in the novel's dialectic to
Signor Jupe's Merrylegs and to Sleary's horses that operate against
the utilitarian forces in *Hard Times*. The research is merely "ration-
alized forms of death . . . in the service of the one species cursed
with the knowledge that it will die" (230). Just as the dogs with
absurdly Russian names within the cages of "The White Visitation"
are victims of human insanity, so the dogs that guard the compound
are "specially betrayed, belted, starved into reflex leaps to kill"
(74) and Octopus Grigori is conditioned by film and food to the
point that Slothrop has the intuition—when he is introduced to
Katje through the absurdly staged scene on the Riviera—to recognize that "his octopus is not in good mental health" (187).

Slothrop is hardly distinguishable from Pointsman's dogs—he is
merely "One, little, Fox" (53) for Pointsman to build his Nobel
dreams upon. Slothrop has been the subject of conditioning experimentation from his infancy and at "the White Visitation" he is
subject to such standard psychological fare as the Minnesota
Multiphasic Personality Inventory—really a test to see whether
one will be "a good soldier or a bad soldier" (81)—and quasi-
Freudian probing by the staff as they try to fathom the coincidence
of his sexual encounters and rocket strikes upon London. If
Slothrop seems to fall on the same side of the dialectic as Pavlov's
dogs and Sleary's horses, then Pointsman is an equivalent to the

utilitarian Bounderby (both of them implosive creatures subject to spontaneous combustion)—Pointsman witnessing "the mad exploding of himself" (143) and finally ending up as a cog in the post-war cartel at "alcoholic luncheons with various industrialists" (533). Thus is born the horror of the contemporary corporate state.

"The White Visitation" is a convenient microcosm for the insane enterprise of the quasi-scientific mind at the service of the establishment and is a non-battlefield parallel to the quest for the ultimate rocket of destruction. Pointsman quickly becomes a mediocre, bureaucratic Faust in his quest to connect Roger Mexico's chart of rocket strikes on London and Slothrop's sexual encounters. Thus "the war itself" (49) becomes Pointsman's own laboratory in his work upon the American who has already been under the control of the Bland/Jamf enterprise, Harvard and the U.S. Army.

To the cartel, war itself is a piece of technology—"a machine of many parts . . ." (130). Through a seance we learn that German technology has developed a ray that will turn populations blind, but that IG Farben has been forced to withdraw the weapon because it would make the international dye market obsolete: business, war, and science are intertwined in their control of the mass population. The scientist Lazlo Jamf, working for a Swiss-based cartel connected to IG Farben, Shell, and ICI, has developed Imipolex G— "an aromatic heterocyclic polymer" (249) that has its origins at Dupont—it is the material worn by the erotic starlet Greta Erdmann, the substance implanted in the infant Tyrone (chosen because of Lyle Bland's connection with Jamf and because of the GE factory in Pittsfield, Massachusetts), and a component of the ultimate rocket. We are told of the myth that the benzene ring was first formulated by Kekule, of whom Jamf was a disciple, after a dream of a serpent swallowing its own tail. Just so, technology turns upon its purpose—to enhance the natural condition—in the mad pursuit of materials in the cause of human destruction. Slothrop's own family business has been sawing down trees to make paper currency so that his heritage is one of complicity with the anti-natural role of the cartel and Tyrone himself is sacrificed by his father to the power of the technological world.

If Pointsman and Weissmann are the most palpable human representatives of the scientific/technological establishment, then the rocket/bomb becomes the omnipresent center of its endeavors. Though the novel begins at an indeterminate time in the aftermath of some urban disaster of immense proportion, we quickly move to a specific past to encounter the less massively destructive "incoming mail" (6) of German rocket-bombs descending on London (it is after these attacks that Pointsman goes looking for dogs upon which to experiment). The German rocket-bombs are an escalation of the war in response to an RAF "terror raid" (215). Late in the narrative we learn that "The White Visitation" contains files of an English steel firm that shares a patent for "an alloy used in the liquid-oxygen couplings" (632) of the super 00000 rocket that becomes the primary object of the epic quests of *Gravity's Rainbow*. Thus, as Tchitcherine perceives, the rocket cartel is international.

We are taken through the history of the V–2 and its progeny via the narrative account of the chemical engineer Franz Pökler, conveniently a fellow student of Kurt Mondaugen from *V*. Through a chance encounter with Mondaugen—who has also been a pupil of Lazlo Jamf—Pökler joins a group of rocket enthusiasts who are taken over by the pre-war Nazi military. The non-political rocketeers comply with the military's need for "practical hardware" in preference to "pushing on in chronic poverty, dreaming of expeditions to Venus" (401). As the scientists achieve guidance in addition to propulsion and they are "invading Gravity itself" (404), their rockets become wartime weapons. Now learning that his wife—the antithesis of his compliance with the Nazis—and their daughter are in "re-education camps," Pökler allows himself to be controlled by Weissmann in return for an annual meeting with a girl—or succession of girls—who claim(s) to be his daughter and with whom he begins to have yearly sex in keeping with the perversity of his occupation and his controllers. Thus, just as the scientists study the trajectory of the rocket through frame-by-frame photography, Pökler is allowed annual summertime frames of his "daughter" at the surrealistic corporate state of innocence, Zwölfkinder. I don't think that McHale makes a convincing case that Pökler's annual meeting with Ilse is Pökler's/Pynchon's fantasy.[4] Of course, it is fantasy in that all the novel is fantasy stemming from the initial nightmare of urban destruction managed, for the collective fear, by Pirate. But I'm not sure that we can term Pökler's encounters with Ilse as fantasy as firmly as we can say that Pirate's giant bananas and banana breakfasts are a particular fantasy of banana-starved wartime Britain (I assume that the "reading" of these bananas by the banana cultivators McHoul and Wills is a sly example of pre-CLT—by the way, they're not the only banana cultivators to read Pynchon).

Pökler's pact with Weissmann puts him in quest of a plastic material that will insulate the propulsion section of a special rocket—the ultimate weapon apparently witnessed both at the beginning and the end of the recurring nightmare/film loop that is *Gravity's Rainbow*. To build or to find this special rocket becomes, in turn, the murky quest of a field of characters—from Weissmann, to Enzian and his Schwarzkommando (as well as the mirror-image death-seeker Ombindi and his Empty Ones), to Tchitcherine and Slothrop. By the book's end, there seem to be two special rockets—one possessed by Weissmann (the 00000), one by Enzian/Ombindi (the 00001)—as though the work continues to strain after a dialectical structure of good and evil, hopeless as that effort may be in the face of narrative entropy.

Slothrop, in search of the secret to his identity, metamorphosizes into the "Rocketman" as he is drawn toward the "Schwarzgerät," the "black" device. In the mad, capitalist "black" market of the post-war Zone, Slothrop's path leads him to "Der Springer," whose emblem—a white chesspiece—also seems to be made of Imipolex-G. When Der Springer himself metamorphosizes into Gerhardt von Göll, the pre-war moviemaker, we are reminded of the use of Imipolex as erotic stimulus in a perverse movie industry. The rocket encompasses all motifs within the book and Slothrop, the predominant "character" in the novel, is last seen staring at a picture of a rocket in the street until interrupted by a real "fire-burst" (694) that perhaps signals the end of any proximity of *Gravity's Rainbow*'s narrative to realism.

The rocket—"that elegant blend of philosophy and hardware" (239)—moves from the concreteness of the initial rocket bomb attacks on London into an engine of a mythic futuristic state. Besides Weissmann's Enzian and his Schwarzkommando, there are other elements that convert the rocket/bomb into fantastical status. There are gnomes, for example, who toil in the underground rocket-works at Peenemunde—a kind of Wagnerian mythic presence. Jessica's dreams of a rocket-monster and Slothrop's travels into the Zone, revealing bizarre, folkloric tunnels, forests and castles, are the ultimate extension of the Faust/Frankenstein myth of science and technology visiting destruction upon the natural order. Weissmann's sadistic performances with Gottfried and Katje are twentieth-century versions of the Hansel-Gretel myth as the death figure Blicero (eventually to exist on the heath of death) lures the two "children" into "the dark oven of himself" (93). While this routine may be nominally a way of shutting out the war, it also becomes a primary symbol of the surrealistic drive toward destruction of western civilization as Gottfried finally enters the ultimate rocket/oven in the ultimate stage of the novel. Technology must subvert the natural order of myth and replace it with a new perverse consciousness. Thus, if Leni and her pre-war revolutionaries will try to establish a folk-consciousness in their battle against fascism, the "War" does not "want a folk-consciousness" (130), but rather a "machine of many parts" that will serve itself, thus engendering the new consciousness of despair rather than of regeneration. If Ensign Morituri, the Japanese aboard the *Anubis,* speaks optimistically of returning to the beautiful city of Hiroshima after the war, Pirate, the fantasist with the power of projection, weeps as he projects himself witnessing "a new Cosmic Bomb" (544).

The entropic nature of western existence is mirrored by the absurd metamorphosis of the Operation Black Wing propaganda into "The Empty Ones" who are bent on a racial, if not universal, suicide through absolute destruction via the ultimate rocket. If Enzian is taught by Weissmann that the rocket is a way of opposing "the entropies of lovable but scatterbrained Mother Nature" (324), Enzian's "hallucination" (732), Josef Ombindi, seeks through the rocket an acceleration of nature's ultimate entropy. Western civilization, or the universe itself, is hurtling towards a Spenglerian entropy, which sees characters in *Gravity's Rainbow* also moving towards disintegration as the narrative itself falls apart. While Slothrop is "being broken down . . . and scattered" (738), recognizable only by a minor figure like Seaman Bodine from *V.,* the novel itself disintegrates into a series of desperate, brief improvisational sequences that leave behind the already unsteady narratives of Pirate, Slothrop, Roger, Katje et al. The entropy of civilization is matched by the author's inability to hold together his story. In his introduction to *Slow Learner,* Pynchon suggests that if the "The Bomb" engenders a gamut of responses from "not thinking about it to going crazy about it," then "somewhere on this spectrum of impotence is writing fiction about it."[5] The breakdown of character and narrative in *Gravity's Rainbow* suggests that this text leans toward the latter end of the spectrum.

The entropy of the West, of mankind if a group such as the Hereroes stretches the implications of human ecology, is evident from the beginning as we are confronted with a far more shattered wasteland than the California of *The Crying of Lot 49.* The Zone in post-war Germany, where Slothrop is both escaping from Pointsman's enterprise and searching for truth about his identity, is the crucible of decay, with global representation in the path toward destruction. It is here where Jessica, once part of that opposition to the sado-masochistic impulse of the establishment, is now part of the destructive enterprise—of the "forces . . . who have opted

for sterility and death" (316). The surrealism of the first two sections intensifies in Part Three, "In the Zone," which is perhaps a
time zone reaching into the present and future as much as a military
area after World War II, as its occupants register "the new Uncertainty" (303). If dogs are the victims of the Pavlovians outside
London, then cows and horses are blown up by mines and other
engines of destruction in the Zone and rats, in a starving Berlin,
must try "to make believe they don't have a nearer and dearer
status among the Berliners" (364).

3

If Pointsman and his colleagues at "The White Visitation" are
our first palpable emblem of the utilitarian world that leads to death
(the ceilings in the building ironically depict pastoral scenes), the
human and animal inmates upon whom the scientists experiment
become, along with the Roger/Jessica bond, their contrary in the
book's early dialectical scheme. Dog Vanya, nose to nose through
wire cages with rat Ilya after a short break from the test stand,
undercuts the purely cause and effect stance of the Pavlovians and
a surrealistic Busby Berkely number that the animals perform,
complete with songs, is stopped by attendant Webley Silvernail
locking them back in their cages and telling them that he cannot
set them free because "it isn't free out here" (230). The animals
are caged to be tortured and killed at the service of an insanely
implosive species whose technology has become a monster coupled with a capitalist bureaucracy that feeds upon the earth like
an immense parasite. This dialectic continues throughout the
book—in Book Three, "In the Zone," for example, when swans,
pheasants, and rabbits exist amid the wasteland of the rocket sites.
Thus too, an early inmate has rushed down to the nearby cliffs and
witnessed "the Lord of the Sea" (73), a Wordsworthian contrast to
the scientists who are too much with the material world—for example, a young Dr. Bligh who will enjoy exploitative juvenile sex in
a pillbox (with connotations of both war and medicine) on the cliffs
after "a difficult lobotomy" (91) on one of the human "patients."
While a series of oppositions is initially offered in the narrative,
the dialectical scheme doesn't always work as smoothly as we
might expect regarding human beings. For example, Katje has been
slow to pinpoint rocket sites for the British and seems as much a
collaborator with German and British fascism as its victim;
Slothrop is not above a perversion in his sexual encounters, so
that he is linked with his controllers. Yet we can generally recog-

nize such characters, including Roger Mexico, as individuals caught in the fact of a totalitarian, technological/military economy that slides from war to peace with little difference in its stance towards existence. In Book Two, Slothrop is stripped of all possessions—"ID, everything, taken" (201)—so that he becomes one of the dispossessed to enter the Zone of Book Three. If Slothrop, identityless at the Casino Hermann Goering, finds himself in a rigged game as the "Firm" controls all of his movements, then Katje is merely an "employee of the House" (208) who is "knocked from one room to another" (209). And Dodson-Truck, who will eventually greet both Katje and Pirate in the establishment's version of hell, also has an "unmistakable aura of the employee and loser" (211). It is Slothrop's quest, a connector to the various scenes and episodes of *Gravity's Rainbow,* to find out the reasons for his early and late victimization that puts him at odds with the officers of the power structure such as Pointsman, Weissmann, or Marvy.

The notion of character, the penetration of the individual consciousness itself, works as a contrary vector to the utilitarian bonding of science, business, and the military. An inside vision of even a Pointsman, via intense indirect free speech—

Feeling a bit megalo these days, nothing to worry about really, never gets worse than, oh perhaps the impression, whilst zooming along through the corridors of "The White Visitation," that all others seem to be frozen in attitudes of unmistakable parkinsonism, with himself the only stable, unpalsied one remaining (269)

—creates a dialectic with his outward fascistic gestures as the narrative is able to penetrate that which the surface consciousness of Pointsman himself is unable to admit.

In fact, besides the dying natural world, the primary opposition to the utilitarian world comes from the language that describes, at times, victim and oppressor alike. For an omniscient narrator, operating very much like Dickens in *Hard Times,* to suggest that "perhaps, Pointsman, there is a kindness-reflex after all" (714) is to set up a direct opposition to the cold science of the Pavlovian; but generally it is the imagistic intensity of Pynchon's descriptions that battles the material world. The doggerel embedded within a prose passage, such as, "And the crowds they swarm in Knightsbridge, and wireless carols drone, and the Underground's a mobscene, but Pointsman's all alone" (167–68), relegates the vivisectionist to the absurdly mundane, but a poem that Pointsman himself writes on Pavlov at eighty-three, exhibits a more profound nature. Yet the public Pointsman must deny this depth as we are told that "[Pointsman never shows these excursions of his to anyone]" (226). They are excursions because they are outside of Pointsman's assumed stance toward the outside world, so that he reveals an example of what Mailer saw in LBJ as the "minority within."

By entering into the consciousness of the dogs, Pynchon is able to expose the shallow nature of the Pavlovian cause and effect mentality. Thus the listing of the scientist's full name and title—"Mr. Edward W. A. Pointsman, F.R.C.S."—competes with what follows, that is the inner processes of a cornered dog:

> He has the memory, or reflex, of escaping into similar darkness . . . once from the pack of children, recently from a sudden blast of noise-light, a fall of masonry that caught him on the left hindquarter (still raw, still needs licking). But tonight's threat is something new: not so violent, instead a systematic stealth he isn't used to. Life out here is more direct. (42)

Jessica, the lover initially outside of the system, projects herself into the consciousness of the trapped dog, as she sees "the poor lost flimsy thing . . . waiting in the night and rain for its owner, for its room to reassemble around it . . ." (43), and the dog, seeing Pointsman's flashlight, recalls the light from the recent rocket strike that has destroyed its house and made it available to Pointsman's "dognapping" excursions: "the light that followed the great blast so seethed through afterward by pain and cold. Light from the rear signals death/men with nets about to leap can be avoided" (45). The rendered processes of animals relegate the endeavors of a Pointsman to the moral level of the destructive rockets of technology. The poetry of the animal, a poetry that a Pointsman can only suppress within himself, is matched by a poetic quality attached early to Jessica, the creature of love. Thus Roger will feel "in his skin each saccade of her olive, her amber, her coffee-colored eyes" (38). The multifarious quality ascribed to her matches the sensibility that informs Pointsman's tortured animals. Slothrop, too, is quickly defined as part of the opposition to the utilitarian world. Thus his care for a young victim of a rocket attack—he holds her hand and gives her a slippery elm lozenge in the absence of gum—puts him within the same sensibility of Roger, the initial Jessica, and dog Vanya.

The texture of imaginative sensibility (or what the first three books of *Gravity's Rainbow* might call the counterforce) used to define contraries to the movers behind totalitarian wartime and post-war existence is not limited to select characters (we've seen it used to render the inner consciousness of even a Pointsman), but, as with *Hard Times,* it is the primary component of the opposition to the fascism of the material world: Tchitcherine's father, engendering Enzian with a Herero girl, feels "something warm and kindly around his penis besides his lonely fist" (351); Pirate, newly arrived in the Firm's living hell, follows a tortuous path that is "like Route One where it passes through the heart of Providence" (537). That is perhaps an absurd image to describe the movement of an Englishman, but it competes against the very conformity in which Pirate is about to find himself. Two shallow doctors about to emasculate Major Marvy—mistaking him for Slothrop—discuss the operation while a distant radio plays the music of "Sandy MacPerson at the Organ" (592)—an incidental piece of realistic detail that undercuts their self-importance (the operation on Slothrop has been ordered by Pointsman) and relegates to the absurd the quasi-scientific endeavor. Thus the primary texture of *Gravity's Rainbow* consists of the way by which a language of sensibility, allied to the natural world, competes with the unnatural power of the utilitarian. Indeed, the struggle of the work itself is between that language of sensibility and the entropy of the social and moral order of the modern world. As the narrative enters into its final defeated condition of fragmentation—a condition in opposition to the positive final resolutions of *Daniel Martin*—our last image of the natural world, fittingly for a novel so parallel in its dialectical structure to *Hard Times,* is of "the last horse," a sacrifice now to the triumph of the technological appetite of the twentieth-century system, but still at one with what remains of the natural world, as his "tail lashes at the clear elusive flesh of the wind" (749).

The macrodialectical system, arising early in the novel and permeating it, between the natural world and the technological/establishment/military conglomerate of repression, would seem to suggest some possibility of opposition to the entropy or gravitational pull of the narrative towards destruction. Pokler's wife Leni joins a movement before the war, which suggests the possibility of a folk-consciousness in opposition to the fascism that is controlling Germany. Thus, too, the intense lovemaking between Slothrop and Katje after they have been set up by Pointsman's operatives indicates a counterforce of possibilities to systems of control which come to be recognized as "They" or "Them;" and Katje, released from "The White Visitation," suspects for a while that she has been naive not to think that "some counterforce would have had to arise" (536). Yet she finds herself, along with Pirate and Sir Stephen Dodson-Truck, in a world of no possibilities and no exit which is indistinguishable from "They." The Counterforce has apparently been co-opted by the Firm so that Pirate is forced to lament that "I defected for nothing, didn't I?" (542). The "counterforce traveling song" (639) is sung in a setting little different from the decadent atmosphere of Pirate's initial townhouse and by the end of the narrative, even the dead Commander Pudding is a member of the Counterforce, as though it were no different from a heavenly version of old-school-tie membership—or a curtain call for vanished characters. Indeed, that the Counterforce has failed seems to suggest that, unlike Dickens in *Hard Times,* Pynchon is finally unable to overcome the weight of twentieth-century oppression. The Counterforce becomes as uncertain as the epigram attributed to Richard Nixon—"What?"—in the final Book Four, "The Counterforce."

Tchitcherine mistakes the various disguised presences of the questing/escaping Slothrop as evidence of "a counterforce in the Zone" (611). But what counterforce that is revealed is incompetent in the face of the matters of great pitch and moment with which it must deal. If Roger, himself finally submitting to forces of conformity, dreams of "the failed Counterforce" (713), the counterforce of the narrative itself is apparently not equipped to maintain a Slothrop as character or to "disarm, de-penis and dismantle the Man" (712)—who is, we assume, "They/Them." As any pretense of narrative reality disintegrates, "a spokesman for the Counterforce" (738) materializes for an interview with *The Wall Street Journal* to explain the function of Slothrop in the text. But apparently that function is murky, Slothrop's role having been the cause of much debate within the Counterforce. Yet it becomes unclear whether this "spokesman" is a true spokesman for the Counterforce (or, indeed, whether we should trust what we read in the *Journal*—it is, after all, an organ that caters to the very forces against which the Counterforce is meant to battle)—and it is also unclear where his interview ceases in the final fragments of *Gravity's Rainbow*— so that it is possible that Slothrop has not, in fact, been atomized as a character, but that the Spokesman, or outside narrator, resurrects him as he tells of Seaman Bodine handing a piece of blood-soaked cloth from Dillinger's shirt to Slothrop (as though an American folk hero is metamorphosed into Slothrop, the folk baton passed on). The Counterforce is apparently as dubious a force against inevitability as is Nora Dodson-Truck's final role as Gravity holding back the rocket's fall.

The Puritan dissenter William Slothrop, preaching a humanistic brand of Puritanism for the non-elect, is perhaps the most positive strain in the novel in opposition to the surrealistic moral void that all but swallows up narrative and character. As Smith and Tololyan point out, William Slothrop's presence in the novel allows for associations with Hooker's sermons on moral order. It also allows for the rocket from Germany that Katje and Tyrone Slothrop witness to be termed "the Rainbow" and "they its children" (209). Despite our sympathies for them, in the Puritan frame of reference, they are "the glozing neuters of the world" (677), unable, unlike Leni, to constitute a serious counterforce to the West's moral decay. Thus the final song of the novel is a hymnal that—even though it is now given a screen presence as we are told to "follow the bouncing ball" (760)—sustains the truth of the mad William Slothrop in predicting the doomsday of our inner-directed civilization. While William Slothrop may offer the possibility of an antithesis to the decadence initially encountered in Pirate's flat (the equivalent to the "whole sick crew" of *V.*), the Puritan emphasis on Doomsday perhaps also suggests the inevitable entropic path of a decadent society toward destruction via the bomb. Passing through the ruins of a bombed London, Tyrone Slothrop sees everywhere "a sermon on vanity" (25) and if a hand will emerge from a cloud onto a Slothropian ancestor's gravestone, that same hand will appear at a rocket's strike. Pynchon uses Puritanism to both oppose twentieth-century decadence (reminding us of the folly of human self-interest) and yet to free up the individual moral will as it recognizes its own inevitable mortality. Thus Smith and Tololyan see *Gravity's Rainbow* as using the form of the Puritan jeremiad to paradoxically "reject the ghost that haunted," and still haunts: that suffocating Puritanism which has so dominated the American temper.[6] While Puritanism offers "horological" pessimism, Smith and Tololyan point out that it also offers a "chronometric" freedom from suffocating acceptance of systems.[7] This latter possibility is mirrored, as Ozier points out, in Leni's embracing the moment of now, $\Delta \to 0$.[8]

4

The pressures created by the competing forces of the macro-dialect of *Gravity's Rainbow* that we've examined in the last two sections of this chapter result in the surrealistic nature of its narrative. Indeed, one suspects that if there existed an American novelist named Saul Green (as in *The Golden Notebook*), he would be writing the schizophrenic narratives of *Why Are We In Vietnam?* or *Gravity's Rainbow* rather than the somewhat tame piece he writes about Algeria. The Burroughs-like surrealism of Pynchon is fed by the novel's multiple drug sequences and their impulse leads to fantastical chase scenes, song-and-dance numbers, and bizarre metamorphoses—for example, a doll that Slothrop is burning becomes human and Katje-like. Scenes such as a super-Felliniesque fashion show with "oddly-colored television images flickering across toenails" (296) tend to deny the validity of preceding or succeeding outer plot, forcing the focus of the narrative back inward and creating an intermingling of inner and outer decadence and surrealism. Thus, too, the intense penetration of character achieved by the narrative's highly charged imagery is countered by intermittent devaluation of the narrative into surrealistic absurdity of stage and screen episode which leads to the final undercutting of both character and narrative.

In describing the connections, American and European, within the parameters of Lyle Bland's empire, the speaker offers us "a paranoid structure worthy of the name" (582) and *Gravity's Rainbow* achieves, on a much wider scale than *The Crying of Lot 49* and its rock group The Paranoids, a worthy paranoid system in its totality: we are offered information from "Paranoid Systems of History (PSH), a short-lived periodical of the 1920s whose plates have all mysteriously vanished, natch . . ." (238) as well as a series of "Proverbs for Paranoids." Fittingly for a Pavlovian-controlled institution, where even the programmatic Pointsman is given to fits of hallucinatory paranoia, "The White Visitation" is termed by Roger Mexico "a great swamp of paranoia" (33) and in Germany, pre-war rocket specialization began when "the bureaus and paranoias moved in . . ." (402).

In Slothrop, who must both escape from the insane science of Pointsman and quest in search of "THE PENIS HE THOUGHT WAS HIS OWN," we have the most concentrated doses of paranoid systems. The hero of the novel—that is, as long as he is sustained as character and not as some foil of the Counterforce—begins to suspect, even as he recognizes voices behind plant ventilation in his hotel room with Katje, that he has been "under their observation—m-maybe since he was born" (286). Slothrop connects his father with his early control by "Them" and, like Oedipa Maas in Pynchon's second novel, sees a super-conspiracy in everything, even in the last-minute rescues that he undergoes—for example, with the convenient escape managed by the fairy-tale-like

Professor Glimpf (Jamf?). The omnipresent Springer asks Slothrop why he has to see conspiracies in everything and, indeed, the authenticity of Slothrop's paranoias is undermined when reference to the deadly animosity of his father and motherly unconcern become increasingly Barthelmean in their smug overtness. Indeed, if Slothrop is eventually told to blame himself only for his condition, perhaps the true source of his paranoias is the overtly plot-manipulating author (perhaps his true father). As with Slothrop, the possibilities of mass conspiracy controlling and limiting the freedom of individual being are diminished as initially plausible possibilities of controlling systems are reduced to the absurd. Thus, consigned to his sedate captivity with a false counterforce, Pirate must persuade Roger of the "creative paranoia" (638) available in erecting "They-systems" and "We-systems," or an auditor of the text who finds an absurd haiku unauthentic is crowned by the voice of the novel: "YOU—are our PARANOID FOR THE DAY!" (691) and a sequence on "LISTENING TO THE TOILET" posits an absurd need to listen to see whether "They" have turned off the water system to prevent the flushing away of contraband (but a finely-tuned, paranoid reader will make the connection with the historically accurate finding of German rocket plans in the toilet pipes of abandoned camps).

Tchitcherine's late, paranoid discovery that "everything is connected" (701) is, in fact, apparent from the start of the novel as an indeterminate opening zeroes into Pirate Prentice apparently waking from a bad dream. If everything thereafter indeed stems from Pirate's consciousness or fantasy-surrogacy, then it is understandable that, Pirate's head feeling made from metal as he awakes from his initial dream, his Russian counterpart Tchitcherine, like the mechanized characters in V., will be composed almost entirely of metal, or that Pirate's lover Scorpia Mossmoon's husband will be a link between multinational industrial corporations and the affairs of "The White Visitation" and will be an important player in the lover Roger's final catastrophe. If the keepers of Pavlov's "Book" will be fascinated with the idea of the opposite, then, everything being connected, the Hereros will see their God as both creator and destroyer so that the child Enzian considers his sex with Weissmann a reflection of that God who is "all sets of opposites joined together" (100). The black-white motif begins with Slothrop's recollected fantasies, under drugs at "The White Visitation," of Roxbury encounters with blacks, one of whom, Red Malcolm, seems to be the younger Malcolm X, later to appear as the novel disintegrates in an absurd digression on the meaning of the term "shit 'n shinola." The same mouth harp that Slothrop fantasizes losing down a Roxbury sewer shows up in the Zone. Similarly, Commander Pudding will associate Katje's droppings as the smell of war death with a "Negro penis" (235) and the continued dwelling on the penis, whether Slothrop's Imipolex–implanted member or another, is associated with the "masculine technologies" (324) of rocketry. While Slothrop, Tchitcherine, Enzian, and Blicero are all in search of the ultimate rocket, all enterprise also is connected to the giant cartel of Euro-American commerce and technology. If Slothrop is set up with a conditioned Octopus Grigori, then the cartel is also an "octopus" (284). Sometimes, the swirling complexities of the novel's narrative ground make the edge between dialectical forces tend to be porous so that reader, character, and perhaps author alike are condemned to reside in vertigo.

The interconnectedness in the work of motif, characters and narrative sequence points to a cosmic reach and fights against that fragmentation that always seems imminent, especially as the work reaches its final stages, or countdown, and that seems to reflect the failure of the artist to contain his field of play. That field of play is immense enough to show the vast extent of intercontinental enterprise. Pirate will wake up from his nightmare of annihilation in London to create an extravaganza of an American breakfast and the book will soon begin to reveal the "interplay of the Anglo-American Empire" (129). By the book's close, Pirate's London nightmare will be transferred to a movieland version of the ultimate disaster in Hollywood. Just as there is a series of connections between the enterprise of nations, so a whole series of characters achieve slippage into other roles. Thus Slothrop, after assuming the identity of the British correspondent Ian Scuffling, becomes another character, Max Schlepzig, who—curiouser and curiouser—was the partner of the actress Margharite Erdmann who herself changes into a variety of characters—from Greta, to Gretel, and to a mysterious child murderess. If Slothrop will fit into the tight boots of Tchitcherine, he will also become the Rocketman and, after sailing down the Spree-Oder, will reach Swinemunde and become Pigman after a description of his swineherding, preterite-preaching ancestor. Slothrop, "a trudging pig in motley" (573), will encounter a real pig, Frieda, and will pass on his costume to a more sinister pig, Major Marvy, only to lose any possibility of costume or character. A description of Geli Tripping, the witch lover of Tchitcherine as well as Slothrop, will give way to that of a Slothropian witch ancestor; Gerhardt von Göll, pre-war decadent/technomaniacal German moviemaker will become Der Springer;

and "the two children Gottfried and Bianca"—Weissmann's lover and Slothrop's lover—are revealed to be "the same" (672) so that perhaps even Slothrop and Weissmann are also the same within the tangled matrix of their author's personality.

If character seems to bleed into character, the system of the work itself seems liable to a contingency that is apparent as early as the opening scenes of the novel where we encounter an indeterminate place, occasion, and time, only halfheartedly clarified by the zoom into Pirate's penthouse. Likewise, we are made to deal with an indeterminate narrative voice that may be authorial, may be Pirate's, or Slothrop's, or other possible "you's." Along with Pökler, the reader is in suspense as to the identity of the Ilse whom he accompanies each year to Zwölfkinder. The indeterminacy of the work's initial setting will be echoed in the uncertain location where Pirate, Roger and Katje are institutionalized, or in the veiled locations and actions involved in the closing sequences of the novel.

The scientist Lazlo Jamf develops a torpedo operated through a space/time warp; so the narrative undergoes a series of changes—from the indeterminate time of the beginning, to the "present" time of 1944 (though we weave back and forth within even that "present" time-frame reference: for example, when we move from Slothrop reacting to a rocket strike, to his earlier visit, with Tantivy Mucker-Maffick, to a rocket-site)—back to earlier, pre-war sequences in Germany, to a present after the war, to indeterminate futuristic times in the novel's closing sequences when Weissmann is delivering his final soliloquy to Gottfried about failed European spiritual enterprise, or to "Cindy Bloth of Carbon City, Illinois" (735) conducting us up a surrealistic future elevator suspiciously like the elevator of Pirate's initial wartime nightmare. But in a work where "EVERYTHING is CONNECTED" (701), the impulse of fragmentation is suggested by our uncertainty of whether narrative consciousness belongs to a virtually omniscient author, to an intermediate consciousness like Slothrop, or to a more internal sensibility like that of Slothrop. Characters, too, like Katje, are broken down into a series of shots and angles and Slothrop, a.k.a. Scuffling or Schlepzig, is "broken down . . . and scattered" (738). Narrative, too, disintegrates into a series of impossible quick cuts, like the fragmentary sequences that precede unification in *The Golden Notebook*. But that unification is denied in this work.

At first glance, character seems to break down under the pressure of the outward forces of utilitarianism. Slothrop himself, having had his clothes, identity card, and everything stolen on the

French Riviera, goes through a series of personalities before losing all character as the narrative disintegrates. Even Max Schlepzig, whose identity Slothrop takes, turns out not to be a "real" name and "Greta" Erdmann will, in turn, claim that the name "Erdmann wasn't mine" (395). We are told that "as early as the ANUBIS era, Slothrop has begun to thin, to scatter" (509) even as he closes in on his quest for identity. As *Gravity's Rainbow* reaches its termination point, Slothrop has been "scattered all over the Zone" (712) so that only an old crony like Seaman Bodine from *V.* can still see Slothrop as "any sort of integral creature any more" (740). Eventually, Slothrop no longer exists as any kind of autonomous character, but only, like Weissmann, as the output of a tarot pack. Increasingly, the failure of character is directly the result of authorial decision rather than the menace of "They" as the reader is withdrawn from engagement with narrative and pitched back out into the world of public and private responsibility.

5

The narrative begins, and continues throughout much of the novel, with an outside, perhaps ironically detached, posture. The epigrams that precede each book—from the quote of Werner von Braun affirming his belief in life after death to a "What?" of Richard Nixon that dubiously introduces the final book, "The Counterforce,"—achieve a distancing similar to the chapter headings of *The Golden Notebook*. And, while there are some songs that display lyric earnestness (such as the folk song that Tchitcherine transcribes in the outer provinces of the Soviet Union or Roger's dream song to his lost love as he drives along the Autobahn), most serve as distancing devices that keep the audience from being immersed in narrative emotion. For example, when Roger takes Jessica's nephews and nieces to the pantomime (fittingly, it's a show about Hansel and Gretel that continues the folk motif established by the Weissmann/Gottfried/Katje routines) an outside rocket blast is followed by Gretel singing, to the audience's accompaniment, about death and the masters of war. It is a worthy Brechtian performance, absurd in its spontaneous interruption of the pantomime fantasy.

The indeterminate opening passage of Book One, with a nonspecific catastrophe, refers to a "he" who is part of a population to be evacuated "to salvation" (3) so that the narrator is a third-person presence viewing his characters. That no salvation is apparently possible—"it is a judgement from which there is no escape"

(4)—indicates that the outside narrator is ironic in posture towards his subjects. Indeed, he can be, at times, a trickster on the order of Doris Lessing when, for example, a conversation between Pointsman and Mexico is terminated with the remark that, "No one listens to those early conversations—not even an idle snapshot survives" (92). That component of the narrative, at least, is detached from its characters. But there are other portions of the narrative that are less clearly detached than such early ironic postures as the undercutting of human endeavor in the initial evacuation scene. A description of the Schwarzkommando in their native land will tell us that, "You were likely to come across them at night. . . . You knew what they feared. . . . And you had business upcountry . . ." (315)—and the "you" presumably refers to a non-Herero, collective European presence to which the novel's voice chooses to attach itself.

Less collective "you" references are seldom clearly definable. Before Slothrop is set up in France with Katje and Octopus Grigori, he settles down for a picnic at the beach with his controllers. Thus: "For a moment you can let the world go . . ." (185). This is apparently Slothrop whom we suddenly go inside and we presumably enter his consciousness at other times, but transitions to such a perspective are not announced. Even less sharply defined is a passage after description of new arrivals (or fantasized new arrivals) at "The White Visitation":

> You impress them with your gentleness. You've never quite decided if they can see through to your vacuum. They won't yet look in your eyes. . . . (50)

Since Pointsman has been the prime subject in previous paragraphs—he has been discussing Slothrop, as subject of experimentation, with his colleague Spectro—we might assume that we are entering into Pointsman's consciousness through a species of free indirect speech; yet an uncertainty remains as to whether we are entering a particular consciousness or whether we are presented with a universal consciousness hazily symbolized in the outside narrative by Pointsman. The "you's" are, in fact, encountered throughout *Gravity's Rainbow*—about as frequently as the "they's"—and it is seldom possible to decide whether we have gone inside a particular character or whether the reader is included in the narrative as an agent with a consciousness identifiable with characters in the fable of the work.

At times, the confusion over "you" becomes particularly acute.

After we are told of water bugs who were "deep in the straw of the manger at Bethlehem," a section closes with:

> The crying of the infant reached you perhaps as bursts of energy from the invisible distance, nearly unsensed, often ignored. Your savior, you see. . . . (174)

Is the "you" the water bugs, or is the collective readership transformed into a condition at one with the same water bugs who will one day, presumably, inherit the earth after the ultimate rocket strike? Whatever the reference, we are at a narrative posture considerably less certain than the outside ironic condition of the book's beginning. Towards the novel's end, a section begins by referring to Enzian, but goes on to question, two pages later, "how you loved" the rocket (726). Though "you" may be Enzian, it is just as possible that we are no longer dealing with particular characters, but with a collective consciousness that has been shaped and prepared by the references to "you" that have permeated the book. Indeed, we might also be entering a "you" who is the author himself—a single character who emerges after the smoke screen of characters within the fable have been eliminated, so that a Dos Passosian "Camera Eye" presence emerges, warped as that eye might be in post-World War II madness.

The "he" of the novel's initial passage is identified as Captain Geoffrey ("Pirate") Prentice, the first character whose consciousness we clearly enter via free indirect speech:

> He takes some time lighting a cigarette. He won't hear the thing come in. . . . What if it should hit EXACTLY—ahh, no—for a split second you'd have to feel the very point, with the terrible mass above, strike the top of the skull. . . . (7)

Free indirect speech becomes a primary way for the narrative to oppose its initial outside ironic posture, so that it is used, as with a Pointsman or a Weissmann, to penetrate even the suppressed sensibilities of totalitarian symbols. Thus there are few characters who are not penetrated through some version of this technique: we are privy to the surreal inner recollections of World War I by Commander Pudding or to the inner being of Katje's twin of masochism, Weissmann's sacrificial lamb Gottfried, just as we are to a Roger who senses that he has lost Jessica: "You're catching the War. It's infecting you and I don't know how to keep it away. Oh, Jess. Jessica. Don't leave me . . ." (177). But it is Slothrop, the Jamesian innocent lost in Europe, who seems to be our primary outside/inside character. The inner rendition of this American searcher—

> s'posed to be a hardboiled private-eye here, gonna go out all alone and beat the odds, avenge my friend that They killed, get my ID back and find that piece of mystery hardware. . . .(561)

—becomes one with a national search for identity in the twentieth century.

Before the war, Tchitcherine has been in the outer Soviet provinces where a prime goal has been to revise the language so that more uniformity will be achieved throughout the empire. Thus a babel of committees has evolved and it is to such a "crew of irredeemables" that Tchitcherine "gravitates" (353) as language seems set to destroy the authenticity of native experience, so that, for example, a singing duel "will be lost" when it is recorded in the "New Turkic Alphabet" (357). A teacher of the new alphabet, Galena, who is garrisoned with Tchitcherine, differentiates between language and silence, which is a natural phenomenon, and, reappearing toward the end of the book as the characters and narrative break down, she meditates on the "chain-link fields of the Word" (705). Again, like Kekule's serpent swallowing its own tail, the text undercuts itself to deliver the reader from the narrative and out into the world of experience. But such devaluation of the word also brings us away from the author's fabulation and directly to the consciousness of the author himself.

In the middle of the text, Slothrop in disguise as Ian Scuffling, British war correspondent, creates a field of assonance when he suggests to Enzian:

> Schwarzgerät, Schwarzkommando, Scuffling: suppose somewhere there were an alphabetical list, someone's list, an input to someone's intelligence arm, say, some country, doesn't matter. (362)

The juxtaposition of two names would be merely "alphabetical coincidence" so that the characters themselves, as well as the intelligence arm, "wouldn't have to be real" (363). Again, the emphasis on what Tanner would term a "lexical playfield" undercuts our close identification with narrative and text—a contrary to the use of free indirect speech to penetrate character. It is as though the text itself as a product of an overt authorial presence has overpowered character and narrative so that the personality of the author finally becomes the primary consciousness of the book, sucking all other presences and plots into its vortex. Lest we forget that language itself is the prime currency in a work about a market where information has "come to be the only real medium of exchange" (258), we are presented with a menu—as the narrative as reality perishes—that considers such paradoxical idioms of the American experience as "shit 'n shinola" and "ass backwards." What occurs, in maneuvering similar to the complex scheme of *The Golden Notebook,* is that character is undermined as authorial participation in the text prevails.

The nightmare of a holocaust seems to end when Pirate wakes from it and reflects upon it—so that what has started as a dream narrative presumes into a real, waking world. But it is questionable that this new narrative condition is any less surreal—with its banana sequences that Mailer cannot get through and bizarre cast of characters, more bizarre, even, than *V.*'s "whole Sick Crew"— than the sequence that precedes it. Pirate's "famous . . . Banana Breakfasts . . ." (5) and his London hothouse with "foot and a half" long bananas—surely a collective English fantasy during the war—are, the previously ironic speaker assures us, "amazing but true" (6). Despite this assertion, it is possible that, while the initial dream sequence ends early, a larger Pirate-related dream remains as narrative impetus, interrupted continually by alienation devices, from which we are not finally free until devaluation of the narrative removes both Pirate and primary inner narrative character Slothrop from this macro-dream.

At the sound of an approaching rocket (we are placed now in a definite time-frame of World War II London), Pirate is able to empty his mind—"a Commando trick" (7)—but his most "amazing" quality is that he can, the speaker "might as well mention here" (11), get "inside the fantasies of others" (12). He is useful to "the Firm" because he can unburden others—very important people in the Firm's scheme—of their "exhausting little daydreams" in his role as "fantasist-surrogate" (12). Thus "much of what the dossiers call Pirate Prentice" (11–12) is this very talent: as a character he exists primarily as a conduit to the inner beings of others. In the last fragmented stages of the narrative, as it reaches new surrealistic vistas, we find a metamorphosis of Pirate's initial assignment in the text for the Firm (the control of Lord Blatherard Osmo's monster adenoid). The final "Adenoid" is Elmo Zhlubb who "suffers from a chronic adenoidal condition," is manager of a Los Angeles movie theater (where the final sequences of a movie of destruction may coincide with a rocket strike upon the movie theater), and whose own fantasy of a freeway death while he is enshrouded with plastic is superseded by an overwhelming siren making way for final scenes of Blicero/Weissmann firing his ultimate rocket with the passive Gottfried, himself enshrouded in Imipolex, on board. It is as though the initial dream/fantasy that Pirate has perhaps managed for someone else—perhaps either author or reader—has asserted itself enough to overwhelm other planes and postures.

It is difficult to know—given that we've been told that much of Pirate is fantasy—what is real about him and what is not real. He recollects an affair with Scorpia Mossmoon, the wife of an Imperial Chemical plastics expert, which seems to be a mirror of the doomed relationship between Roger Mexico and Jessica Swanlake. No wonder that Roger must pass through the chapel sinister of Mossmoon's office before his fall. If what follows Pirate's initial nightmare (a collective fantasy of the current readership of *Gravity's Rainbow*) is a wider dream, then apparently Pirate also reaches inside the condition of a rounded character such as Slothrop. It is as though the [ap]prentice pirate[r] (writer/printer) is an authorial surrogate as the novel, which considers a surrealistic public world hurtling towards its own destruction, must also present the inner beings of a series of figures under the pressure of that public world.

Pirate's fantasies seem to be the key to the phantasmagoric transitions in the narrative. If we are told of Pirate's Mendoza gun, on the next page we will zoom back to the seventeenth century to consider an ancestor of Katje shooting dodoes to extinction with his haakbus. And if it seems inappropriate for, say, a Pointsman to be assigned an inner consciousness that reaches poetry, we may attribute it to the reverie of Pirate/Pynchon. The rendition of Pointsman's "mad exploding of himself" (143) belongs less to that "scientist-neutral" Pointsman first identified by Jessica, than to that inner sensibility reached by Pirate's old commando trick: it is the achievement of the novelist to manage and display the consciousness of others (his characters).

If much of *Gravity's Rainbow* seems to stem from Pirate, the fantasy surrogate, we note times when a more overt authorial presence emerges. It is a presence that devalues the initial narrative in much the same way as the intrusions in *Why Are We In Vietnam?* or in *The Golden Notebook* occur—as author overtly displaces character as primary link with reader. There is an authorial playfulness, for example, in a "Yes, old Africa hands" (316) during a digression on Herero etymology, which is similar to the tone of

authorial intrusions in *Why Are We In Vietnam*. As the narrative
falls apart, the outer narrative voice will tell the reader in a perfunctory nod to any possibility of narrative completion, "You want
cause and effect. All right" (663). It is as though the author, slipping
away from the fantasist-surrogate Pirate, is able to admit his presence in the consciousness rendered by the totality of the novel and
it is this presence within the dream narrative of *Gravity's Rainbow*
that is able to act as some approximation of William Slothrop's
Providence; is able, say, to rescue Tyrone Slothrop from a series
of impossible situations, to save him for further phantasmagoric
adventures, or to appear as a pointing finger above the graves of
Tyrone's New World ancestors. Indeed, it is this presence that is
able to have his characters, human or not, break into song or dance
at will. Toward the end of the novel, as all strands implode into a
single rocket-conscious vortex in the Zone, the authorial consciousness will emerge even as characters within the text have
"scattered." That amid the global reach of the novel exists the
inner consciousness of the author is apparent when the voice of
the "Holy Text" refers to itself as "one of the scholar-magicians
of the Zone" (520). If the "Text had to be the Rocket," to be "picked
to pieces, annotated, explicated, and masturbated" (520), then the
display of authorial consciousness is camouflaged under a guise
such as Pirate. The Text that the author is "riding through right
now" (520) is a piece of "incoming mail," a banana/rocket that the
author is "decoding . . . coding, recoding, decoding" (520–21).

By the end of the novel, the Counterforce spokesman has undercut Slothrop as authentic character and has denied Jamf's existence as primary agent of Slothrop's troubles. If Jamf doesn't exist,
then Slothrop's troubles, and by extension global troubles, are
inside the paranoid individual's head; and yet if Slothrop himself
is denied existence as the work achieves Absolute Zero, then he
is under an authorial control equivalent to that of his initial manipu-
lator from "The White Visitation." The entropy of the narrative
indicates that the late twentieth-century narrative's hand of providence is considerably less secure than that of William Slothrop,
whose Doomsday is less imminent than Pynchon's and our own
global self-annihilation.

To recognize the presence of the author in his text, to see that
he weaves in and out of his narrative in a like operation to that of
the authors in *The Golden Notebook*, *Why Are We In Vietnam?*,
and *Daniel Martin*, and to see that the primary relation of the
novel is between author and readership, is to see that the dialectical
systems of *Gravity's Rainbow* are contained within the gestalt of

authorial consciousness. Just as Slothrop seems to share some of the faults of his adversaries, Pynchon admits both sides of the novel's primary dialectic into his moral personality. If he presents this vast novel in judgment of contemporary Western civilization, he must also include his own hardly bearable weaknesses. The ultimate rocket, this work, is also on a journey to the inner limits of current being. Thus if decadence seems to permeate the novel, it is not a condition from which our primary narrator separates himself. If Pirate Prentice is conduit to the fantasies of others, he is himself the product of the author's decadent fantasies as he fixes his hothouse banana breakfasts for his "whole Sick Crew." The party at Raoul de la Perlimpinpin's at which Slothrop effects his temporary escape from the Firm's control is an increase in the narrative's decadence and, although it takes place near the narrative's World War II time frame, it is as though the decadence has been reinforced by the novel's more contemporary closing sequences—as though authorial time-present mingles with narrative time-past. The decadence on board the *Anubis,* an ultimate ship of fools, reveals the "same old shit that was going on back at Raoul de la Perlimpinpin's" (463)—a mad excess of drugs and sex—and it is a condition that increasingly fills the narrative so that author and reader alike become enmeshed or implicated in the insanities of characters' lives, indeed replacing characters who scatter from the text.

Given the continuing tensions between the natural order and "that succession of the criminally insane who have enjoyed power since 1945"[9]—and apparently even before then—and between outside narrative posture and personal, authorial presence within the existence of his characters, it is no wonder that the narrative is swept up in a series of absurd or surreal episodes under the pressure of those tensions. And given the surrealistic turns of the narrative, it's no wonder that a number of critics have been unable to bear witness to Pynchon's presence in his text—just as others, we've seen, have failed to recognize Mailer's extreme presence in *Why Are We In Vietnam?* or Lessing's in *The Golden Notebook.* Thus Mendelson suggests that Pynchon's books "take little interest in the interior psychological labyrinth" and that "self-consciousness" is only a problem in his "early works."[10] Frank McConnell associates Pynchon's dislike for public or critical attention with an invisibility which is an "essential context of the books."[11] Thus, too, Schwarzbach considers that Pynchon is "compelled to 'hide' himself in his fiction as he does in life."[12] I would suggest, however, that the intrusions of the author, through and beyond Pirate's fantasy management, signal that Pynchon's personality is one with the surrealistic excursions, those very perversions, that permeate the narrative. Indeed, the narrative survives only by a series of absurd chase and escape scenes that undercut the validity of character as action, except to assume that the action of the narrative takes place within the author's phantasmagoric self. Perhaps there is a connection between Pynchon's craving for privacy and the courageous self-revelation displayed in his fiction, especially in the inner investigation that makes up the texture of *Gravity's Rainbow*—beginning as early as Slothrop's fantasies of the Roseland ballroom and Roxbury sewers.

Tony Tanner sees Pynchon's novels as an examination of the relationships between the historical and the personal[13] and Smith and Tololyan, while endorsing Mendelson's view that Pynchon isn't interested in interior investigation, note that the jeremiadic form of *Gravity's Rainbow* contains a study of both personal and national (American—though we might extend this to Western) history. Pynchon himself suggests that his fiction exhibits a consideration of whether "history is personal or statistical."[14] The epic quests that propel the narrative—the multiple searches for the rocket, Slothrop's simultaneous quests for the secret to his sexual identity and to return to native ground—parallel the quests of Stencil in *V.* or of Oedipa Maas in *The Crying of Lot 49*. But perhaps more than in those works, *Gravity's Rainbow*'s compulsive absurdities reveal the author's own quest for a mode of personal conduct in a world that seems to have lost its reason.

Hellman includes Pynchon among "a large group" who "turned away from realism to write fables that clearly made no attempt to represent American life."[15] Thus he considers that "Pynchon describes a World War Two that never happened in *Gravity's Rainbow*."[16] Tololyan, however, demonstrates that Pynchon's third novel is rooted in the history of pre-war Germany and in the precise international details of the war and its aftermath.[17] The personal and historic tensions precipitate an insanity more intense than the surreal, penultimate episodes of *The Golden Notebook*.

History, our outside narrator tells us, misinterprets the true nature of war by concentrating on "battle after battle" (105) rather than revealing its true economic nature in enhancing the international cartel. Thus the "mass nature of wartime death is useful in many ways," for example "as diversions from the real movements of the War" (105). History ignores those "routes of power our teachers never imagined, or were encouraged to avoid . . ." (521). In fact, those "academic hookers" in the field of history—at

Slothrop's Harvard, Pynchon's Cornell or elsewhere—are accomplices in the enterprise to cover the nature of war and of history itself. True history, according to the gospel of the Holy Text of *Gravity's Rainbow,* must reveal that the historical process of twentieth-century Western civilization is dominated by that illuminatus which seeks to protect its profit margin. Pynchon's history, similar to *The Golden Notebook* in its Brechtian distancing techniques, forces the reader to reject stock notions of history. Yet, just as the possibility that Tyrone Slothrop's existence has been controlled from the beginning by parental and industrial/technological fascism is eventually undercut by his reduction as character and by a voice which suggests that he is responsible for his own moral self-reliance, so the narrative focuses eventually upon the individual and his existence, given the inevitability of individual death. Pynchon's self-investigation within his own extended nightmare gives credibility to the hand, which he points down to his own time.

5

In Penelope's Arms:
From Lyric to Epic in *Daniel Martin*

1

In JOHN FOWLES'S *MANTISSA* THERE ARE CASUAL EPIC REFER-
ences—a robe should be "wine-dark"[1] rather than green and the
muse of the author Miles claims to have written what became
known as the *Odyssey* to spite her sister Calliope. In *Daniel Martin*
the narrator/author's seduction by a British film starlet (described
as if she were a version of Diana Dors) is presented in the mock-
epic terms of Circe and Ulysses; but Fowles' most extensive discussion of the epic comes, surprisingly, in the text which accompanies Fay Godwin's photographs of the Scilly Islands. That
Islands was published just a year after *Daniel Martin* might suggest
that there is a close connection between the speculations on the
epic embedded in the seemingly slight, nonfiction work and the
thematic and technical nature of the novel that I consider to be
Fowles' variation of the contemporary epic.

Fowles suggests that there is "strong circumstantial evidence"
that "mysterious strangers" were familiar with southwest Britain
"from at least Homer's time."[2] Thus Odysseus' visit to Tiresias and
the land of the dead after his escape from Circe may be connected
to the "Scillies or Cornwall, since it is also a place of perpetual
cloud and mist."[3] Thus *Daniel Martin* bypasses Arthurian epic and
reaches back to Homer for its impetus as well as its "archipelagic
structure."[4] In fact, the *Odyssey* is the "*sine qua non* of all serious
study or practice of fiction" and has had "a greater influence on
subsequent storytelling, both thematically and technically, than
any other single book in human history."[5] Accepting this, we may
assume that the key to the heart of *Daniel Martin* may be found
in Homer.

When Miles's muse in *Mantissa* claims that she has written the
Odyssey, she claims that she called it *Men, Will They Ever Grow*

Up? She wrote about one of Calliope's "rotten hero characters" to "show his sort up for what they really are."[6] This claim follows closely the line in *Islands,* where Fowles—following Dante's condemnation of the reckless hero and Dryden's version of the *Aeneid* where the hero is "dire and insatiate Odysseus"—terms the hero "the least attractive character of them all" and, in modern terms, translates the name of this figure of "quintessential maleness" as "the paranoiac."[7] Odysseus' own "incapacity to do anything but undergo the experience"[8] is paralleled by the tragedies visited upon the house of Agamemnon and caused by "male stupidity and arrogance, that inability to be satisfied with what one has, that perpetual lust to amass more, possess more, score more"[9] and by the Aeolus episode again caused by "male greed."[10]

While the hapless Miles claims that "every classical scholar since scholarship began knows Homer was a man,"[11] Fowles follows Samuel Butler and Robert Graves in announcing that "the *Odyssey* must have been written by a woman."[12] His initial reasoning is a little shaky; for while the writer may seem more "knowledgeable about domestic matters . . . than about nautical ones,"[13] this might mean that the rhapsodist is a land-bound male—blind or not. But Fowles joins the author of the *Odyssey* with Penelope, the patient wife in opposition to reckless husband, by translating the Greek word "for a recited epic, rhapsody" as "stitched song"[14]—thus linking the epic with Penelope's activity as she avoids her suitors and wards off acceptance of widowhood. Fowles connects the *Odyssey* with the writings of Marie de France and Christine de Pisan as he sees each concluding a male journey of "self-discovery" with a conclusion that "true wisdom always lay at home."[15]

While Fowles claims that the massacre of the suitors, the hanging of maids and the mutilation of Melanthius are examples of Odysseus' continuing paranoia, I suspect that his interpretation is the imposition of twentieth-century sensibility upon ancient (surely the detail regarding Melanthius is too strong for Fowles's wise authoress). Nevertheless, Fowles sees the force of the work coming from that wisdom shared by Penelope and the goddess Athene. Indeed, he sees the climax of the *Odyssey* not in the slaughter of suitors, et al., but in the domestic triumph of Book Twenty-three. Thus:

No man who has ever risked or provoked the ship-wreck of a marriage by his own selfishness has ever doubted the profound affirmation of *female* wisdom in that climactic passage; or for that matter had to wonder why the ancients personified wisdom as a woman.[16]

Indeed, Odysseus' one virtue is his longing to return home to Penelope and wisdom. As in Fowles's own epic, the wandering hero reaches wisdom through the heart and mind of the mature woman.

Beneath the fabulous mythology of Homer, Fowles sees "ordinary men and women with practical social problems"[17] so that it is not surprising that he can so easily connect the Homeric epic with the novel. It is Odysseus' sojourn with Calypso and the struggle between his desire to remain with her and the call back to Penelope, which apparently is the most compelling theme infiltrating Fowles own novels: "I know how much I owe, as a writer of fiction, to the Calypso-Penelope dilemma; it has haunted my own and countless other novels, and always will."[18] Certainly, we can see that *The Magus* is written "under the vast aegis of the *Odyssey*"[19] as Nicholas must chose between the phantasms of the god-game and the patient Alison. But the *Odyssey* is not merely an inspiration for subject matter in Fowles' work; it is also a source of technique. For Odysseus is also "the voyage of the mind . . . is every artist who sets off into the unknown of his unconscious. . . ."[20] In fact, Odysseus is the fledgling novelist Daniel Martin who must leave the secure haven of Hollywood. The fragmentation of the early parts of the novel reflects the man without wisdom who must reach back to the wisdom of a contemporary Penelope to find himself, though it is from a contemporary Calypso that the hero will first learn enough "home truths" to set him on his voyage. If much of the "cunning structure of the *Odyssey,* is told in flashback,"[21] then the screenwriter will borrow a technique from his forsaken trade to tell the story of himself. The screenwriter Dan, who has succumbed to the lure of the symbol of the decline of the West—he challenges his old classmate to "Reject Spengler, then, if you can"[22] after he has told him of his life in Hollywood—uses the tricks of his trade as he sets out on the initial stages of his "voyage of the mind." Indeed, while Robert Huffaker finds *Daniel Martin* to be without the trickery that he sees permeating Fowles's other novels,[23] I would suggest that it resembles the other primary examples of the epic novel discussed in this book in its often abrupt interplay of narrative stances.

Especially like *Gravity's Rainbow,* the shifts in the nature of *Daniel Martin*'s narrative rely upon its close alliance to film techniques. Thus the tricks of dissonance and fragmentation that Dan/Fowles uses are closely related to what we might call the epic stooge of the epic novel in progress—the movie script that Dan is commissioned to write about the British general Kitchener. It is from the movie world that Dan must break away, so that film influences the form or struggle of the early stages of the novel. The film would represent to the Hollywood hack what Fowles terms in *The Aristos* the "Nemo . . . man's sense of his own futility and ephemerality,"[24] so that the technical complexities of the first half of *Daniel Martin* are very much the result of the milieu that Dan is attempting to forsake. "Games," the second chapter, places our hero at a window looking out at Los Angeles' "endless plain of trivial light" glistening through "the infamous city's artificial night" (12). The boy of the first chapter, "The Harvest," is now the middle-aged screenwriter of the 'seventies, feeling himself a failure and empathizing with the homesickness of the recently arrived Scottish actress, Jenny McNeil—the novel's Calypso. Though it was in London that Dan first let himself "be dazzled by the gilt chimeras" (71) of the film world, Hollywood seems to become the primary symbol for the decadent, false world that Martin and the members of his generation have reached at mid-life. The old set of *Camelot,* where Daniel epiphanizes the hollowness of his life, parallels like symbolic sets in Nathanael West's *Day of the Locust* and F. Scott Fitzgerald's *The Last Tycoon.* Like those works (as well as more recent Hollywood novels such as Mailer's *The Deer Park* and Joan Didion's *Play It As It Lays*), *Daniel Martin* offers Hollywood as an emblem for Spenglerian intimations that "the racial geist is . . . mortal" (393).

The chapter sequencing of *Daniel Martin* stems from Dan's film craft. If Chapter One takes us back into the lush Devon of 1942 and Chapter Two brings us to an arbitrary Hollywood present, Chapter Three situates Dan as a terminal student at Oxford and Chapter Four propels the situation of the second chapter forward into the final, sustained narrative that will lead to the writing of the book about itself by Dan. The movie writer turned fledgling novelist is playing with a sequencing he has learned at the studios: chapters that take us "Forward Backward" or into "Future Present," while they might define the *Odyssey* as the first film as well as the first novel, belong to a grammar comparable to the script-writer's strategy for his final film project, for which he will "use a flashback inside a flashback, and possibly a flashback inside that as well; a Chinese-box gimmick, but with possibilities" (416). Besides that filmic structuring, certain experiences are rendered with a visual intensity akin to the sweep that film can achieve. Just as Fitzgerald attempted to present a film-like order of experience more intense than the nominal outside narrative of Cecilia Brady might allow (thus achieving, in the scenes between Monroe Stahr and the elusive Kathleen, an effect demagnetized only by the inter-

ruptions of Cecilia "taking up the narrative again"), so the process
of *Daniel Martin* hinges on passages that sweep into the narrative
like dynamic film gestures: the call that will take Daniel home from
Hollywood is introduced by the image of a door opening in a wall;
when two chapters later, this phone conversation is resumed, Dan
is a "surfer, suddenly caught in the crest" (46); a "dissociated hand
on the final lock" (93) will signal the end of a first brief affair with
Jane; an "empty half-bottle sitting on her desk" (144) will signal
the beginning of an affair with Andrea; a touching of hands across
a white tablecloth affords the promise of a reconciliation with Jane.
Like film, the novel progresses by gesture.

The lush recollective images of the first chapter—of an order
with those powerful rustic passages in *The Magus* (when Nicholas
and Alison climb up to a Parnassus bower), *The French Lieutenant's Woman,* and *A Maggot*—give way to new angles of vision
and a new narrative starting point, from the recent rather than
early history of Daniel Martin. Dialogue from a different world
than the "hoy . . . whoy . . . jok-jok" (5) of Devon leads into a
mirror reflection of Jenny from "A new angle; nicest because no
lens . . . could get it" (12) so that the extent of Dan's drift from
his early being is emphasized. Indeed, while Dan and Jenny agree
that they feel outsiders in California, their relationship tends to be
defined in film terms. Thus, while Dan will attack Hollywood mor-
als, he will initiate his first lovemaking with Jenny by suggesting
that they are "wasting footage" (40). And Dan, the narrator of his
own novel, will define his own life by the terms of film. Thus, when
his daughter, Caro, announces that she is having an affair with her
father's Oxford classmate and is moving to her own flat, he will
close the episode with a self-deprecating "Cut" (125). His decision
to buy his farm in Thorncombe is a "cutting job," a "script" (130)
to be formalized. The filmic term will deprecate that to which it is
attached, so that, when Dan's adolescent affair with Nancy Reed
has been described, the degree of Daniel's fall from that Edenic
state is symbolized by a recent meeting with her introduced by
"One last shot. *Many years later,* as they used to say in the old
sub-titles" (379). Even the umbrella Daniel's father keeps with him
receives the overkill of "my Rosebud" (89). If Jenny will confi-
dently tell Dan, as he broods about the difficulties of writing a
novel, "All you have to do is put down exactly what we've just
said" (16), Dan will realize that the present, or near present, moment is the language of film. Thus, "Film excludes all but now;
permits no glances away to past and future; is therefore the safest
dream" (155). In that safe dream of the present, Jenny is able to

make her contributions without needing to consider the more dangerous terrain of Dan's past. If the word is imprecise, then the film or photographic image is precise (87). Thus the true nature of the English temper—"the continual evasion of the inner self, the continual actual reality of saying one thing and thinking another" (274), that which can only be plumbed by the serious novel—cannot be captured by the camera. The dichotomy of film and novel becomes a keynote to the form of *Daniel Martin*.

As he wanders through a Hollywood studio, Dan comes upon an old set of *Camelot* where he realizes that his true artistic mission, which is to arrive at "the real history of what I am" (15), cannot be captured by film or stage. Later into the enterprise that will become the book, he fears those "bits between" (390) that are beyond the craft of cameras and angles. While he is not a "literary experimenter," Dan realizes that his quarrel with the film industry is that it "put so much more value on the craft than the code-breaking side," so that "even the smallest departure from the cinematic established and sanctified had to be so fiercely fought for" (207). The novel promises to allow the possibility of breaking codes just as life itself does in the call back to England that Dan receives from the dying Anthony. This process of reality itself opposes obedience to the rules of the game demanded by the film industry. The novel will allow Daniel Martin relief from the burden of his parasitic endeavors and a pathway to understanding who he is.

Barney Dillon, another of Dan's classmates at Oxford and now a media personality who is soon revealed to be the lover of Dan's daughter, suggests that the screenwriter's current project on Kitchener is an "epic" (102). Barney uses the term in its popular, adulterated sense—Daniel will later refer to the project as "cast-of-thousands work" (278). But the structure that Dan plans—"to catch Kitchener somewhere in mid-career and at some central focus geographically; and then rally from that point in flashback and then flash-forward to the rest of his life" (279)—approximates the structure of that first novel and inspiration of all others, the *Odyssey*, and certainly of *Daniel Martin* and the other three novels discussed at length in this study. What Daniel and his producer wish to achieve is an image of human complexity through the juxtaposition of Kitchener as public figure and as private man. The interactions of those public and private worlds in the life of Daniel himself make up the version of the contemporary epic kind exhibited by *Daniel Martin,* though the subject is not a classically epic hero like Kitchener, but is, like the Romantic epic figure, a representative writer/individual of a generation who learns the way to sing himself.

2

As Daniel picks up the "Crimes and Punishments" narrative of his early days in the film industry and of the breakup of his marriage, he ponders the mysterious "effect of public on private history" (156). Perhaps the impetus for such conjecture comes from his time in America, for in *The Aristos* Fowles considers that the fabric of the American temper is derived from the struggle between the drive for individualism and the call for social equality. That duality between private and public is also considered in a work that Dan begins to read, through the good offices of his Penelope/ Athene figure, Jane, on his return to Oxford. In *Selections from the Prison Notebooks of Antonio Gramsci,* Dan finds that the follower of praxis (that is, the philosopher of social action) is considered both as individual and as component of social group. Listening to the humorist Sabry in Egypt, Dan sees political establishments as a conspiracy that emphasizes "man as a product of history, not of his true, inner, personal, nature" (470). But notions of duality also arise in the last phase of the novel, as the German papyrologist Kirnberger explains that, to ancient Egyptians, the" 'ka' and 'ba' were ways of seeing man first as an individual . . . and then as one" (513). Thus "Your story. Your real history of you" (17), as Jenny calls Daniel's budding project, must not only seek "the bitter and repressed child [who] once hid in green Devon countryside" separated from the natural world around him, but must also reveal ways by which the modern world has shaped the emerging man.

The mirrors in the young bohemian Daniel's rooms at Oxford represent the "overweening narcissism" of his generation, whose "liberal scruples, the concern with living right and doing right, were not based on external principles, but self-obsession" (593). Dan at Oxford is like Nicholas Urfe of *The Magus,* the self-centered rebel of Conchis's *The Midcentury Predicament.*[25] If the mirrors represent the inner-directed, personal aspect of existence, a series of airplanes represent the ways by which the public world barges hard into and tempers that personal existence. A Luftwaffe shatters the adolescent Dan's pastoral scene in Devon as, "The long combe is flooded with the frantic approach, violent machinery at full stretch, screaming in an agony of vicious fear" (7). Later, an American Flying Fortress flies over the Isis and is connected with the strangled girl whom Dan and Jane have just found—"Perhaps . . . it carries the murderer: he chews gum, in a baseball hat, watching a panel of instruments, up there" (27). The "strange . . . all-invasive" roar (308) of a Concorde seems to spell doom for the Tory England of Andrew's Compton so that the plane becomes a symbol of intrusion of a country that now "has only itself to live for" (391), unable to adjust to a world which has "jumped forward three decades in one" (49). Thus *Daniel Martin* becomes very much an elegaic novel about "a country drifting slowly into oblivion" (391). No wonder that the dying Anthony Mallory reminds Dan of another Anthony: the prime minister during Suez, the crisis which seemed to signal the final eclipse of the British Empire. It is a country perhaps waiting for a new kind of visionary, prophetic Daniel, like he from the Old Testament who denounced the falling from moral purpose of his contemporaries. Yet the emphasis on empire symbolically represented by Kitchener's public self is itself "the great disease . . . and profoundly un-English" (423), for the true character of England, under the imposed nineteenth-century layers of Victorian patriotism and repression, calls for freedom to follow one's personal temperament. The imposition of a false England has dominated Daniel's childhood—for example, his adolescent, prelapsarian affair with Nancy is repressed "by convention, by respectability, by class, by Christianity . . ." (377). Thus the English are in a state of perpetual past or future, unable to live in the present. Beyond our vision of public life in England and its effect upon the individual, we are also afforded visions of the new empire—through Jenny's contributions, which first condemn the American temper but then offer a more positive assessment: "perhaps all the stupidity and the tastelessness and the inequality and the violence and the conformity are just the price of keeping a national energy alive" (235). That positive view is later somewhat tempered by Kirnberger, the East German expert on an older empire, who informs Dan and Jane that to the Egyptians the West was the land of death, and by their encounter on the Nile cruise ship with the young Americans, Mitchell and Marcia Hooper. Kirnberger offers a view of the mind set of the Soviet bloc (complementing Jane's Maoist-Marxist theorizing from her Oxford involvements) when he suggests that the difference between East and West is in differing views of the contrary of freedom: chaos versus authority. Certainly there is enough geographic scope within the "archipelagic structure" of *Daniel Martin* to give us a view of the global situation's shaping of individual existence and the representative author/individual must understand his relationship to that global situation in order to come to terms with his own being.

Although Dan sees at least one component of his novel—"Inter-lude"—as an "exorcism by the written word" (253), and though he certainly elevates the novel above film in terms of its ability to depict the self in relation to society, he yet senses that the novel might simply afford him another mode of retreat from the outside world (a theory of the novel that is offered not only in the introduc-tion to the revised version of *The Magus*, but in *The French Lieu-tenant's Woman*, *A Maggot*, and *Mantissa*). He fears that the possibility of self-accounting through the novel could be countered by the compulsion to use the mode for escape. Recognizing his penchant for escape, in London after Anthony's funeral, he sees the possibility of writing a novel about his own representative Odyssean condition: "A character who must be seen in flight, like a bird who has forgotten how to stop migrating" (276). This note is followed by a question: "What makes him stop?" We are to see a domestic swallow (unless it is another Martin, the kingfisher of the Nile) join song with the prophetic, public voice of a Daniel to make up the polyvocal narrative of this novel. Perhaps what makes Dan stop is the death of his friend, together with Anthony's charge to care for the soon-to-be widowed and soon-to-be lover-unshod Jane; though perhaps it is also Jenny—responding to Dan's film industry nausea and to his desire to write "the real history of what I am" (15)—who, through her first and second "contributions," gives Dan the impetus for an accounting of himself and his genera-tion. Jenny will recognize that the clearsighted young Dan of the novel's opening chapter now has "faults of perception" (231) so that he needs "his eyesight tested" (14): thus Dan's quest is to respond to the corrective angle of vision by tracing his own fall from the grace of "The Harvest." Although sometimes that self-analysis verges on the amateur—a description of his initial sexual experience includes the freeze-frame observation that Nancy Reed's "body was his lost mother's" (358)—Dan's triumph is the sincerity by which he is able to locate the circuits of his life and to direct them toward the modest commitments (like *The Golden Notebook*'s Anna Wulf, Dan is seen at the end of his narrative joining the Labour Party) of maturity.

The impulse of the early stage of the novel is lyric—we witness the rustic ritual of stooking and are reminded of the lush descrip-tions of the Undercliff and Ware Commons in *The French Lieuten-ant's Woman*—and is undercut only by the shame that the young Danny has of his educated dialect in opposition to the natural dia-lect of Devon. That awkward sense of self converts to the narcis-sism that we witness in the mirror obsessed narcissist at Oxford—

a perversion of the novel's initial lyricism, but which itself gives way to a humanistic maturity where will is tempered or coupled with compassion. Thus a new kind of "whole sight" is established as Dan, in the novel's final chapter, identifies with Rembrandt's self-portrait where the eyes of the artist look out at the world with a balance of inner and outer understanding. To reach that state, to become a mature artist, Daniel Martin must come to terms with the dislocation by class and cultural repression which has haunted him since his childhood as the out-of-place son of a minister amid the folklife of Devon. Thus the novel exists on a loop similar to that of *Gravity's Rainbow* as Daniel, mature enough to achieve his novel, offers the first words of *Daniel Martin* to Jane in the book's penultimate sentence. The lyric voice gives way to a more epic posture as the narrative moves about the globe only to arrive at its own lyric beginning back in Devon. In fact, the global reach of the novel is considerably more muted than that of *Gravity's Rainbow, The Golden Notebook,* or even *Why Are We In Vietnam?* Our primary view of World War II is the two bombers that fly over Dan (in Devon and with Jane on the Cherwell after the war); the U.S. involvement in Vietnam is given swift treatment through the Hoopers—is dealt with more significantly in the brief illustrations within *A Maggot;* the most intensive analysis of the third world comes in Sabry's comic turn. Fowles is more concerned with his own narrator's attempt to render his sense of place and sense of a people's temper (and thus by implication why their political situation is so) than he is concerned directly with immersion in the interface of politics with individual history. Clearly, if Fowles believes that the novel's prototype is a domestic epic, then his own contemporary epic novel will tend to emphasize the domestic, with the journey tending to be more a symbol of emotional flight than viewpoint for political purchase.

3

One of the primary voices of *The French Lieutenant's Woman* is a collective contemporary "we"—a sensibility that is defined by its difference and similarity with the nineteenth century it describes, and that is closely related to the "I" who freely admits that he manipulates his nineteenth-century tale. That secure narrative stance is achieved in *Daniel Martin* only after an extreme struggle of less secure narrative stances. The camera's eye and microphone's ear that describe the novel's initial scenes of the wartime harvest in Devon gradually focuses on the boy Dan who becomes the "he" of the novel. After the slaughter of rabbits at the end of the initial harvest scene, "his heart turns, some strange premonitory turn, a day when in an empty field he shall weep for this" (9)—it will be the mature artist rendering his past whose whole sight will weep for this past moment. But a more complex narrative stance infiltrates when "I feel in his pocket and bring out a clasp-knife" (11): a self-conscious speaker intruding upon the objective lens just as "I" will "seem to remember" details of "Dan's" room at Oxford (52). Through its first two-thirds, the novel will tend to swing back and forth between "I" and "Dan" as narrator. For example, recollecting his own past in the chapter symbolically titled "The Umbrella," Dan begins with: "My mother died just before my fourth birthday, and I really cannot remember her at all . . ." (75). But even in this early recollective passage, a distancing will take place when, though referring to himself at the present moment of recollection as "I," the speaker will yet refer to himself in the past as "the small boy" and "he" (81). The chapter that follows describes the punting scene between Dan and Jane before Dan marries her sister and Jane marries their friend Anthony. We start off with "Dan" in present—"the now of then" (90)—flying into New York on his way to Oxford from Hollywood. But he soon becomes "I" as he begins to contemplate the past, then again becoming "Dan" as we reenter a past episode. As the novel moves into more and more difficult old ground to be covered, the interplay between first-and third-person becomes more and more intense. Thus "Breaking Silence"—describing the failure of the marriage of Dan and Nell and the beginning of Dan's misadventures—switches continually between "Dan" and "I" as discomfort in confronting the past and self becomes acute. Only when past and present selves can be integrated is a more sustained narrative stance available. In contrast, to Dan's achievement, "The Loneliness of the Long-Distance Runner" reveals a continual undercutting of its narrative ground precisely because the character/speaker Smith is unable to reconcile his present and past selves. While both *A Maggot* and *The French Lieutenant's Woman* are primarily interested in comparing past and present, integration of those two aspects of individual existence is achieved in *Daniel Martin* only after a narrative uncertainty as intense as that of Sillitoe's still misunderstood, lying hero.

On his way to the Los Angeles airport, from where he will set out for England and a contemplation of his own past, Dan is "reduced to watching himself, as if he were indeed a fiction, a paper person in someone else's script . . ." (62). The third-person narrative even reports that Dan tried out a sentence in first-person—"I missed my flight (or I nearly missed my flight)"—but rejected the "sound and feel" of this stance (63). An "I think they learned rather more . . ." (68) or an "I will not make her teeter on the windowsill" (103) will less frequently, but much more casually, invade *The French Lieutenant's Woman* than will the "I was also very tired that morning" (63) enter the narrative of *Daniel Martin* after being initially rejected. Here and elsewhere—"But my major sin was still to come" (164)—the first-person signals a confessional sincerity which reaches back to the romantic epic. This shifting in voice is paralleled by the confusion in Jenny's contributions, where an attempt to treat Dan objectively will be undermined by a slippage into personalized reference. Thus: "(. . . but it was strange, Dan, I *did* feel something was going to happen to us). When you, I mean he, talked of chasms" (34); or, "We've talked a lot about him, by the way," followed by "I'm more than half writing to myself, you know that" (236) in her second contribution. If, in the first of the book's two primary movements, switches in person seem to signify a tenuous hold upon detachment and narrative authority and if, in the body of the book, the shuttling of narrative stances signifies both the interaction of private and public worlds and Dan's efforts to come to terms with his past, then the primary gesture of the novel's first half will be the struggle between the two voices to gain control of the narrative. By the time that Dan has physically returned to "the Orchard of the Blessed" in Devon, the third-person is beginning to overpower the "I" who remembers his past, for Dan has traveled through his past and is becoming the author of his life: "He was still bare of a story or characters in any practical sense, but he began to see, dimly, a kind of general purpose or drift . . ." (401).

Just as first- and third-person stances interchange during accounts of Dan's earlier past, so will they interchange during accounts of recent times. His former sister-in-law and soon to be life-partner Jane recognizes that Dan "has always been two people" (265). Looking back early in the novel, in "Phillida," Dan must painfully recall his adolescent affair with Nancy Reed and he zigzags back and forth in referring to himself back then both as "Daniel/he" and "I": "I was terribly scared of being laughed at . . . "; "He was head over heels in love with her . . ." (348); "Daniel felt vaguely disappointed . . ." (370); "we decided it must have been Bill Hannacott" (373); "He thought she would stop and give him his wages . . . "; "I went up to my room and lay on my bed . . ." (375). Past tense is described from both postures as it is in the sequence of chapters describing the breakup of his relationship with Nell. Both in past and present, the duality of voice is most manifest at times of crisis, so that the meeting between Dan and the dying Anthony (his former college friend and estranged brother-in-law) will culminate in switches back and forth between "Dan" and "I" and the same shifts are present during the inquest after Anthony's suicide and on both the arrival of Jenny's contribution to the writer's own story and Dan's resultant separation from her. The shifting narrative ground during Dan's transatlantic flight together with the television celebrity Barney Dillon will foreshadow the more intense narrative shifting when Dan must confront his classmate's affair with his daughter, Caro. At such times, third-person stances seem a kind of evasive objectivity maneuver, like the voice switches in the early sections of *The Ginger Man,* where the protagonist/narrator/author seeks to escape from himself.

The recollective/confession of his adolescent encounter with Nancy the farm girl—about two-thirds into the book—marks the last major passage of the interchange between "Dan" and "I," for, in the final third of the novel, the third-person begins to override, in a sustained way, first-person intrusions. When, after Dan's seduction by the "British Open" film starlet, we are told that, "It was very clear to him that he had done something wicked and he must not let it happen again" (138), the early third-person stance is sardonic towards its subject—there is an ironic detachment between Dan the narrator and Dan the subject. Thus too, as Dan goes to sleep after returning to Oxford, a nineteenth-century ironic omniscience is executed with, "Mr. Specula Speculans snores there now" (208), and a, "Which leaves our hero caged behind his window above, obliged to smile to himself, like an inefficient god . . ." (230) perhaps reaches back to Thackeray and before in achieving a detachment approximate to a film fade. The third-person must mature with the hero of the novel, must work through its uncertainty to the secure status equalled by the union of Dan and Jane. Thus "one can't dissociate the kind of man he is from the vulgarest kind of vanity, the Casanova aspect of the beast" (238) offers a more realistic approach to detached self-assessment. The collective voice that is achieved by the novel's end—"We are civilized adults; but Dan felt a million miles from civilized adulthood" (604)—offers the maturity of empathetic humanism.

As the case for the third-person develops, a phone call from Jenny announcing the imminent arrival of her third "contribution" to the novel will characteristically bring back the unsteady ground of narrative interchange; but the cementing of Dan's relationship with

Jane is accompanied by an almost exclusively third-person narrative. An early gesture in the relationship—"Dan hesitates, then reaches across the white cloth and touches her hand lightly" (192)—tends to be no more than a view for the camera's lens. But as Dan and Jane set out on their journey, they are "both carefully objective," so that "he talked about himself as he talks here, in the third-person . . ." (491). Even Dan's difficulties in wooing Jane do not rate an intrusion of the first-person. Private and public worlds are wedded into the steady voice of the mature novelist who is not as intrusive as the author who draws attention to himself at key points in *The French Lieutenant's Woman* and toward the end of *A Maggot,* but is an author at one with character and audience.

When Dan says that Miriam and Marjory, the cockney sisters with whom he takes up after the breakup of his marriage, possessed "a courage of the kind Brecht immortalized" (251), it is difficult not to believe that Fowles himself provides a rather shallow reading of Brecht's attitude towards his character. But when we consider a reference in *The French Lieutenant's Woman* to "an unconscious alienation effect of the Brechtian kind,"[26] or that Lily-Julie in *The Magus* imposes "a disconcerting alienation effect"[27] upon Nicholas, then the presence of distancing techniques may be discernable in the narrative switches of *Daniel Martin.* Thus Dan will say of his first major success as a playwright: "I had only the sketchiest notion at the time of what Brecht was getting at" (139). Certainly there is an intense distancing in *The French Lieutenant's Woman,* where the narrator will intrude upon his narrative to the extent of invalidating his characters and plot: "They begat what shall it be—let us say seven children"[28] But just as Dan is able to distance himself from a past embarrassment by referring to himself as Ulysses and a British starlet as Circe, he will distance himself from a contribution of Jenny by a "this was yet to come, of course" (236) reference to the manipulated time sequencing of his narrative. The lyric impulse of the narrative's early Devon and Cherwell sequences gives way to a field of technical trickery very much akin to the alienation devices in the first-and third-person theater of the Brechtian epic, or to the "disintoxification" process which is the final movement of *The Magus.* For *Daniel Martin,* it is a process that will make way for the steady third-person of Dan matured through injections of Jane.

When Dan says that Jenny's "Second Contribution" was "yet to come," he not only makes us aware of the "chronology of this reconstruction" (239), but he also increases our awareness of the narrative as fabrication, our awareness of the relationship between author and narrator. In *The French Lieutenant's Woman,* both reference to twentieth-century matters (for example, a quote from Manchester's *Death of a President* heads a chapter) and the narrator's increasingly frequent references to his manipulation of the plot—indeed his very presence as a manipulating character within the plot—become the book's primary mannerism in a similar fashion to self-reference in *Mantissa.* Though *Daniel Martin* is about the actual writing of a traditional novel, the self-reference is more gradual than in Fowles's other works (though Sue Park makes a strong case for Fowles's dominance of his narrator in considering the initial name for Dan's central character—S. Wolfe—as an anagram for Fowles). When Dan tells Jenny that "One day I shall make you up" and she replies by asking, "What makes you think you're not doing that already?" (252) we enter into the realms of *Mantissa;* but back in Devon Dan is able to refer comfortably to himself as conscious writer at one with his past and present selves.

4

The chapter "Interlude" begins with an outside narrator—before Dan's recollective first-person recalls a relationship with the two young cockney girls—who tells us, "A novel is written in two tenses: the present perfect of the writer's mind, the concluded past of conventional fiction," and who then slips into a "cramped and myopic fictional present" (239) to analyze the accuracy of Jenny's assessment of Dan in one of her contributions. In fact, like *The French Lieutenant's Woman* and *A Maggot, Daniel Martin* delves into the relationships between past and present as it switches back and forth between time perspectives almost as diligently as it switches back and forth in voice. Like the earlier and later novels, *Daniel Martin* will zoom into the present from a narrative chugging along in the conventional past, a Dickensian technique particularly appropriate for a novel by and/or about a technician of movie scripts. Of course, the narrative moment exists on three planes— the actual moment of narration (presumably back at Thorncombe both before and, especially, after the final bonding with Jane); the "NOW OF THEN" (90), which tells of the recent events leading to the writing of the novel; the more distant, confessional past, which is recalled alongside the recent past (I ignore for the time being the true narrator, the mirror image of S. Wolfe, who invents Jenny and her contributions even as he discusses their merits in "Interlude"). The narrative moves comfortably back and forth between these planes and, like a movie camera, will enter into the present of a moment initially recalled in the "concluded past of conventional fiction." Thus several scenes during the courtship with Jane have a film-like zoom into the present: "She left a pause. . . . A long moment. He whispers . . ." (60). But the technique is not simply a rendition of the eternal present of film; if changes of voice tend to echo the struggle of private and public worlds, tense moves tend to exhibit the present's struggle to come to terms with the past of self and the historic past. Only when present and past selves can be integrated will a sustained voice of the novel become possible.

Daniel Martin's epigram from Gramsci's *Notebooks*—"The crisis consists precisely in the fact that the old is dying and the new cannot be born; in the interregnum a great variety of morbid symptoms appears"—suggests that the condition of modern man is a fissioned consciousness resulting from the sudden cultural leaps of the twentieth century. In *The Aristos* these morbid symptoms might include the trickeries of inner-directed nemoistic art,[29] while in *Daniel Martin* we might see the struggle appearing in such a parallel mannerism to the movement between narrative stances as the interplay between vectors of past and present. For the character and frequent narrator Daniel Martin, the representative member of his generation, the call back to Oxford for reconciliation with the dying Anthony is a "re-entry into the past" (207) and a means to discover himself in terms of Gramsci's notion that the "individual is a synthesis not only of existing relationships, but of the history of those relationships" (104). Anthony's dying and the family gatherings after his death provide a means for the "prodigal son" (220) to move again in family "crosscurrents" (221). Daniel's path into maturity and the novel is an escape from the eternal lyric present moment of the film world into a recognition of "that vile, stupid and inhuman pretense that our pasts are not always our presents" (381). Like the former inhabitants of Tsankawi in New Mexico, Daniel is able to reach a condition that includes past and future in present consciousness.

Whereas Dan's reentry into his past discloses the interplay between an individual's past and present, early passages of the book afford glimpses of the old and new worlds. In "The Harvest," Babe the poacher is "an ancient presence, and quasi-divine . . ." (9). Yet the shrill modern violence of a warplane penetrates the old world of Devon. The last two centuries have been confounded by abrupt transformations of existence, and Dan's generation has been especially dislocated by that sudden cultural change, one of the "most abrupt . . . in the history of mankind" (86), which followed the

Second World War. Thus "a great chasm in twentieth-century history" occurred when the century "jumped forward three decades in one" (49). So Daniel's pasts are not easy to reenter despite the conveniences of plot. Only the union with Jane will allow a mutual "heightened sense of personal present and past" (493).

Schisms between past and present are manifested by the jumping back and forth among narrative sequences of Dan's text: his Devon narrative beginning with the novel's initial chapter, "The Harvest"; his undergraduate/postgraduate narrative beginning with the novel's third chapter, "The Woman in the Reeds," and moving through his career up to his affair with Jenny; his narrative of the recent past beginning with the novel's second chapter, "Games"; the parallel narrative of Jenny's corrective and distancing contributions. The novel's early fragmentation by sequencing is similar to the way in which the various parts of *The Golden Notebook* reveal the fission that exists up to and after the dissolving of separate components into the penultimate section—the inner golden notebook. And there are confusions even within the nominally separate components so that, for example, Dan will include a contribution from Jenny in advance of its reception by him in the time frame of his recent narrative. Although three chapters are devoted to Jenny's three letters, another fragment—presumably from the second letter—is included in what is nominally Dan's own chapter, "Tsankawi." In fact, Dan admits that he recasts Jenny's contribution into this chapter, which yet gives way in its last few paragraphs to Jenny's own voice so that these seemingly separate components spill back into each other.

In a sense, we are aware of a writer in current operation still struggling with competing past and present, inner and outer impulses. Thus there is another narrative shadow involved in a plot parallel to that of Dan's most recent past. Although the narrative ends securely with a matured Dan renouncing Jenny for Jane and gazing with understanding at Rembrandt's self-portrait, another action takes place in the process of the novel itself: Daniel, who presumably is writing this novel after the narrative has reached the point of the final page, is still practicing—experiencing rather than merely technically manipulating—fragmentation as he reaches toward the integrated voice and narrative of what will be the book's final movement. Thus, while the narrative reports on the progress of the novel in terms of its origin in Hollywood and the development of the idea of the novel in England and Egypt, there is also another time frame for the novel's process: the actual construction of the novel at Daniel's home in Thorncombe, Devonshire—"where I write now" (379)—by the novelist who is trying to execute "what this book is trying to be . . ." (331). It is this currently creating novelist who is writing the history of the growth of what he is writing and who is recording a stage when it was "still bare of a story or characters in any practical sense," but contained "a kind of purpose or general drift . . . a site, if not yet the house" (401); and who yet continues to try to complete the process of the book's beginning.

5

Although the chronological beginning of the novel is the wartime Devon harvest, the immediate process of Dan's novel begins in Los Angeles where, having confronted his own failure on the old *Camelot* set, Dan speaks with Jenny McNeil about writing his own true history. Jenny suggests that the novel can begin "here," that all Dan needs "to do is to put down exactly what we've just said" (16). Although Dan, as mature novelist, will finally sequence "Games" after "Harvest," for Jenny the scene in Los Angeles prior to the summoning phone call "*is* the first chapter" (17), so that she finds a name, "Simon Wolfe," for him because one can't use one's own name in a novel. Later, Jenny will even write what is titled in the novel "An Unbiased View," which, she considers, is the beginning of the novel. But, though for Jenny the beginning of the novel seems not a difficult affair, the process is not so easy for Dan—if not quite as difficult as it is for the author/character of *Mantissa*. If Dan and his Hollywood colleagues have difficulty in fathoming Jenny—"it was hard to tell what was genuine and what was being tried out in pursuit of a working persona in a very alien environment" (65)—Dan himself seems to mirror the uncertainty of his initial muse as he works toward establishing a persona for his fledgling novel. A third of the book is over before he will tentatively confess to his daughter that he is "thinking of trying a novel" (267), and it is almost another third of the book before he will say the same thing to his enduring muse, Jane—"I might try a novel" (389). Back to his beginnings in Devon, the story of himself begins to take firmer shape: "He was still bare of a story or characters in any practical sense, but he began to see, dimly, a kind of general purpose or drift; in architectural terms, a site, if not yet the house . . ." (401). He becomes more secure when he compares his project to that of Barney Dillon who is himself thinking of writing "a sort of autobiography" (451).

The quest toward the novel involves the rejection of his career as a film writer—the craft of film, as opposed to the mature artistry of fiction, "reeked of safety" (276). Thus Dan will push aside his epic Kitchener script in order to "start assembling a few notes on why he should leave the sanctuary of a medium he knew for the mysteries and complexities of one he didn't" (269). In fact, *Daniel Martin* is a more direct version of the growth of a novelist than *The Magus*. In that novel, the failed poet Urfe, encounters the "novelist *sans* novel,"[30] Conchis, and is able finally to escape Conchis's empowerment over his existence by becoming his own novelist *sans* novel as he directs Alison into his own game of hazard, which becomes the ultimate incident of Urfe's narrative.

The development of a mature relationship with Jane, ironically to grow on a scouting trip up the Nile for the Kitchener movie, allows the form of the final third of the novel to escape confusions of contemporary existence into an achievement of the secure overview of the traditional novelist. The debate which begins on Dan's way to the Los Angeles airport about whether to write in first-or third-person is resolved through Jane's influence into third-person. The journey up the Nile will see Dan's "new medium . . . at last begin to brew, to grow rich" (516). While he will still have concerns about "not being his own master, of being in someone else's play" (542), the journey of the novel is able to reconcile its time frames. Gazing at Rembrandt's self-portrait, Dan recognizes a new kind of artistic persona at the very point that his actual process of writing reaches a like stance: "—even though, with the abruptness of that dash, he had hardly thought this before he saw himself saying the thought to the woman who would be waiting for him . . ." (628). Time sequences have merged as narrative and the process of the novel reach the same point.

Jane, the woman waiting, is Dan's guide into the mature novel which supersedes the narrative about the reach toward maturation and away from narcissism represented by film. Jane becomes the primary emblem/muse in that stage of the novel when it is able to resolve the fragmentation of its earlier reaches. As opposed to Jenny, whose character is refined—especially through her third contribution—into representation of the surface world of film, "this psychologically obscure creature belonged, or had grown to belong, to another art, another system, the one he was trying to enter" (414). Thus, more than Jenny's corrective vision, Jane will allow Dan to gain an objective persona as he is able to "look at himself through her eyes" (414). No wonder that the couple who once punted along Cherwell and Isis in Oxford twice behold, on their Nile excursion, those super propagators Isis and Osiris. Thus in the Temple of Karnak, the statue of the two fertile deities is "a green fuse" (477) mirroring the flowering of the reborn relationship between Dan and Jane. The narrative will slip into a collective "they" as the "I" of Dan's earlier narrative disappears—even their reestablishment of that sexual relationship first achieved but quickly set aside as undergraduates will be "in the third," though Dan "had craved the first and second" (599). Jane becomes the figure of wisdom—Penelope/Athene—replacing Jenny who has been metamorphosized into Calypso.

Like Fowles's vision of the *Odyssey,* there is a geographic progression into maturity as the novel, first conceived in the false world of Hollywood, wi'l "brew" during the pilgrimage to the ancient past world of Egypt and to "The End of the World" in Syria. Thus the "homeless, permanently mid-Atlantic" (33) artist will be able to find a more stable permanence, in the Devonshire "Garden of Eden" of his early days, writing about the growth of a novel and novelist. It is a growth from an experimental, "code-breaking" work (paradoxically reflecting the technically stagnant world of Hollywood) with radical shifts in narrative stance, into a narrative that will accommodate what Jane would term "our moral tradition" (392). If Miles, the author of *Mantissa,* will lecture his elusive muse that the novel is "a *reflexive* medium now,"[31] then the concluding third of *Daniel Martin,* via Lukács, is a return to the "sixty years dead" reflective novel.[32] It offers a "counter-hegemony" to the "ideological hegemony" of bourgeois principle that is the result of "what Marxists call mystification" (392)—apparently a more successful counterforce than that of *Gravity's Rainbow.* Luckily the brewing novelist has had Jane, widow of a don and ex-mistress of another, teach him what he hadn't picked up as an Oxford undergraduate or thereafter.

Perhaps even more than allowing him to discover Gramsci, the major service provided by Dan's companion on the Nile is the filling of a gap in his knowledge of twentieth-century literary criticism. Thus, when he confides his fear that the writing of a novel will be just another form of self-indulgence for him, she is able to offer "an anthology, *Lukács on Critical Realism,* issued by some small left-wing publishing house . . ." (458), in exchange for a Blue Guide to Egypt. It is a fitting gift from one who reminds Dan "of the far more famous Jane" (473)—that figure of narrative steadiness and control whom Fowles links with Marie de France in *The Ebony Tower* in that both "set a new standard for accuracy over human emotions and their absurdities."[33] No wonder that, on the morning after first reading the Hungarian, Dan, though skeptical of the public consequences of Lukacs' premises (as he is skeptical of Jane's neo-Marxism) will begin again to talk of himself in the third-person. Thus the self-indulgence of shifting narrative stances in the earlier sections of the novel will give way to an acceptance of "the great and progressive literary traditions of realism in preference to formalistic experimentation" (500), allowing Dan "the emotional attempt to see life totally" (501). Through Lukács's dicta of literary conservatism, the novelist finds "both his world-view and his own being as a writer enlarged and redefined" (501). The lyric "whole sight" of the book's initial childhood camera's eye becomes the mature whole and steady sight of the master artist who looks and speaks with self-knowledge (enough to have recognized himself as that "mediocre, average English gentleman" whom Lukács sees in Scott's novels), with both will and compassion, to his audience of fellow humans. This is geographically fitting since Dan learns from Professor Kirnberger, who will speak of his own life "quite objectively, as if he were a site, not himself" (520), that Egyptian "art" was a means of control. Thus, despite misgivings about Lukács, Dan will decide that the "passive third-person" is best (516).

In fact, the novel's final stance isn't entirely passive. In the early stages of the novel, the traditional fictional technique of free indirect speech is used to render Dan's discomfort with his father amid the Devon natives: "We have a car, an ancient Standard Flying-12, but on some days my stupid father will use his rotten old bicycle like this" (88). And in the middle of the novel, this technique will describe difficult moments between Dan and Nancy Reed. As the novel moves into a steady third-person, free indirect speech tends to provide a transition from more experimental maneuvers of voice and tense. For example, we hear Jane with: "It wasn't her fault, it was Oxford's: the Socratic method, seeing all the rest of the world as students . . . it was awful, she hadn't realized" (497). This is a sympathetic rendering of Jane, while the Hoopers, the young American table partners of Dan and Jane during the Nile cruise, tend to be negated along with American culture, through a linguistic strategy such as:

> They liked Cairo, Egypt, and Egyptians. You just had to learn their methods. Like the man said, if you had no patience when you came, you learned it; and if you came with patience, you lost it. . . . You had to learn to live with it. . . . (487)

And, "Beirut, Damascus, Byblos, Palmyra . . . the latter especially, it was incredible, the strangest one hell of a place on earth

. . it was such a pity Mitch hadn't brought some fantastic shots
e took" (507) manages to obliterate any positive image of America
emaining after the book's early Hollywood negativity. The writer
n Thorncombe aligns himself with the traditions of Flaubert and
he more famous Jane and thus achieves an ironic detachment to-
vard characters who come to be emblems for the worst of the
Vest. But if *Daniel Martin* seems to end up as a traditional novel,
)an's partial rejection of total "authorial responsibility" and "total
:onsciousness" (516), together with his regard for Rembrandt's
elf-portrait as an example of the simultaneous presentation of
)ersonal and public selves, suggests that his final narrative stance
s more a merging of first-and third-person stances than purely a
ejection of the former.

In a sense, the other narrative strands (including the reports of
he writer writing) are fused by novel's end at the expense of
enny's contributions, which must be rejected as emblematic of
hat "enormous proliferation in styles and techniques" of private
ind obscure nemoistic art.[34] The novel's ultimate gesture is to
.chieve that simultaneously inner and outer posture of Rem-
)randt's self-portrait—certainly a condition far different from con-
emporary anxiety and fragmentation. The danger is that obedience
o the demands of the traditional novel will overcome what Dan
ias associated with successful art: "the breaking of established
odes" (207). Other novelists I've examined have tended to move
rom the complexities of voice in their representative contempo-
ary epics to more muted narrative textures in ensuing works (per-
iaps Pynchon's *Vineland* might be an exception, though I don't
hink that an argument could hold that it approaches the complex-
ty of *Gravity's Rainbow*). *Daniel Martin* attempts, to a greater
legree than other contemporary epics, to work through and to
)vercome its own initial dissonance, and that attempt endangers it
o the kind of limitation in authenticity that Denis Donoghue found
n it soon after publication. Donoghue suggests that while the "rela-
ion between social structure and individual feeling is a major
heme in itself . . . it does not exert any pressure on *Daniel
Martin*."[35]

What is possible is that the dynamic interplay of fragmented
oices and narratives in the first movement of the novel is too
asily snuffed out in the attempt to make way for the final "passive
hird-person" (516). Perhaps the manipulation of character and plot
nvolved in a reach toward a traditional narrative posture smothers
he conscious artist Daniel Martin's ability finally to mirror the
ertiginous nature of his age as do Anna Wulf, Ronald Jethroe, or

that narrator who may be Pirate Prentice. The door in the wall of Dan's life, which is finally opened by the phone call from Oxford at the end of "Games," provides a striking filmic image of an existential situation. But as the Dan-Jane relationship falls neatly into place—with endorsements from Nell, Caro, Roz, and all—that "chink in the door widening a centimeter" (422) has become an image of rather mechanical contrivance. Luckily, Jane's affair with her late husband's colleague—"one of those Iris Murdoch situations" (204)—has been terminated—"My ex-friend, Dan" (384)—and the Dan-Jane relationship will be finally reconsummated through the fortunate machinery of a leaky kerosene stove at the Hotel Zenobia. Like an "ordinary writer," Dan abolishes "randomness . . . hazard" from his "finished text" (271). While Dan continues to believe with "the inmost grain of conviction" that "whatever else the sacrifice, it must not be of complexity of feeling" (526), he is, despite his solitary childhood and difficulties at sustaining relationships, against the grain of contemporary art in that he enjoys "life too much to make a convincing case for any real despair or dissatisfaction" (402). Thus, the too happy humanist is in danger of permanent incarceration inside what threatens to be "an adamantly middle-class novel" (229). While the omniscient narrator of *The French Lieutenant's Woman* claims, "It is only when our characters and events begin to disobey us that they begin to live,"[36] Dan's path to maturity demands that he fit into a novel that fits into the tradition that Iris Murdoch herself, despite all her own complexities of plot, has espoused for these times and any other.

While the geographical expanse of the novel tends at times to verge on a smug travelogue—for example, "She sent her letter of resignation from a drowsy little port, charmingly free of the vulgar mob, called St. Tropez" (139)—and while the modern temper may be dismayed (if Sue Park is correct that we should closely connect John Fowles with S. Wolfe/Daniel Martin) at the political conservatism of Dan seeing "privilege as something evolutionary and preordained" (470), the achievement of *Daniel Martin* should not be quickly dismissed, nor should we exclude it from among the major novels of our time. Still, the narrative eccentricities which reflect Dan's early fragmentation are less organically worked through than mechanically overcome by the novelist in Thorncombe, or, I should say, by John Fowles. While Fowles has eloquently defended Dan's rejection of Jenny and his linkage with Jane[37] and while *Islands* indicates Fowles's strong reasons for replacing a Calypso with a Penelope, there is at least an appearance that character is diminished and reduced to symbols of the novelist's movement from fragmentation and inner-directedness into wholeness and compassionate humanism. Although Jenny may well provide the impetus for the novel, her three contributions—the last especially together with the phone call where she speaks of having sex with her co-star under the influence of marijuana and/or tequila—provide a means to shuffle her off as an immature representative of the stage/film/West Coast world of artificiality. She is reduced to the stoogery of *Kitchener* or of a Richard Portmain. Her dismissal is made too easy by the supposedly pot-induced fancy of her final contribution, so that it is not difficult to connect her with the naive arrogance of the Hoopers on the ride along the Nile (if the free indirect speech rendition of the Hoopers tends to indicate that Fowles's version of Americans is less fortunate even than Lessing's, their perfunctory discussion of Vietnam with Jane is inferior art to the vivid vision of that war in *A Maggot*). On the other hand, Jane emerges, varicose veins notwithstanding, as emblematic of Dan's epic muse—she is his Beatrice. Emblematic of "another art, another system, the one he was trying to enter" (414)—certainly a less difficult and more stable muse than we find in *Mantissa*—she is "to be solved; tamed and transcribed" (404) just as Jenny is to be rejected as representative of Dan's own pre-novelist limitations.

Perhaps because, unlike most artists of his age, Dan has been "to happy to be tragic" (402), his becoming sole or whole cannot involve his being rent like the protagonists of *The Golden Notebook, Gravity's Rainbow,* or *Why Are We In Vietnam?* Somehow, then, the epic hero's quest for wholeness is too easily accommodated, as though the final third of the novel tends to ride on coattails of those dynamic forces at play in its earlier segments—as though the brewing mixture of early narrative interplay is, like Dan's good, unblended whiskey, finally watered down. Unlike the three other novels I've discussed, neither the public nor private worlds of *Daniel Martin* are subject to surrealistic episode. At its worst, the novel will slip into a kind of bubble-bath of comfort in the aristocratic world of Compton—as though we are in a twentieth-century equivalent of a Walter Scott elegy. At its best in its final movement, *Daniel Martin* will capture the cadenced gesture as similar to Dickens as passages in *The French Lieutenant's Woman:*

She withdrew her hand, but they did not turn; sat in silence again in the dappled shade. Three snow-white egrets flew across the river, but

Dan saw them without thinking. It had been in that downward look at the joined hands. It had been a declension, out of the theater of their behavior on the cruise into something undeclared not only between them, but also in each separately; and describable in the other sense of declension . . . a feminine look, not a neutrally companionable one. Almost reluctant, admitting nothing but its brief existence; yet there. (528–29)

Such serene eloquence, indeed, perhaps indicates why *Daniel Martin* stands only on the verges of the contemporary epic, as a work about the twentieth-century temper rests on pinnings of an earlier century's great, if sentimental, art.

6

The Epic and Beyond

EACH OF THE FOUR NOVELS DISCUSSED CONTAINS A PRIMARY NARrative texture consisting of a particular approach to the display of complex impulses that constitute a field of radical inner and outer interplay. Their simultaneous reach for authenticity in dealing with contemporary history and integrity in personal investigation marks the state of epic fiction in the third quarter of the century. Each author, in the seriousness of their global scrutiny and self-scrutiny, reaches to accommodate, as did Whitman's epic, both the "simple separate person" and the "En-masse" of the age—though the resultant complexity of each narrative is a far distance from that of the romantic epic.

If the romantics found in the natural world their version of what the pre-Platonic epic critics agreed was special inspiration, recent epic novelists have claimed little inspiration outside of their own frail, if courageous, selves. Even in *Daniel Martin,* the most stable and perhaps less far-reaching either externally or internally of the four novels, the natural world is treated in a fashion close to the elegiac (Devon seems to represent a lost pre-war world even if Dan seems to circle back there as the narrative ends). In *Why Are We In Vietnam?* what is left of the natural world is close to destruction and that condition is even more imminent in the present of *Gravity's Rainbow,* which seems about to become a more intense version of the wasteland of the post-war "Zone." In *The Golden Notebook* the natural world of Mashopi must be dismissed as nostalgia in the narrative's devaluative process.

These novels add to Aristotle's description of the epic's narrative form as containing numerous simultaneous events in that they also contain a range of voices, although the experience conveyed by the interaction of those voices is essentially ad hoc. Wilkie compares epic poets to the succession of Hebrew prophetic writers who rejected contemporary orthodoxy while rooting themselves within the traditions of the prophets of the covenant.[1] What Marcus

Smith and Khachig Tolyolyan would term the jeremiadic nature of *Gravity's Rainbow*[2] aligns this novel to the tradition Wilkie invokes. Mailer, too, opposes the corrupt belief and practices of the age even as character and, by implication, author participate in them, and the standards of Anna Wulf in *The Golden Notebook* require distancing not only from the conservative world represented by Portmain, Maitland, and the television hacks, but from the political party to which Anna herself belongs. While the struggle of *Daniel Martin* is to escape from the world of Hollywood and pretense, it is far more successful than the other three novels in reaching the firm ground of traditional narrative structure as Daniel, via June, is able to find accommodation in traditional English values.

The Marxist/humanist tradition that Mailer and Lessing share and with which Pynchon is certainly in sympathy and to which Daniel Martin is introduced by June, tends to require devaluation—certainly as practiced by Brecht who, Kenneth Tynan claims, borrowed the term "Epic Theatre" from Piscator and continued to redefine it for the rest of his life—or undercutting of the narrative's cathartic effect as the artist must promote a certain amount of transference of the audience's immersion in the "unreal" world of the work to that world of social reality that the outer gesture of the work promotes. Certainly, Lessing's adaptations of Brechtian epic definitions and devices demand devaluation of most texts within *The Golden Notebook* and Pynchon's absurdities, including his perennial gag songs and episodes such as the story of Byron the Lightbulb, also seem to suggest the Verfrumdungseffekt, although their devaluative role might lend itself to that aspect of the novel operating as perverse Judy Garland movie. Wilkie claims that *Don Juan* is an "epic of negation" in that it is "deliberately and in every sense inconclusive" because Byron "wanted to show life itself as ultimately without meaning."[3] What perhaps counters that devaluative process of the mock-epic kind in *Why Are We In Vietnam?* is, in addition to the high seriousness of its subject as implied by the title, the counter-gesture against implosion by the narrative's surging, existential style. What might be termed the achievement of *Daniel Martin* is its successful overcoming of devaluative, evasive tendencies, although Dan perhaps encounters considerably less difficult terrain than characters in other novels.

While epic intent in each of the novels remains a serious matter, the product of that intent frequently verges on self-parody, with resultant non-celebrative documents dealing with failures of society—for example, the radical left, the new managerial class, the surrender of the individual to technological oppression—and with basic flaws in national and international systems analogous to personal turmoil. What ameliorates both the hostile stance toward society and the parodic element involving self-awareness of the work as literary endeavor in the contemporary epic novel is the authenticity of confessional element that the complex turns and counter-turns in narrative voice encourage the reader to recognize. What these works reveal about the nature of the particular artist is painful to that writer to the extent that exercises in disguise compete with the attempt to relate personal experience with contemporary social experience. Thus elaborate systems of camouflage must be spun and unspun in *The Golden Notebook* and narrative ground remains uncertain in *Why Are We In Vietnam?* and *Gravity's Rainbow* as clues to identity are offered and withdrawn. This difficult enterprise in sincerity recognizes what Lukács insisted was the "organic, indissoluble connection between man as a private individual and man as a social being, as a member of a community."[4] For Lukács it was the job of the modern novelist to investigate and display that connection. And for the modern epic novelist another component of the artistic transaction—the reader—must become dynamically active in the engagements of the work. Thus in *Why Are We In Vietnam?* the epic patron/addressee/inspirer becomes the auditory "young America" itself, prone to receive the shock treatment of the abrasive narrating character/author, to be reprogrammed; and in *The Golden Notebook* and *Gravity's Rainbow* several distancing techniques provide a series of exits from the continuing pull of narrative immersion. Only *Daniel Martin,* finally governed by Dan's brushes—via the new Oxford of Jane—with the relatively secure cultural premises of Lukács, offers the reader a traditional, sustained position of engagement with the narrative as Dan only of the four novels' primary characters is able to achieve some return to a traditional role amid contemporary circumstance.

Other works, contemporaneous with the four novels I've discussed in separate chapters, contain narrative strategies that signal like forms of endeavor. While they contribute to what constitutes a field or kind in the path of the novel, they afford less compelling characteristics of the contemporary epic. For Pascal, who suggests that free indirect speech can only flourish within the realm of an "authoritative third-person narrator," Saul Bellow remains one major writer who "powerfully continues a tradition."[5] But the transference of tense and person in *Herzog* is greater than that which Pascal requires from traditional free indirect speech. Tony Tanner considers the novel a monologue "'written' by a man lying on a couch in an empty room."[6] In fact, the novel begins and stays mostly in the third-person; but first-person infiltrations suggest that the narrative participates in Moses Herzog's consciousness, choosing, at times, to share in the academic philosopher's guilt and anxiety. While Tanner finds that Herzog arrives by the end of the novel "at a state of inertia,"[7] the book, I think, arrives at, and then passes through, the narrative point of its initial images so that the approximation of epic framework signals that Herzog, along with narrative disorder, has moved toward the process of recovery.

Chirantan Kulshrestha claims that *Herzog* is a Menippean Satire "mainly directed against . . . Moses Elkanah Herzog,"[8] so that "the author . . . is distanced from any stances that the protagonist may self-righteously assume."[9] But the strategy of *Herzog* is to draw one's stance out of satire and into sympathy as voices fuse and we come to know Moses Herzog through more dear eyes than those which saw him from the distant perspective in the early stages of the novel. Author and reader share Herzog's experience through a process of narrative fusion that begins to take place in the midst of Herzog's letters to his fellow scholar Shapiro and to the lawyer Himmelstein as well as during Herzog's "reported" recollections of his childhood. Thus Herzog recollects the hijacking of his father's bootleg whiskey truck: "That was how he entered the dark kitchen on Napoleon Street. We were all there. It was gloomy March. . . ."[10] Gradually, the early objective stance toward Herzog—"thought Moses Herzog," "Herzog said," "Still, Herzog considered"—breaks down until the narrative voice takes part directly in Herzog's experience. By the time that the narrative returns to initial circumstance, the omniscient voice of "But if I am out of my mind it's all right with me, thought Moses Herzog"[11] has given way to the shared voice of "But if I am out of my mind, it's alright with me."[12]

Joseph Heller's *Something Happened* begins with narrator Bob Slocum's confession that "I get the willies when I see closed doors."[13] He explains this condition by suggesting that "something must have happened to me sometime."[14] Soon that "something" is revealed to be perhaps a moment in childhood when he walked in on his older brother who was with a young girl and who claimed afterward that "something happened, all right."[15] Later in the novel Slocum, the father of a healthy boy and girl and a retarded younger son, confesses a fear that "something terribly tragic is going to happen to my little boy."[16] Indeed, something does happen when Slocum squeezes and smothers to death his son who has been bleeding, nonfatally, after an auto accident. If those "closed doors" become emblematic of the novel's primary narrative gesture, with parenthesized information operating to a degree like that in *Notes From Underground,* Slocum's act of physical suffocation becomes a counter-gesture of true expression amidst all the evasion, suffocation, and suppression of Bob Slocum's self-accounting.

The something that happened also becomes a signal for the primary theme that we see in so many contemporary American novels: the loss of the American dream. While *Something Happened* tends not to contain the overt political awareness of, say, *The Golden Notebook* or *Gravity's Rainbow,* it does have an epic reach in its reflections upon the American condition—particularly through the extensive descriptions of the company for whom Slocum works and which operates, as he realizes in discussing the sales department, only to make money. He is an emblematic American character like Willy Loman and the novel has a symbolic outer reach toward mirroring the American tragedy through that large scale metaphor employed also by *Goodbye, Columbus* and by most of Vonnegut's works.

In an interview shortly after the publication of *Something Happened,* Heller claimed that the novel's structure was something new in that "first-and third-person are fused in a way I've never seen before."[17] This fusion is signalled by the continued use of parentheses within Slocum's confessional, so that two voices are present in the narrative, one of them separate from that of Bob's formal confessional. It is as though the parentheses allow an authorial voice to enter into the condition of the character. If the Slocum of the outer narrative seems unaware of events happening as the novel progresses, that other narrative presence exists in a compressed time frame where all is already known. The primary tension of the work is between the narrative as a process of evasion, suffocation, and the counter gesture of narrative as opening door.

Whereas the self-reference of *Something Happened* is balanced by its social impulse, the outer impulse of John Barth's *Chimera* is of minor significance in comparison to the examination of personal endeavor. Thus, while it would be an error to term Pynchon a fabulator, it's a term that well fits Barth's fiction, just as it would describe Nabokov before him and Barth's contemporary, Robert Coover, or the charming but socially narrow polyphony of Mario Vargas Llosa in *Aunt Julia and the Scriptwriter.* The elusive shifts of voice in Barth's tripartite narrative structure may tend to reflect the idea that "no one who sees entire the scope and variety of the world can rest content with a single form,"[18] but Barth's attempt to impose overt mythic structure upon the chaos of contemporary consciousness falls short of the epic reach of Lessing, Mailer, or Pynchon. The overt literary references offer us the novelist as genie, the novelist as ancient mythic hero-elect who is at times somehow located in Maryland marshes (somewhere to the north and east of Johns Hopkins), and as a character, Jerome Bray, whose work has been adulterated by a character with like initials. Bray even gives lectures on "his" own previous works—*Giles Goat-Boy* and *The Sot-Weed Factor*—and explains how critical interpretations of his work have led to the mythic overlay of this current work. Bray also lectures to his class on literary techniques—such as "unreliable narrator"[19]—which will render complexity. We find that *Chimera*'s mythic structure—perhaps like the intended destination of Fowles's *Mantissa*—is a reach for dislocation from a forty-year-old writer's block symbolized by the failure of Pegasus to fly. Self-scrutiny, Barth/Bray seems to tell us, is affordable through mythic distance; but the attempt of the artist/hero to parallel the myth of the wandering hero with current concerns, to transform his existence, like the mythic hero, "into the sound of his own voice, or the story of his life"[20] is susceptible to the smug, ironic authorial referentiality that we find in Barthelme and in the more global orientation of Vonnegut's work.

Alan Sillitoe's *The Loneliness of the Long-Distance Runner* is an example of a work with a narrative complexity reflecting the dual impulse of the best examples of the contemporary epic novel, though its middle-distance brevity rather limits its outer social reach more so than with *Why Are We In Vietnam?*, the shortest by far of those novels. Sillitoe's short masterpiece has tended to be misunderstood by critics, who seem to be swayed a priori by Tony Richardson's film treatment, which grossly distorts the work, because Smith's narrative word in the story seems to be taken as gospel even though he warns the reader of his cunning. One neglected part of the work's texture is its series of dislocations in time perspective: at times, Smith writes or thinks in a "trot-trot-trot, puff-puff-puff" bower of actual running; at times he is in a general present Borstal, for example when he says that "they're training me up fine for the big sports day";[21] but at times, and certainly at the story's end, we are in a present of long after the big race, in fact well after Smith has left Borstal. As with the story's complex time structure, there are multiple levels in its metaphoric system. Smith quickly makes a wordplay joke about running—his family has made a habit of running from the law. Soon we have a metaphor that extends throughout the story: running is life. But running and thinking are also equivalents—especially during those endorphinic passages within the bower of actual running—and this connection extends to writing, especially Smith's writing of this story for which he is his own cagey narrator.

From the relatively outside perspective of Smith recollecting time past, his claim that he deliberately lost the race (as interpreted by Richardson's film) seems particularly hard to swallow, though critics have taken that bait without question. In fact, the evidence of the description of the later stages of the race suggests that Smith is in acute physical distress before collapsing short of the winning post. The claim that the loss has been a deliberate act of rebellion is post-race bravado, a shared fantasy of all not-quite-great athletes. In fact, despite his cunning, Smith remains in a limbo between innocence and experience, investing far too much meaning in the governor's trivial words about the race and unable to accept the loss of an event in which he has invested disproportionate importance. After the report of the race, Sillitoe separates himself from his middle-distance loser, exhibiting a readiness to stride into those complex traces of contemporary long-distance narrative reflecting the dual impulse achieved in *The Widower's Son.*

A recent version of the contemporary epic would be Salman Rushdie's *The Satanic Verses,* which bears similar tendencies to those of Pynchon (for example, Slothrop-like metamorphoses and a song sequel from a surrealistic musical, *Friends,* from Dickens's *Our Mutual Friend*) so that it is no wonder that the most sympathetic and interesting review of the somewhat critically mauled *Vineland* came from Rushdie. (Ken Kesey's *Sailor's Song* also pays strong homage to Pynchon.) Nor is it surprising that this novel has occasioned such political response—for the totalitarianism of Rushdie's would-be assassins belongs to a cultural pre-twentieth-century mind set unable to grasp those complex ironies that exhibit "the conflicting selves jostling and joggling within these bags of skin"[22] and the relativity of personal, social, and cosmic engagement. Less able to accommodate the subterranean nature of character, in fact in opposition to the primary inner gestures of Nabokov and Coover, is Robert Stone's *A Flag For Sunrise,* which refrains from entering the complexities of inner being and its relation to outer existence. Graham Swift's *Waterland* melds public and private twentieth-century histories as the reader is student auditing lectures on historiography and tale of teller in the marshy narrative of inner and outer voices. Toni Morrison's *Jazz* provides that authentic history demanded by Pynchon toward the end of *Gravity's Rainbow* as the outside narrator, revealed at the book's end to be living in the present and looking at photographs of characters living in Harlem of the 'twenties, interacts with those characters just as past and present, inner and outer, existences interconnect. Charles Frye's *The Peter Pan Chronicles,* with shifting terrain between the surreal inner voice of a maddened federal undercover agent/marine and a kind of folk narrative outside voice, reveals the intense interaction of public and private African-American worlds in the 'sixties and 'seventies. We see the contemporary "epic kind" continuing in such a diverse range of work from the South African Bessie Head's Lessing-like dialectics and in the narrative presences of such contemporary writers as William Vollmann.

Perhaps it is not accidental that three of the novels discussed at length offer orthodox versions of psychiatry at work for central characters even as they explore contemporary psychic terrain those characters might find orthodox psychiatry ill-equipped to encounter. *Daniel Martin,* which does not have that overt struggle between psychiatry and contemporary experience, is also the novel arriving at a stable narrative stance. Those novels carry a reciprocity between intense self-analysis and outer public statement on the condition of the western world. And this interactive perspective, with concomitant narrative experimentation, constitutes the state of the epic novel in the second half of the century. For Fowles, *Mantissa* seems to be a purgation of all those insecurities siphoned off from the last third of *Daniel Martin.* The telescopic, distant-past stance of the later *A Maggot* shares the secure relationship to the present achieved in Lessing's space fiction. Mailer followed a decade of nonfiction after *Why Are We In Vietnam?* with the muted free indirect speech authorial presences in *The Executioner's Song* and with *Ancient Evenings'* secure narratives of generational ghosts also a fair distance from present earth. In *Harlot's Ghost,* the primary narrative mode is first-person; but character lacks the depth of earlier novels where primary character fuses in voice with authorial presence. Because the privileged speaker Harry Hubbard and his epistolary companion Kittredge lack contact with that second, subterranean river of American experience demanded by Mailer thirty years ago, possibilities of that experience may only be glimpsed through secondary, real or fictional characters.

Clearly, authorial presence remains in these works; but only Pynchon's *Vineland* continues the emphatic dual impulse of *Gravity's Rainbow;* in fact, we might term the latter novel the former novel gone west and into the eighties and nineties. While optimistic signs have been found in the book's ending by reviewers, the tone of the work is primarily elegiac for the "spilled, broken world"[23] of experience, and the primary forces at work in *Gravity's Rainbow* remain. The novels discussed in separate chapters will remain, I think, the major achievement of each writer. Certainly they've achieved the sympathies necessary for this work to identify a major movement in recent fiction.

Notes

Chapter 1. Two Rivers of the Modern Novel

1. Stephen Spender, *The Struggle of the Modern* (Berkeley: University of California Press, 1963), 104–5.

2. Stephen Spender, *World Within World* (New York: Harcourt, Brace, 1951), vi.

3. Wayne C. Booth, *The Rhetoric of Fiction* (Chicago: University of Chicago Press, 1961), 389.

4. Roy Pascal, *The Dual Voice* (Manchester: Manchester University Press, 1977), 132.

5. Robert Kellogg and Robert Scholes, *The Nature of Narrative* (Oxford: Oxford University Press, 1966), 278.

6. Austin Warren and Rene Wellek, *The Theory of Literature* (New York: Harcourt, Brace, 1955), 33.

7. E. M. W. Tillyard, *The Epic Strain in the English Novel* (London: Chatto & Windus, 1958), 117.

8. Ibid., 196.

9. Mark Spilka, "Fielding and the Epic Impulse," *Criticism* 11 (Winter 1969): 76.

10. Ibid., 72.

11. Brian Wilkie, *Romantic Poets and the Epic Tradition* (Madison: University of Wisconsin Press, 1965), 10.

12. Ibid., 11.

13. Ibid., 10–11.

14. M. M. Bakhtin, *The Dialogic Imagination: Four Essays by M. M. Bakhtin,* ed. Michael Holquist and trans. Caryl Emerson and Michael Holquist (Austin: University of Texas Press, 1981), 15.

15. Ibid., 3.

16. Ibid., 13.

17. Ibid., 15.

18. Tillyard, *Epic Strain,* 15–17.

19. Lionel Abel, *Important Nonsense* (Buffalo, N.Y.: Prometheus, 1987), 34–35.

20. Roland Barthes, "The Death of the Author," in *Modern Criticism and Theory: A Reader,* ed. David Lodge (London: Longman, 1988), 170.

21. Ibid., 171.

22. Michel Foucault, "What Is An Author?" in *Modern Criticism and Theory: A Reader,* ed. David Lodge (London: Longman, 1988), 202.

23. Paul de Man, "The Resistance to Theory," in *Modern Criticism and Theory: A Reader,* ed. David Lodge (London: Longman, 1988), 362.

24. Abel, *Important Nonsense,* 34.

25. Ibid., 36.

26. Ibid., 40–44.

27. Ibid., 142.

28. M. H. Abrams, "The Deconstructive Angel," in *Modern Criticism and Theory: A Reader,* ed. David Lodge (London: Longman, 1988), 269.

29. Denis Donoghue, "Deconstructing Deconstruction," *The New York Review of Books,* 12 June 1980, 37–38.

30. Ibid., 41.

31. Ibid., 39–40.

32. Jeffrey T. Nealon, "The Discipline of Deconstruction," *PMLA* 107 (October 1992): 1276.

33. Jacques Lacan, "The Insistence of the Letter in the Unconscious," in *Modern Criticism and Theory: A Reader,* ed. David Lodge (London: Longman, 1988), 86.

34. Nealon, "Discipline," 1271.

35. Ibid., 1268.

36. Ibid., 1272.

37. Sherry Turkle, *Psychoanalytical Politics: Freud's French Revolution* (New York: Basic Books, 1978), 76.

38. Ibid., 238.

39. Alec McHoul and David Wills, *Writing Pynchon: Strategies in Fictional Analysis* (Urbana: University of Illinois Press, 1990), 10.

40. Ibid., 6.

41. Ibid., 13.

42. Alvin Kernan, *The Death of Literature* (New Haven: Yale University Press, 1990), 83.

43. Ibid., 41.

44. Michiko Kakutani, "Critic's Notebook," *The New York Times,* 27 July 1993, national ed., B8.

45. George Steiner, *Real Presences* (Cambridge: Cambridge University Press, 1986), 7.

46. Ibid., 19.

47. Kernan, *Death of Literature,* 82.

48. Brian McHale, *Postmodernist Fiction* (New York: Methuen, 1987), xi.

49. Brian McHale, "Modernist Reading, Postmodern Text: The Case of *Gravity's Rainbow,*" *Poetics Today* 1, no. 1–2 (1979): 91.

50. Catherine R. Stimpson, "The Postmodern Element in the Postmodern Humanities," *Weber Studies* 10 (Spring/Summer 1993): 41.

51. Thomas Mann, *Death in Venice and Seven Other Stories* (New York: Knopf, 1930), 10–11.

52. David Lodge, *Language of Fiction: Essays in Criticism and Analysis of the English Novel* (New York: Columbia University Press, 1966), 261.

53. Brian McHale, "Free Indirect Discourse: A Survey of Recent Accounts," *PTL* 3 (April 1978): 249–50.

54. Pascal, *Dual Voice,* 136–37.

55. Ibid., 137.

56. John Hersey, "The Legend on the License," *The Yale Review* 70 (October 1980): 17.

57. Pascal, *Dual Voice,* 17.

58. Ibid., 271.

59. Hugh Kenner, *Joyce's Voices* (Berkeley: University of California Press, 1978), 16–38.

60. Pascal, *Dual Voice,* 125, 148.

61. Kenner, *Joyce's Voices,* 104.

62. Booth, *Rhetoric of Fiction,* 181.

63. Tom F. Driver, "Beckett by the Madeleine," *Columbia University Forum* 4 (Summer 1961): 23.

64. Samuel Beckett, *Molloy* (New York: Grove, 1959), 230.

65. Samuel Beckett, *Malone* (New York: Grove, 1959), 291.

66. Samuel Beckett, *Murphy* (New York: Grove, 1957), 53.

67. Samuel Beckett and Georges Duthuit, "Three Dialogues," *Samuel Beckett: A Collection of Critical Essays,* ed. Martin Esslin (Englewood Cliffs, N.J.: Prentice-Hall, 1965), 17.

68. Israel Shenker, "An Interview with Samuel Beckett," *The New York Times,* 6 May 1956, section 2.

69. Donald Pizer, "The Camera's Eye in *USA:* The Sexual Center," *Modern Fiction Studies* 26 (Autumn 1980): 429.

70. F. Scott Fitzgerald, *The Last Tycoon* (New York: Scribner's, 1970), 138.

71. Ibid., 77, 98.

Chapter 2. Real People:
Character and Author in *The Golden Notebook*

1. Frederick Karl, *A Reader's Guide to the Contemporary English Novel* (New York: Farrar, Straus and Giroux, 1972), 313.

2. Irving Howe, *Celebrations and Attacks: Thirty Years of Literary and Cultural Commentary* (New York: Horizon, 1978), 113.

3. Doris Lessing, *The Golden Notebook* (New York: Bantam, 1973), xi. Subsequent quotations from this work are cited parenthetically in the text.

4. Doris Lessing, *A Small Personal Voice,* ed. Paul Schlueter (New York: Vintage, 1973), 65.

5. Ibid.

6. Doris Lessing, *The Four-Gated City* (New York: New American Library, 1976), 131.

7. Lessing, *Small Personal Voice,* 70.

8. Ibid., 80.

9. Ibid., 5.

10. Ibid., 14.

11. Ibid., 17.

12. Ibid., 6.

13. Ibid., 7.

14. Mark Spilka, "Lessing and Lawrence: the Battle of the Sexes," *Contemporary Literature* 16 (Spring 1975): 218–40.

15. Lessing, *Small Personal Voice,* 81.

16. Bertolt Brecht, *Brecht on Theatre,* ed. and trans. John Willett (New York: Hill and Wang, 1966), 23.

17. Martin Esslin, *Brecht: The Man and His Works* (New York: Doubleday, 1960), 134.

18. Brecht, *Brecht on Theatre,* 23.

19. Ibid., 277.

20. Spilka, "Lessing and Lawrence," 230.

21. Doris Lessing, "The Eye of God in Paradise," in *The Habit of Loving* (New York: Thomas Y. Crowell, 1957), 274.

22. Doris Lessing, *The Summer Before the Dark* (New York: Bantam, 1974), 42.

23. Spilka, "Fielding and the Epic Impulse," 74–75.

24. Lessing, *Small Personal Voice,* 81.

25. Ibid., 63.

26. Ibid., 66.

27. Ibid., 5.

28. Howe, *Celebrations,* 117.

29. Ibid.

30. John Carey, "Art and Reality in *The Golden Notebook,*" *Contemporary Literature* 14 (Autumn 1973): 440.

Chapter 3. A Physician Half-Blind:
Implosion and Public Address in *Why Are We In Vietnam?*

1. Norman Mailer, *Why Are We In Vietnam?* (New York: G.P. Putnam's Sons, 1967), 24. Subsequent quotations from this work are cited parenthetically in the text.

2. Tony Tanner, *City of Words: American Fiction, 1950–1970* (New York: Harper & Row, 1971), 369.

3. Ibid., 370.

4. Ted Kerasote, *Bloodties: Nature, Culture and the Hunt* (New York: Random House, 1993), 110–12.

5. Norman Mailer, *Cannibals and Christians* (New York: Dell, 1965), 131.

6. Norman Mailer, *The Executioner's Song* (Boston: Little, Brown, 1979), 15.

7. Ibid., 985.

8. Ibid., 1019.

9. Fredric Jameson, "The Great American Hunter, or, Ideological Content in the Novel," *College English* 32 (November 1972): 191.

10. Spilka, "Fielding and the Epic Impulse," 68–69.

11. Norman Mailer, *Barbary Shore* (New York: New American Library, 1951), 6.

12. Ibid., 132–34.

13. Tillyard, *Epic Strain* 15.

14. Ibid., 16.

15. Ibid., 15.

16. Richard Poirier, *Norman Mailer* (New York: Viking, 1972), 152.

17. Ibid., 150.

18. Ibid.

19. Norman Mailer, *The Idol and the Octopus* (New York: Dell, 1968), 255.

20. Ibid., 266.

21. Mailer, *Cannibals,* 5.

22. Norman Mailer, *Armies of the Night* (New York: New American Library, 1968), 241.

23. Ibid., 245.

24. Ibid.

25. Ibid.

26. Robert Solotaroff, *Down Mailer's Way* (Urbana: University of Illinois Press, 1974), 182–83.

27. Poirier, *Normal Mailer,* 152.

28. Ibid., 155.

29. Oriana Fallaci, "An Interview with Norman Mailer," *Writer's Digest,* December 1969, 46.

30. Norman Mailer, *Existential Errands* (Boston: Little, Brown, 1972), 104.

31. Ibid., 117.

32. Ibid., 92.

33. Ibid., 123.

34. Paul Carroll, "An Interview with Norman Mailer," *Playboy,* January 1968, 84.

35. Ibid.

36. Ibid.

37. Norman Mailer, *Advertisements for Myself* (New York: G.P. Putnam's Sons, 1959), 379.

38. Norman Mailer, *The Naked and the Dead* (New York: Holt, Rinehart and Winston, 1968), 658.

39. Mailer, *Advertisements,* 106.

40. Norman Mailer, *The Presidential Papers* (New York: G.P. Putnam's Sons, 1963), 38.

41. Philip Roth, "Writing American Fiction," *Commentary* 31 (March 1961): 227.

42. Jameson, "Great American Hunter," 186.

Chapter 4. Hard Times for Innocence: Utilitarianism and Sensibility in *Gravity's Rainbow*

1. Norman Mailer, *Pieces and Pontifications* (Boston: Little, Brown, 1982), 157.

2. Robert Hellman, *Fables of Fact: The New Journalism as New Fiction* (Urbana: University of Illinois Press, 1981), 59.

3. Thomas Pynchon, *Gravity's Rainbow* (New York: Viking, 1971), 58. Subsequent quotations from this work are cited parenthetically in the text.

4. Brian McHale, "Modernist Reading: Postmodern Text: The Case of *Gravity's Rainbow,*" *Poetics Today* 1, no. 1–2 (1979): 92–93. Ì

5. Thomas Pynchon, *Slow Learner* (Boston: Little, Brown, 1984), 19.

6. Marcus Smith and Khachig Tololyan, "The New Jeremiad: *Gravity's Rainbow,*" in *Critical Essays on Thomas Pynchon,* ed. Richard Pearce (Boston: G.K. Hall, 1981), 179.

7. Ibid., 180–81.

8. Lance W. Ozier, "The Calculus of Transformation: More Mathematical Imagery in *Gravity's Rainbow,*" *Twentieth Century Literature* 21 (May 1975): 196–98.

9. Pynchon, *Slow Learner,* 18.

10. Edward Mendelson, "Gravity's Encyclopedia," in *Mindful Pleasures: Essays on Thomas Pynchon,* ed. George Levine and David Leverenz (Boston: Little, Brown, 1976), 1.

11. F. D. McConnell, *Four Postwar American Novelists: Bellow, Mailer, Barth and Pynchon* (Chicago: University of Chicago Press, 1978), 159.

12. F. S. Schwarzbach, "A Matter of Gravity," in *Pynchon: A Collection of Critical Essays,* ed. Edward Mendelson (Englewood Cliffs, N.J.: Prentice Hall, 1978), 65.

13. Tony Tanner, "Caries and Cabals," in *Mindful Pleasures: Essays on Thomas Pynchon,* ed. George Levine and David Leverenz (Boston: Little, Brown, 1976), 54.

14. Pynchon, *Slow Learner,* 18.

15. Hellman, *Fables of Fact,* 10.

16. Ibid., 12.

17. Khachig Tololyan, "War as Background in *Gravity's Rainbow,*" in *Approaches to Gravity's Rainbow,* ed. Charles Clerc (Columbus: Ohio State University Press, 1983), 31–67.

Chapter 5. In Penelope's Arms: From Lyric to Epic in *Daniel Martin*

1. John Fowles, *Mantissa* (London: J. Cape, 1982), 100.

2. John Fowles, *Islands* (Boston: Little, Brown, 1978), 11.

3. Ibid., 66.

4. Ibid., 51.

5. Ibid.

6. Fowles, *Mantissa,* 169.

7. Fowles, *Islands,* 54.

8. Ibid., 73.

9. Ibid., 58.

10. Ibid., 62.

11. Fowles, *Mantissa,* 170.

12. Fowles, *Islands,* 51.

13. Ibid.

14. Ibid., 52.

15. Ibid., 58.

16. Ibid., 54.

17. Ibid., 58.

18. Ibid., 72.

19. Ibid., 73.

20. Ibid., 74.

21. Ibid., 66.

22. John Fowles, *Daniel Martin* (Boston: Little, Brown, 1977), 183. Subsequent quotations from this work are cited parenthetically in the text.

23. Robert Huffaker, *John Fowles* (Boston: Twayne, 1980), 19, 136.

24. John Fowles, *The Aristos* (Boston: Little, Brown, 1964), 37.

25. John Fowles, *The Magus* (Boston: Little, Brown, 1965), 439.

26. John Fowles, *The French Lieutenant's Woman* (Boston: Little, Brown, 1969), 66.

27. Fowles, *Magus,* 289.

28. Fowles, *French Lieutenant's Woman,* 348.

29. Fowles, *Aristos,* 39.

30. Fowles, *Magus,* 214.

31. Fowles, *Mantissa,* 118.

32. Ibid., 117.

33. John Fowles, *The Ebony Tower* (Boston: Little, Brown, 1974), 120.

34. Fowles, *Aristos,* 39.

35. Denis Donoghue, "Only Disconnect," *The New York Review of Books,* 8 December 1977, 45.

36. Fowles, *French Lieutenant's Woman,* 105.

37. Carol Barnum, "An Interview with John Fowles," *Modern Fiction Studies* 31 (Spring 1985): 199.

Chapter 6. The Epic and Beyond

1. Wilkie, *Romantic Poets, 10–11.*

2. Smith and Tololyan, "The New Jeremiad," 172–79.

3. Wilkie, *Romantic Poets,* 211.

4. György·Lukács, *Studies in European Realism,* trans. Edith Bone (London: Hillway, 1950), 8.

5. Roy Pascal, *The Dual Voice* (Manchester: Manchester University Press, 1977), 140.

6. Tony Tanner, *City of Words* (New York: Harper and Row, 1971), 66.

7. Ibid., 300.

8. Chirantan Kulshrestha, *Saul Bellow: The Problem of Affirmation* (New Delhi: Heinemann, 1978), 114.

9. Ibid., 116.

10. Saul Bellow, *Herzog* (New York: Viking, 1964), 31.

11. Ibid., 1.

12. Ibid., 315.

13. Joseph Heller, *Something Happened* (New York: Ballantine, 1975), 1.

14. Ibid.

15. Ibid., 3.

16. Ibid., 364.

17. Sam Murrill, "An Interview with Joseph Heller," Playboy, June 1975, 74.

18. John Barth, *Chimera* (New York: Fawcett, 1973), 307.

19. Ibid., 158.

20. Ibid., 207.

21. Alan Sillitoe, *The Loneliness of the Long-Distance Runner* (New York: Knopf, 1960), 8.

22. Salman Rushdie, *The Satanic Verses* (New York: Viking, 1989), 519.

23. Thomas Pynchon, *Vineland* (Boston: Little, Brown, 1990), 267.

Bibliography

Abel, Lionel. *Important Nonsense*. Buffalo: Prometheus, 1987.

Abrams, M.H. "The Deconstructive Angel." In *Modern Criticism and Theory: A Reader*, edited by David Lodge, 265–76. London: Longman, 1988.

Bakhtin, M.M. *The Dialogic Imagination: Four Essays by M.M. Bakhtin*. Edited by Michael Holquist. Translated by Caryl Emerson and Michael Holquist. Austin: University of Texas Press, 1981.

Barnum, Carol. "An Interview With John Fowles." *Modern Fiction Studies* 31 (Spring 1985): 187–203.

Barth, John. *Chimera*. New York: Fawcett, 1973.

Barthes, Roland. "The Death of the Author." In *Modern Criticism and Theory: A Reader*, edited by David Lodge, 167–72. London: Longman, 1988.

Beckett, Samuel. *Malone*. New York: Grove, 1959.

———. *Molloy*. New York: Grove, 1959.

———. *Murphy*. New York: Grove, 1957.

Beckett, Samuel and Georges Duthuit. "Three Dialogues." In *Samuel Beckett: A Collection of Critical Essays*, edited by Martin Esslin, 16–22. Englewood Cliffs: Prentice-Hall, 1965.

Bellow, Saul. *Herzog*. New York: Viking, 1964.

Booth, Wayne C. *The Rhetoric of Fiction*. Chicago: University of Chicago Press, 1961.

Brecht, Bertolt. *Brecht on Theatre*. Edited and translated by John Willett. New York: Hill and Wang, 1966.

Carey, John. "Art and Reality in *The Golden Notebook*." *Contemporary Literature* 14 (Autumn 1973): 437–56.

de Man, Paul. "The Resistance to Theory." In *Modern Criticism and Theory: A Reader*, edited by David Lodge, 355–71. London: Longman, 1988.

Donoghue, Denis. "Deconstructing Deconstruction." *The New York Review of Books*, 12 June 1980, 37–41.

———. "Only Disconnect." *The New York Review of Books*, 8 December 1977, 45–46.

Draine, Betsy. "Nostalgia and Irony: The Postmodern Order of *The Golden Notebook*." *Modern Fiction Studies* 26 (Spring 1980): 31–48.

Driver, Tom F. "Beckett by the Madeleine." *Columbia University Forum* 4 (Summer 1961): 21–25.

Esslin, Martin. *Brecht: The Man and His Works*. New York: Doubleday, 1960.

Fallaci, Oriana. "An Interview With Norman Mailer." *Writer's Digest*, December 1969, 41–47, 81.

Fitzgerald, F. Scott. *The Last Tycoon.* New York: Scribner's, 1970.

Foucault, Michel. "What Is An Author?" In *Modern Criticism and Theory: A Reader,* edited by David Lodge, 197–210. London: Longman, 1988.

Fowles, John. *The Aristos.* Boston: Little, Brown, 1964.

———. *Daniel Martin.* Boston: Little, Brown, 1977.

———. *The Ebony Tower.* Boston: Little, Brown, 1974.

———. *The French Lieutenant's Woman.* Boston: Little, Brown, 1969.

———. *Islands.* Boston: Little, Brown, 1978.

———. *Mantissa.* London: J. Cape, 1982.

———. *The Magus.* Boston: Little, Brown, 1965.

Heller, Joseph. *Something Happened.* New York: Ballantine, 1975.

Hellman, Robert. *Fables of Fact: the New Journalism as New Fiction.* Urbana: University of Illinois Press, 1981.

Hersey, John. "The Legend on the License." *The Yale Review* 70 (October 1980): 1–25.

Howe, Irving. *Celebrations and Attacks: Thirty Years of Literary and Cultural Commentary.* New York: Horizon, 1978.

Huffaker, Robert. *John Fowles.* Boston: Twayne, 1980.

Jameson, Fredric. "The Great American Hunter, or, Ideological Content in the Novel." *College English* 34 (November 1972): 180–97.

Kakutani, Michiko. "Critic's Notebook." *The New York Times,* 27 July 1993.

Karl, Frederick. *A Reader's Guide to the Contemporary English Novel.* New York: Farrar, Straus and Giroux, 1972.

Kellogg, Robert and Robert Scholes. *The Nature of Narrative.* Oxford: Oxford University Press, 1966.

Kenner, Hugh. *Joyce's Voices.* Berkeley: University of California Press, 1978.

Kerasote, Ted. *Bloodties: Nature, Culture and the Hunt.* New York: Random House, 1993.

Kernan, Alvin. *The Death of Literature.* New Haven: Yale University Press, 1990.

Kulshrestha, Chirantan. *Saul Bellow: The Problem of Affirmation.* New Delhi: Heinemann, 1978.

Lacan, Jaques. "The Insistence of the Letter in the Unconscious." In *Modern Criticism and Theory: A Reader,* edited by David Lodge, 80–106. London: Longman, 1988.

Lessing, Doris. "The Eye of God in Paradise." In *The Habit of Loving,* 235–311. New York: Thomas Y. Crowell, 1957.

———. *The Four-Gated City.* New York: NAL, 1976.

———. *The Golden Notebook.* New York: Bantam, 1973.

———. *The Real Thing.* New York: Harper Collins, 1992.

———. *A Small Personal Voice.* Edited by Paul Schlueter. New York: Vintage, 1973.

———. *The Summer Before the Dark.* New York: Bantam, 1974.

Lodge, David. *Language of Fiction: Essays in Criticism and Analysis of the English Novel.* New York: Columbia University Press, 1966.

Lukács, Gyorgy. *Studies in European Realism.* Translated by Edith Bone. London: Hillway, 1950.

————. *The Theory of the Novel.* Translated by Anna Bostock. Cambridge: MIT Press, 1971.

Mailer, Norman. *Advertisements For Myself.* New York: G.P. Putnam's Sons, 1959.

————. *Barbary Shore.* New York: New American Library, 1951.

————. *Cannibals and Christians.* New York: Dell, 1965.

————. *The Executioner's Song.* Boston: Little, Brown, 1979.

————. *Existential Errands.* Boston: Little, Brown, 1972.

————. *The Idol and the Octopus.* New York: Dell, 1968.

————. *The Naked and the Dead.* New York: Holt, Rinehart and Winston, 1968.

————. *The Presidential Papers.* New York: G.P. Putnam's Sons, 1963.

————. *Why Are We In Vietnam?.* New York: G.P. Putnam's Sons, 1967.

McConnell, F.D. *Four Postwar American Novelists: Bellow, Mailer, Barth and Pynchon.* Chicago: University of Chicago Press, 1978.

McHale, Brian. "Free Indirect Discourse: A Survey of Recent Accounts." *PTL* 3 (April 1978): 249–87.

————. "Modernist Reading, Postmodern Text: The Case of *Gravity's Rainbow.*" *Poetics Today* 1, No. 1–2 (1979): 85–109.

McHoul, Alec and David Wills. *Writing Pynchon: Strategies in Fictional Analysis.* Urbana: University of Illinois Press, 1990.

Mendelson, Edward. "Gravity's Encyclopedia." *Mindful Pleasures: Essays on Thomas Pynchon,* edited by George Levine and David Leverenz, 161–95. Boston: Little, Brown, 1976.

Morgan, Speer. "*Gravity's Rainbow:* What's the Big Idea?" *Critical Essays on Thomas Pynchon,* edited by Richard Pearce, 82–98. Boston: Hall, 1981.

Mulkeen, Anne M. "Twentieth Century Realism: The 'Grid' Structure of *The Golden Notebook.*" *Studies in the Novel* 4 (Summer 1972): 262–74.

Murrill, Sam. "An Interview With Joseph Heller." *Playboy,* June 1975, 59–76.

Nealon, Jeffrey T. "The Discipline of Deconstruction." *PMLA* 107 (October 1992): 1266–79.

Ozier, Lance W. "The Calculus of Transformation: More Mathematical Imagery in *Gravity's Rainbow.*" *Twentieth Century Literature* 21 (May 1975): 195–99.

Park, Sue. "John Fowles, Daniel Martin, and Simon Wolfe." *Modern Fiction Studies* 31 (Spring 1985): 165–71.

Pascal, Roy. *The Dual Voice.* Manchester: Manchester University Press, 1977.

Pizer, Donald. "The Camera's Eye in *U.S.A.:* The Sexual Center." *Modern Fiction Studies* 26 (Autumn 1980): 417–31.

Poirier, Richard. *Norman Mailer.* New York: Viking, 1972.

Pynchon, Thomas. *Gravity's Rainbow.* New York: Viking, 1971.

Roth, Philip. "Writing American Fiction." *Commentary* 31 (March 1961): 223–33.

Rushdie, Salman. *The Satanic Verses.* New York: Viking, 1989.

Schwarzbach, F.S. "A Matter of Gravity." *Pynchon: A Collection of Critical Essays,* edited by Edward Mendelson, 56–67. Englewood Cliffs: Prentice Hall, 1978.

Shenker, Israel. "An Interview with Samuel Beckett." *The New York Times,* 6 May 1956.

Sillitoe, Alan. *The Loneliness of the Long-Distance Runner.* New York: Knopf, 1960.

Smith, Marcus and Khachig Tololyan. "The New Jeremiad: *Gravity's Rainbow.*" *Critical Essays on Thomas Pynchon,* edited by Richard Pearce, 169–86. Boston: G.K. Hall, 1981.

Solotaroff, Robert. *Down Mailer's Way.* Urbana: University of Illinois Press, 1974.

Spender, Stephen. *The Struggle of the Modern.* Berkeley: University of California Press, 1963.

———. *World Within World.* New York: Harcourt, Brace, 1951.

Spilka, Mark. "Fielding and the Epic Impulse." *Criticism* 11 (Winter 1969): 68–77.

———. "Lessing and Lawrence: the Battle of the Sexes." *Contemporary Literature* 16 (Spring 1975): 218–40.

Steiner, George. *Real Presences.* Cambridge: Cambridge University Press, 1986.

Stimpson, Catherine R. "The Postmodern Element in the Postmodern Humanities." *Weber Studies* 10 (Spring/Summer 1993): 41–56.

Tanner, Tony. "Caries and Cabals." *Mindful Pleasures: Essays on Thomas Pynchon,* edited by George Levine and David Leverenz, 49–67. Boston: Little, Brown, 1976.

———. *City of Words: American Fiction, 1950–1970.* New York: Harper & Row, 1971.

Tillyard, E.M.W. *The Epic Strain in the English Novel.* London: Chatto & Windus, 1958.

Tololyan, Khachig. "War as Background in Gravity's Rainbow." Approaches to *Gravity's Rainbow,* edited by Charles Clerc, 31–67. Columbus: Ohio State University Press, 1983.

Turkle, Sherry. *Psychoanalytical Politics: Freud's French Revolution.* New York: Basic, 1978.

Warren, Austin and Rene Wellek. *The Theory of Literature.* New York: Harcourt, Brace, 1955.

Wilkie, Brian. *Romantic Poets and Epic Tradition.* Madison: University of Wisconsin Press, 1965.

INDEX

DATE DUE

MAR 14 ~~~~			
DEC 02 1999			
JAN 0 6 2003			